This book is due for return on or before the last date shown below.

Media Life

MARK DEUZE

polity

First published in 2012 by Polity Press
Reprinted in 2013

Polity Press
65 Bridge Street
Cambridge CB2 1UR, UK

Polity Press
350 Main Street
Malden, MA 02148, USA

ISBN-13: 978-0-7456-4999-3
ISBN-13: 978-0-7456-5000-5 (pb)

A catalogue record for this book is available from the British Library.

Typeset in 10.25 on 13 pt FF Scala
by Servis Filmsetting Ltd, Stockport, Cheshire
Printed in the USA by Edwards Brothers Malloy

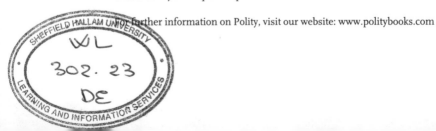

In Memoriam

Jan Deuze (1932–2010)
Twannie Deuze (1962–2011)

Contents

Overview: In Media

where who you are is what media are

You live *in* media. Who you are, what you do, and what all of this means to you does not exist outside of media. Media are to us as water is to fish. This does not mean life is determined by media – it just suggests that whether we like it or not, every aspect of our lives takes place in media. Part of this kind of life is coming to terms with a supersaturation of media messages and machines in households, workplaces, shopping malls, bars and restaurants, and all the other in-between spaces of today's world. Over the last few decades, the key categories of human aliveness and activity converged in a concurrent and continuous exposure to, use of, and immersion in media. It must be clear that media are not just types of technology and chunks of content occupying the world around us – a view that considers media as external agents affecting us in a myriad of ways. If anything, today the uses and appropriations of media can be seen as fused with *everything* people do, *everywhere* people are, *everyone* people aspire to be. There is no external to media life – whatever we perceive as escape hatch, passage out, or potential Delete key is just an illusion. In fact, we can only *imagine* a life outside of media.

In terms of what media communicate, it is tempting to point to governments, companies and corporations for pushing an unrelenting, ever-accelerating stream of content and experiences into our lives. However, most mediated communication comprises of work done by you and me: through our endless texts, chats and e-mails, with our phone calls from anywhere at any time, and through our online social networks that function as the living archives of social reality. With the majority of the world population owning a mobile phone, telecommunication networks spanning almost every inch of the globe, sales figures of any and all media devices growing steadily worldwide, time spent with media up every year, and any and all media by default integrated into an always-on real-time live mode of being, an almost complete mediatization of society seems a somewhat self-evident observation.

A media life includes much more than media hardware,

software and content – it is also everything we do with and in response to media: how we build and sustain relationships and family ties, how we derive cultural status and social currency from the kinds of media we use (the music we listen to, the shows we follow, the games we catch live), and the various ways we more or less deliberately manipulate time and space by checking our e-mail on mobile devices, listen to audiobooks with noise-cancelling headphones, and record our private participation in public proceedings (weddings, concerts, the weekend soccer game) with networked devices that simultaneously *immediatize* and *immortalize* our lived experience as they mediate it. As we merge our perception of ourselves and others with what can be mediated about us, media competencies, literacies and fitness become paramount to the human condition. Media benchmark our experience of the world, and how we make sense of our role in it. A media life reflects how media are both a *necessary* and *unavoidable* part of our existence and survival.

It certainly seems media multiply in everyday life. Media are *ubiquitous* – they are everywhere – and *pervasive* – they cannot be switched off. Furthermore, our near-complete immersion in media constitutes the majority of time spent in waking life. Research in countries as varied as the United States, Brazil, South Korea, the Netherlands, India and New Zealand consistently shows that most of our time on any given day gets spent using media, and that being concurrently exposed to media has become a mundane mark of existence. The media life perspective further recognizes that media, as much as the human brain (or the cosmos), are *indeterminate*. Media are not finished, nor static – but essentially plastic, and pliable. Media evolve, and have creative agency. As hardware and software, they act upon each other next to their interactions with us. We emotionally invest ourselves into media as much as our media become an affective part of us. As platforms for communication, media constitute as well as reproduce the world we live in.

Throughout this book, I use "media" interchangeably with "information" and "communication technologies," and with "machines" more generally insofar as relations with humanity and society are involved. Media, thus broadly conceived, are any (symbolic or technological) systems that enable, structure or amplify communication between people. Life, on the other hand, is not just about surviving – it is about living a *live* life, a life worth living, and a form of liveness that goes beyond simply making it work from day to day. At the heart of the project in this book is the question of what a good, passionate, beautiful and socially responsible media life looks like. A dichotomous reading of the mixing of media and life identifies and maps ways in which human beings and behaviors steer the development of media to make sense of people's everyday life and what can be done about it. Such media-centrism and technological determinism often boils down to benevolent or malevolent mechanistic fascination with the machinery of media and the technique of technologies. It tends to obscure rather than unveil the interdependency of humanity and technology – as it keeps insisting on finding ways of making sense of the world outside of media, of attributing primacy to the social over the technological.

In essence, media-centrism (and its attendant arguments about the real or perceived influences of media on ways of being alive) is a product of a live lived in media: it is an illusion we maintain in order to convince ourselves and each other that we exist not just next to, but in an intrinsically more central and indeed privileged relationship to our media. Maintaining an outside to media makes us, as human beings, feel *special*. As French philosopher Jean Baudrillard remarked in response to the way his work featured as inspiration for the popular *The Matrix* film franchise (in an interview with *Le Nouvel Observateur*, July 2004): "*The Matrix* is surely the kind of film about the matrix that the matrix would have been able to produce."[1] Correspondingly, media-centrism and technological determinism can be considered to be the kind of theoretical stopgaps a media life perspective would produce in order to mask itself. The illusion that we can comprehensively control our media (for example by pulling the plug, pressing the off switch on a remote control, by becoming *mediawise* and developing sophisticated media literacies) in fact preserves media as the primary definer of our reality. If we let go of this deception – this dualist fallacy of domination of man over machine (or vice versa) – it may be possible to come to terms with the world we are a part of in ways that are less about effects, things and what *happens*, more about process, practice and what *can be done*.

The key to this book is the question of how we can understand ourselves and the world we live in if we accept, if only for a moment, that we do not live *with*, but *in*, media. Media, to most people, belong to the realm of the unreal, or less real. What if this exclusive orientation to the alterity of (reality in) media acts as a crutch rather than a tool for living our lives more ethically and aesthetically? Instead of fusing the horizons of media and life, it seems as if we invest all our time in keeping them separate. By way of a first step and chapter in this book, I therefore unpack the history of man–machine separation, while at the same time highlighting how media life was always already firmly established in our sensemaking practices of the world and our role in it.

The second issue I faced was how to bring media back into our awareness without simply stating that one needs to look more closely at media – which would maintain their otherness. By adopting an archaeological approach to media in conjunction with a social history of dominant media species – the television and the mobile phone – I suggest in the second chapter that the key to understanding media is to emphasize not their *difference* but their *disappearance* from our lives. This amounts to a paradox: the more media dematerialize, the more people seem to be talking about media and what they mean to us. From a media-life point of view I engage this enigma by emphasizing how, through our apparent

need for media in order to express anything about media, the intense discussions about the role of media in people's lives are symptomatic of the mediatization of both individuals and society.

As we lose ourselves to technology, what happens next? The conflation of technology with technique, and of media with being mediated tends to be viewed with apprehension. Surely, the cold machines of media are alien to all that we consider as life? Yet, our media come very much alive in accounts of what it is like to live among them. Such an existence engulfed in media seems to mean we are perpetually caught in what has been aqueously described as a communicational *bubble* filled with the *foam* of media.[2] Indeed, "we swim in an ocean of media," as a headline in the *Christian Science Monitor* (of September 28, 2005) reads in a report on people's expanding media use. Splashing around in open water makes it hard to notice what is going on around you, on shore and elsewhere, let alone to take in the plights of other human beings. These liquid lamentations pervade much of the otherwise prudent thinking on media and everyday life. I try to take up this challenge in chapter 3 by arguing that there is no *necessary* relationship between the technological and the social. The relations that do exist are clearly both structural – machines are always *social* as much as they are *technical* – and highly dynamic; living in media is not the same for everyone.[3]

Just like human beings, media have both traits and states. One of the key qualities of our media is their uncanny capacity for recording and storing everything we do with them. A media life can be seen as living in the ultimate archive, a public library of (almost) everything, embodying a personalized experience of all the information of the universe. At the same time, in media life the archive is alive, in that it is subject to constant intervention by yourself and others. In the absence of all-seeing librarians or neatly categorized compendiums, the only way we can make sense of ourselves and each other in media is by carefully, and continuously, checking each other out. This is the theme of the fourth chapter, as the age-old premise of a *Big Brother*-like surveillance society comes full circle in a media world of massive mutual monitoring, where everyone is (or can be expected to be) watching everyone else.

If we live in media, we are in the process of co-creating a society particular to the media of our time that are always already remediations of earlier technologies and societies: never the same, always similar. In chapter 5, I address the constituent elements of a society in media by suggesting that it resembles a world after the zombie apocalypse. Like zombies, we lose our sense of ego and individuality, as we are collectively lost in our technologies. Whether through watching the same or similar television shows regardless of where we are in the world, or simply by logging on to the global grid of the "network of networks" that is internet, we are – again, much like zombies – irreducibly plugged into a worldwide flow of data, information, techniques and technologies in which distinctions between private and public, as well as between social isolation and cohesion, become symbiotic rather than dichotomic. Like zombies, we cannot seem to get enough of media – even though there does not seem to be a collective or consensual agenda as to where we are going. As Sonia Livingstone suggests with regard to the motivation of a society in media: "First, the media mediate, entering into and shaping the mundane but ubiquitous relations among individuals and between individuals and society; and second, as a result, the media mediate, for better or for worse, more than ever before."[4] Zombies are similarly driven – even the amputation of limbs does not tend to stop them – yet seemingly without creative impulse (other than feasting on our brains). Beyond metaphor, thinking about media zombies is instrumental to digging deeper, going beyond the surface of media and life: looking for ways in which we can theorize conjunctions of humanity and technology that highlight how a society in media is at once individual and interconnected as it is both embodied and virtual. This would hopefully open social reality up for the kind of plasticity and malleability of a world we are used to in media: whether by wielding a remote control or by re-arranging hardware, by clicking a mouse or by re-programming software, reality (in media) is open source.

If our sense of the real is experienced in media, how can we think of media as elements of our lives that can help us to get closer to reality? This dilemma is at the heart of the sixth chapter, where I question the kinds of connections we have with each other and ourselves in media, and try to move beyond either postmodern or existentialist frames for what is (or may be) real. Our lifeworld – the world we experience most directly, instantly and without reservation – is irreversibly mediated. It confronts us with endless versions of ourselves and everyone else. There certainly seems to be too much information available – to us as well as about us. In media life it is pertinent to explore how one can derive value from mediated oversharing and overexposure. Such value may not only be affective or perceptual. The seventh chapter explores evolutionary readings of media life, showing how contemporary discourse about the skills and competences one needs to navigate a mediated lifeworld signposts multiple media literacies as *survival* values. The solution is not, as has been suggested as far back as in the immediate response to Charles Darwin's *On the origin of species* (1859), to wage war on machines to prevent them from evolving beyond us. It is by *becoming* media we enhance our fitness for survival.

In the eighth and final chapter, I tie together all the elements of my exploration of life as lived in media through the diagnosis of a Truman Show Delusion by American psychiatrists Joel and Ian Gold, who suggest that classical syndromes such as narcissism and paranoia in combination with pervasive information technologies, in the context of a media culture where the boundaries between the physical and virtual world are blurring, have produced a new type of psychosis. What makes their analysis fit this book is the conclusion that this delusion can best be understood as an extreme manifestation of what most people feel. In media life, the world can certainly seem like a television studio as in the *Truman Show* movie (from 1998), with the significant difference that there is *no exit*. The question is therefore not how to avoid or destroy the media in our lives – we should rather investigate what Truman Burbank could do if he decided to stay inside of his fully mediated life. For one, he would be able to see himself live – and, if need be, adapt and evolve accordingly. This evolutionary process necessarily involves an awareness of how we are interconnected (in media), and therefore requires a sense of responsibility towards each other and ourselves that necessarily moves beyond the real or perceived manifestations of our divine machines. In other words: as Truman, we do not just have to perform for the cameras – the cameras can also perform for us. Whether we like it or not, I think we are slowly but surely becoming information players and creators rather than simply those who are expected to work with the information that is given to us. We can indeed create art with life. In media, that is.

Regarding art, please note the artwork in this book, designed by Dutch multimedia artist and web developer Miek van Dongen (miek.org). Miek is a lifelong friend with whom I share many sources of inspiration. When starting the media life project, I asked her to do the same in a series of drawings that would be independently featured throughout the book. Her pieces do not necessarily illustrate specific points in my argument, and should be seen as autonomous artworks reflecting elements of life as lived in media.

Notes

1 www.ubishops.ca/baudrillardstudies/vol1_2/genosko.htm. For all URLs cited in this volume, the date last accessed is February 1, 2012.
2 These terms for example used by Patrice Flichy in his *Une histoire de la communication moderne* (Paris: La Découverte, 1991), and in Adrian Mackenzie's *Wirelessness* (Cambridge, MA: MIT Press, 2010).
3 Source: Gilles Deleuze and Claire Parnet, *Dialogues II* (New York: Columbia University Press, 1987).
4 Sonia Livingstone, On the mediation of everything. *Journal of Communication* 59(1) (2009), 1–18.

Media Life

where we go beyond human–machine differences and focus on living a good media life

Wandering through the streets of Amsterdam, Johannesburg and Los Angeles, one cannot help but witness media life everywhere. The way people move through public space while wearing or wielding private media (such as mobile phones, digital cameras, and portable music players). How town precincts, historic buildings, parks and monuments get signposted by brightly colored maps urging onlookers to visit websites for more information. Restaurants that label their menus with pictures of delicacies next to clothing stores that blare out tailor-made soundtracks to match their fashion profile. Explorers who navigate the urban jungle by moving from wireless internet hotspot to hotspot – coffeeshop, public library, pop-up store, hotel lobbies. Drivers in cars passing by interacting with talkative personal navigation systems, children on back seats dividing their attention between the images of the city whizzing by and a movie playing on front-seat-mounted screens. A street vendor conducting her business while tunes from a small transistor radio play in the background, the sounds competing with those from a group of busking guitarists across the street – amplified by mini portable electric loudspeakers.

Even though it may be possible to disentangle the tighly woven web of humans and machines at work in this scenario, none of these practices, activities and forms of communication takes place without media. The place of the city has become the space of media – not completely, not without problems, and most definitely not outside of such natural conditions as the sun in the sky and the concrete pavement under our feet. What guides our experience of this world are the ongoing interactions between their constituent elements: people, places and spaces, all of which both produced and consumed in media. This is a life as lived *in*, rather than *with*, media.

The world in media resembles what British media scholar Roger Silverstone (2007) appropriately labels a *mediapolis*: a comprehensively mediated public space where media underpin and overarch the experiences and expressions of everyday life. "The mediapolis . . . signals the presence in everyday life, both empirically and potentially, of that mediated space within which as participants we confront the world, and where, as citizens, we might confront each other" (111). In this space, media have become infinitely intertwined with every single way of being, seeing, moving and acting – without replacing the world of lived experience. It is one thing to describe a media life in terms of the kind of media people use, how people generally go about doing things with media, and how all of these practices are oriented around media. It is another thing, as Ien Ang articulates, to clarify and understand "what it means, or *what it is like*, to live in a media-saturated world" (1995: 72; italics in original). This is not a life simply lived with more media than before the age of internet and mobile telephony. It is a way of living that fuses life with material and mediated conditions of living in ways that bypass the real or perceived dichotomy between such constituent elements of human existence.

A media life is much more than just having an endless variety of electronic gadgets at our disposal, spending a lot of time watching television and surfing the web, and being confronted with networked technologies when we check-out at the store or when we drive new cars. What Russian new-media artist and theorist Lev Manovich headlines as "the practice of everyday (media) life" (2009: 319) has all kinds of consequences for the way we look at the world, and how we are inclined or supposed to make sense of it. Manovich suggests this is a life of constant communication and conversation, part of a reality that is supposedly hackable and remixable by everyone, that is therefore always dynamic, unpredictable and permanently under construction. It forces each and every one of us to reconstruct our lifestyles to adapt to a world where the results of our actions are almost impossible to foresee, given that we live in a world that is inextricably networked, confronting everyone with an almost limitless supply of fragile forms of reality and truth – simply by switching on a radio or television, by consulting a website or opening an e-mail. As German philosopher Peter

Sloterdijk (2004) argues, the bubble of everyday life in media is instantly globalized as well as deeply provincial, where people – because of what colleague and countryman Ulrich Beck sees as a process of "ironic-tragic" (2009: 54) individualization – have to figure everything out on their own, fend for themselves, and are left to their own devices to find the social in an otherwise seemingly fragmented and atomized world.

Continuing with the theme of a suggested or expected malleability of the individual in everyday media life, Danish media scientist Lars Qvortrup (2003) proposes that our media life takes place in the context of a *hypercomplex* world in which social complexity is the cardinal challenge of our current society. It is not just that the world is complex – people observe their own lives and those of people around them (including those whose lives they witness in media) as ever more complex. The only way to survive, Qvortrup states, is to strive for a global dynamic state of equilibrium in which mechanisms and procedures for mutual observation and communication are developed. Italian feminist theorist Leopoldina Fortunati adds that the ever expanding range of choices people have in their communicative contexts – switching back and forth from body-to-body communication to mediated forms of interaction – "is intimately connected to management of complexity of everyday life. This complexity makes it increasingly necessary for us to resort to artificiality and to underdeveloped 'naturalness' of mediated communication" (2005: 56). In this world digital media operate as complexity-management mechanisms that are instrumental both in promoting the complicated and often problematic aspects of a globalized, individualized and networked world, and in providing the tools necessary to tackle such difficulties. The profound role media play in managing life's complexities disappears in this process. The embrace of multiple realities (and ontologies) as the byproduct of media life – as the inevitable consequence of a worldview articulated with media – is reminiscent of Jean Baudrillard's treatise "Simulacres et Simulation" (1981), in which he poses that people, when faced with the ubiquity and pervasiveness of a massively mediated reality, cannot meaningfully take on such a system with something *outside* of media. As Fortunati signals, once we turn to media "to patch up the rips and holes in the net of our social relations" (2005: 57), at some point it becomes impossible to disentangle whether we use media, or media use us. All of this does not necessarily mean there is no more truth or reality, or that our world today is unavoidably multifarious or complex. A media life suggests that the ways we experience, make sense of and act upon the world (including ourselves) are always already tied up in media. In this process we *become* media.

Caught in the grip of the immediate

If everyday life can be seen as a moral and social space where people create and sustain a common humanity, writes Silverstone, the interactive, live and immediate nature of contemporary media and their profound role in shaping and being shaped by the relations between fellow human beings "not only preserve separation in the same breath as they appear to deny it, but such illusory connection has significant consequences for how we understand the world, and above all how we relate to the mediated other in a world where more and more of our significant others are indeed mediated" (2002: 769). John Tomlinson comes to similar conclusions in his discussion of *telemediatization*, which he defines as the more or less immediate "reach of global connectivity into everyday experience, and the 'accessing of the world' by locally situated individuals" (2007: 156). For Tomlinson our teleme-diated practices are both discrete – texting, calling, watching television, surfing the Web – and integrated with lived experience. Such immediacy does seem to be the benchmark for understanding our time in media. In the second volume of his trilogy on "Technics and Time" (2009[1996]), French philosopher Bernard Stiegler proposes that the essential nature

of instantaneity and speed in digital communications profoundly disorientates us, as it dislocates our experiences from
temporal and spatial contexts, reducing all daily situations in
the context of mediated interaction to a direct and real-time
present governed by technology.

What thinkers such as Stiegler and Tomlinson advocate
is a kind of detachment from the seductions and desires of
the here-and-now so readily supplied in media. Perhaps
we are, as Paul Auster subtly notes in his short story "The
Locked Room" (1990[1986]), living "too fully in the grip of
the immediate" (251) to truly appreciate and take responsibility for the wants and needs we act out in media. American
writer and poet Hakim Bey proposes a counter-philosophy of
immediatism, suggesting that the mediation of all experience
alienates us increasingly from the directness of "smell, taste,
touch, the feel of bodies in motion," suggesting that media
"make great toys, but terrible addictions" (1994).[1] Ironically,
his portrayal of a life experienced direct and unmediated, for
which "the past [and our imagination regarding the future]
can be ransacked," resembles the very qualities of the immediate that a media life requires, or at least exemplifies. In the
words of Spanish sociologist Manuel Castells (2010[1996]),
part of the material foundation of media culture is our experience of *timeless time* – where simultaneity and timelessness
both benchmark social reality:

> On the one hand, instant information throughout the globe,
> mixed with live reporting from across the neighborhood,
> provides unprecedented temporal immediacy to social
> events and cultural expressions . . . On the other hand, the
> mixing of times in the media, within the same channel of
> communication and at the choice of the viewer/interactor,
> creates a temporal collage, where not only genres are mixed,
> but their timing becomes synchronous in a flat horizon, with
> no beginning, no end, no sequence. (491–2)

Beyond problematizing or celebrating the timeless time
of media life, the premise of living immediacy should not

be seen as uniquely produced by our current immersion in media. If anything, living in media exposes us to a real-time rendering of life, at times collapsing or expanding the boundaries between past, present and future. Friedrich Nietzsche, in the second of his series of essays titled *Untimely meditations*, forcefully distmantled the notion of humanity as created by its history. Instead, the German philosopher passionately argues for a life based on "a principle of mediated immediacy" (Safranski, 2003: 131), in which one would live unshackled and unsubdued by the forces of a "consumptive historical fever."[2] In his essay, published in 1874, Nietzsche indeed seems to predict (and, dare I say, prefer) media life:

> The time will come in which people wisely refrain from . . . the history of mankind, a time in which people in general no longer consider the masses but individuals once again, who construct a sort of bridge over the desolate storm of becoming. These individuals do not set out some sort of process, but live timelessly and contemporaneously; thanks to the history which permits such a combination, they live like the republic of geniuses.

Life in the media city

The themes of instantaneity, connectedness, (spaceless) space and (timeless) time as constituent elements of media life get taken up by Alex de Jong and Marc Schuilenburg of Dutch urban design platform Studio Popcorn in their book *Mediapolis* (2006), discussing how "the geographical space of the city must be regarded as an open field or as a medial infrastructure that can constantly actualize itself" (15). With over 60 percent of the world's population expected to be living in urban areas by 2030, it is safe to say the mediapolis of De Jong and Schuilenburg represents the dominant context for life for human beings on this planet. When coupled with statistics on the global use of mobile phones, this context of media life seems somewhat paradoxical. Urban life on the one hand suggests being particular to a physical place and proximate location, while at the same time the mode of mediated existence for most people seems more and more mobile, dynamically connected in virtual or otherwise placeless space. Brazilian media scholar Adriana de Souza e Silva (2004) talks about the way people experience this kind of mobile media life as producing a hybrid space, because mobile devices stretch connections between physical and digital spaces, embedding media in everyday outdoor activities and vice versa. In subsequent work, De Souza e Silva (with Daniel Sutko, 2009) expand the notion of hybrid space to consider urban settings broadly as digital cityscapes: places where one's experience of buildings, neighborhoods and the hustle and bustle of street life cannot be seen as separate from a direct engagement with media. One can think of countless everyday encounters with media that somehow seem to structure the way we move through the world – from ubiquitous surveillance cameras in public areas to the use of radio-frequency identification tags on our groceries and identity documents; from more or less interactive screens everywhere (telling us where to go and what to do) to the way people navigate the world using the textual (SMS), visual (maps) and aural (music and voice) features of mobile devices.

A mediated life is not just structured symbolically by omnipresent and pervasive media – it is also arranged through the technological infrastructures in our lives. The history of urban architecture is a poignant example of the ongoing convergence of medial and structural interfaces in the planning, design and execution of people's private and public living environments. As society got increasingly mediated, the twentieth century saw a rapid rise of *urban containers* as the prime areas for working, living and playing in cities around the world, embodying a near-complete convergence of such foundational elements of everyday life into a singular space (sometimes even a single building). Swiss architect Le Corbusier (real name: Charles-Édouard Jeanneret) coined such completely self-contained living communities as *living machines*, combining "living, working, moving and exercising the body and the mind" in the same space.[3] In his 1923 manifesto "Towards a new architecture" Jeanneret considered not just the city, but also each and every house as a machine for living, emphasizing functionality (often associated with machines and technology) as well as beauty. For the modernist architect, technologies and machines were full of ethical and aesthetic promise, enabling a more efficient and both physically and spiritually engaged society.

In 1967 American architect Charles Moore explored the emergence of a technological society and its impact on architecture in an essay exquisitely titled "Plug it in, Rameses, and see if it lights up, because we aren't going to keep it unless it works," hinting at the impermanent and instantaneous nature of life in the context of (new) media. Referring to the work of media theorist Marshall McLuhan, Moore suggested that "We have, as we all know, instant anywhere, as we enjoy our capacity to make immediate electronic contact with people anywhere on the face of the globe. . . . Our new places, that is, are given form with electronic, not visual glue" (2004[1967]: 152). Similarly, Luxembourgian urban planner Léon Krier in 1977 called for the reconstruction of cities into urban quarters, which he called cities within the city. Such ideas have been taken up by contemporary urban developers to indeed create cities within a city: complexes of one or several buildings, generally consisting of shopping, entertainment and recreational facilities, offices, restaurants, hotels and residential space linked via concrete pathways and electronic access points.

Designing cities within cities is a form of urban planning popular throughout Asia. The Japanese enclave of Akiba, part of Tokyo, is a particularly salient example of urban media life in action.[4] Akiba is known as Akihabara Electric City, a district that is dominated by stores dedicated to consumer electronics and all forms of Japanese pop culture, with bars named after (and designed as) watering holes famous from television, film, anime and comic books, and where locals and visitors routinely dress up like characters from video games. Lonely Planet's Matthew Firestone describes the bewildering experience of traversing this place: "With its street touts hawking cheap goods, electronic bells ringing with inimitable sound and fury, geeks of all ages decked out in anime garb, and a frenetic street scene of lights, beeps and endless pedestrian traffic, Akihabara can quickly overwhelm the senses" (2008: 67).

Akiba is most decidedly a physical place – yet everything it refers to exists in media. In this sense, the example of Akiba is an extreme reflection of German philosopher Friedrich Kittler's observation that the city itself is a medium, considering that the primary purpose of the city is to record, transmit and process information (about its locations and networks, its culture, its people and things). None of its inhabitants still has a comprehensive, direct or lived experience of the city as a whole – by and large its existence gets exclusively established through media. "Only an observer from an airplane or skyscraper . . . can recognize once more behind the universal discrete street machine, that analog or continuous flow of vehicles, which once was called traffic, but since has come to be known as frequency" (1996[1988]: 723–4). To Kittler, the city is the formatting of its traffic patterns (for example, through red, yellow and green lights), the distribution of information about itself (think about street signs, directories and maps), and eventually becoming the realization of Lewis Mumford's original proposal for an "invisible city": one that exists only in the imagination and on the screens of the newly established mass medium of his time – television. Mumford witnessed the demise of the city, writing in 1961, and foresaw how this disappearance would come with an expectation of elasticity of its (lived) reality:

> [the Invisible City] is itself an expression of the fact that the new world in which we have begun to live is not merely open on the surface, far beyond the visible horizon, but also open internally, penetrated by invisible rays and emanations,

responding to stimuli and forces beyond the threshold of ordinary observation. Many of the original functions of the city, once natural monopolies, demanding the physical presence of all participants, have now been transposed into forms capable of swift transportation, mechanical manifolding, electronic transmission, worldwide distribution. (563)

Even though urban containers like Akiba can be seen as largely ephemeral and frenetically unreal, there are still people living there, buildings stand tall, and power lines connect everyone in both physical and virtual space. The city vanishes, yet remains. The city or urban district of today is thus perhaps best understood as at once contained and boundaryless. As media are used both to police its physical perimeters and to extend its digital horizon, it becomes possible to make the case that living in a city and urban region can be seen as both a condition and consequence of media life. As a condition, media supply the necessary framework for the urban container to exist, and as a consequence, the destabilizing lack of boundaries that media inspire can only be contained in the "walled garden" of a city within a city.

In a direct reference to media life, German urban sociologist Frank Eckardt and his colleagues suggest we should look at this at once virtual and physical urban space as a *media-city*, because "the social settings and spaces of the city are created, experienced, and practiced through the use and presence of new media" (2008: 7). In fact, the media-city is becoming a well-established form of urban planning and design, for example in the MediaCityUK complex of Salford City (started in 2007),[5] the development of Dubai Media City in the United Arab Emirates (from 2005 onwards),[6] mediacities in Qatar, Jordan and Egypt, as well as in Leipzig[7] and Berlin[8] in Germany. The plan for most of these places often seems exclusive to a group of people generally labeled as a creative class: professionals, generally young, middle-class and well educated, working across creative industries (including but not limited to fashion, design, software, television and film, computer games, and so on). In *The rise of the creative class* (2002), Florida suggests – with an uncanny reference to media life – that cities should transform themselves into *plug-and-play communities* in order to accommodate this affluent social group, allowing them to settle in quickly and without much effort.

Florida's influential advocacy of the contemporary media city as a plug-and-play community that caters to specific social groups belies the fact that most people living in urban areas are not necessarily part of any effortlessly mobile and creative clique, but are more likely to provide the hard labor required for them to do what they do. These people – frequently minorities, women and otherwise underpaid or even unpaid workers – cook, clean, build and demolish, repair and maintain, and provide care for offspring and the elderly. As the rapid movement of a global economy co-determines their work and lifestyle, they too get swept up in the transformation of cities taking place all over the world. Urban sociologist Saskia Sassen is careful to point out these and other critical issues in her discussion of global cities, illustrating how today's cities must be seen as transnational urban systems incorporating many different sociopolitical networks that contribute both to the centralization of international corporate power, as well as to promoting a diversity of alternate and critical supranational agencies. Such urban systems consist therefore not just of a range of distinct places within provincial regions and nation-states, but also of "an emergent horizontal multisited globality" (2006: 194) that stretches across such traditional boundaries, amplified by the very same telecommunications networks that provide the global economy with its power to shape the life of cities, and thus affect the lives of most people on the planet. Sassen's work on cities comes to conclusions similar to those of Tomlinson and Stiegler: our experience of space and place is both locally fixed and globally stretched by virtue of (and as a consequence of) media.

The digital and the physical

The way through and beyond the digital and the physical of everyday encounters can be found in media – in what urban planners such as Christian Licoppe (2009) coin as *hybrid ecologies* of contemporary cities, weaving together mobility and sociality, proximity and hospitality. William Mitchell offers how the interconnection of physical and digital lived experience has the potential to change the design strategies for urban settings to bring about new groundings and a renewed sense of place in the context of a constantly changing environment:

> Not so long ago, the inhabitants of cities physically searched for physical things, and electronically surfed for online information. Today, in addition, they may employ physical exploration and location-sensitive devices to get to geocoded digital information and take advantage of electronic guidance to assist in efficient location of physical things. (2004: 125)

In other words, it is crucial to understand media in this context as providing the grounding as well as groundlessness of lived experience. Urban computing scholar Malcolm McCullough is among those advocating that architecture should intersect with interaction design working towards what he calls a *digital ground*, arguing that the increasing pervasiveness of technology does not negate "the basic human need for getting into place" (2005: 172). In his later work (from 2010 onwards), McCullough suggests that architecture and media studies converge in an *ambient commons*: a way of conceptualizing and designing architecture based on media becoming so prevalent as to seem ambient (as in: contextual, tangible and persistent) – "as architecture becomes layered with media, and urbanism becomes an important frontier in information technology, is information environmentalism a reasonable concern?"[9]

The cross-linkage and mutual implication of the physical and the digital – what MIT's Beth Coleman (2011) articulates as *X-reality*: our experience of being in two places at once – can be established architecturally through designing deliberate interfaces between people, their portable devices and actual buildings. The N Building near the Tachikawa subway station in Tokyo provides a case in point. The building contains offices and shops, and features a barcode on the outside façade that people can take a picture of and upload to the building website, which then projects real-time information about the people and places inside the building onto the mobile phone screen. Qosmo – the company providing this *media architecture* – describes its vision as "one where the facade of the building disappears, showing those inside who want to be seen . . . we display information specific to the building in a manner in which the virtual (iPhone) serves to enhance the physical (N Building). Our goal is to provide an incentive to visit the space and a virtual connection to space without necessarily being present."[10]

The specter of realizing the city (or any other form of life for that matter) in real time through media haunts French urbanist and philosopher Paul Virilio, who in his work outlines an objection to a mediatized world determined by virtuality, variability and velocity up to the point of arriving everywhere and nowhere at the same time: "This is what the teletechnologies of real time are doing: they are killing 'present' time isolating it from its here and now, in favor of a commutative elsewhere that no longer has anything to do with our 'concrete presence' in the world, but is the elsewhere of a 'discreet telepresence' that remains a complete mystery" (1997[1995]: 10–11).

When the mediated real-time presence of the user gains the upper hand over the milieu of real space, Virilio predicts a disturbing architectural regression, a gradual disappearance of objects and places, making people oblivious to the world around them as they roam around the virtual. However, being everywhere virtually still requires people to be somewhere physically. Media life, in this context, can be seen as a perspectival attempt to bridge the gap between the supposed *nowhere* of media and *somewhere* of life. The places we inhabit, both physical and virtual, are not just temporary assemblies of people and things in a specific place, nor should they be considered to be exclusively disembodied practices existing somewhere in cyberspace. Space and place are best understood as under permanent construction (like any site online): something continuously and concurrently made, sustained, remixed and taken apart by the very people and things that make up that ecosystem. Until not so long ago, this was primarily a normative idea, a social theory for the way to critically consider the relationship between the individual and modern society, such as, for example, is presented in the work of German sociologist Georg Simmel, who in 1895 wrote that "Society, in its broadest sense, is found wherever several individuals enter into reciprocal relations" (54), thereby introducing a sense of *vitalism* into the social system of society. Simmel's account of society as the product of social action is significant for contemporary considerations of media life – where British media sociologist Scott Lash articulates that "Simmel's societalization . . . seems increasingly in the information age to be displaced by mediatization" (2010: 38).

Partly in response to metropolitan sprawl, less than adequate living conditions in mass cities and the seeming indifference of philosophers to the everyday predicaments of individuals in such contexts, Henri Lefebvre (1974) put forward the notion of space as being socially produced – with reference to both material and ethical conditions of (media) life. For Lefebvre, the city is an "information-based machine," consuming "truly colossal quantities of energy, both physical and human, and which is in effect a constantly burning, blazing bonfire" (1991[1974]: 93). The social space of the city is not just the neat sum of its parts (people and things), argues Lefebvre: it is continually made and unmade, always changing, and never necessarily the end product of the intentions of its architects, builders or planners. In contemporary plans and designs for cities and urban living ecosystems, such ideas are put into practice, based on the notion of situational particularity (making places fit with the people and things that come together there), embedded media (with sensors, microchips and other artifacts integrated in building materials) and networked connectivity (hybrid spaces enabling interactions between people and things regardless of place), all in the context of an expectation of elasticity extending well beyond the role of human interaction to include our fusion with the living machine of the (urban) environment.

The paradox between living in a place and living in media is not a contradiction at all – if we just proceed to make whatever we consider to be a place subject to the same rules that media abide by. These are the groundbreaking rules outlined by Lev Manovich, making reality subject to negotiation, hackability and remixability. Paraphrasing the work of American communication scholars Gina Neff and David Stark, a media life seems to be premised on an experience of reality that is in a *permanently beta* state, affording "the possibility of influencing which values are encoded into organizations and technologies – and for users to incorporate their values into the structures around them" (2004: 186). A media-life reality brings the dynamic, unpredictable and underdeterminedness of any reality into sharper focus.

Anthropotechnologies, humachines, inforgs and the posthuman

Refrigerators with television screens included so you can watch high-definition TV in your kitchen, toothbrushes with built-in music players so you can literally hear tunes in your head when cleaning your teeth, and sneakers that post "step" to microblogging site Twitter every time you take a step[11] are not science-fiction products that people marvel at – they are cute examples of embedded technologies that seem quite common in the present framework of life. In a speech in September 1999 entitled "Regeln für den Menschenpark"

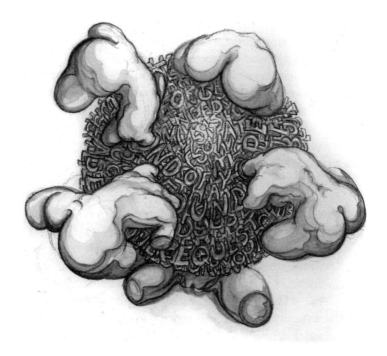

(my translation: "Regulations for the human zoo"), Peter Sloterdijk warns against such extreme levels of comfort with media and machines. Sloterdijk sees the ongoing integration of people and their media as a slippery slope towards an ecology of *anthropotechnologies* wherein human beings in the end decide – without much care or reflection – about natural selection through the intervention of biotechnologies. American songwriter, science-fiction author and media theorist Paul Levinson observes the same phenomenon with optimism, declaring how success in the evolution of media is premised on their anthropotropic development – that is, media necessarily becoming increasingly human in their performance, which in turn produces newer, and better, media (2009: 187–8).

Levinson and Sloterdijk may see nothing but hope or despair in the ongoing fusion between people and technologies, but

both recognize the inevitability of such synthesis. When thinking about the context and consequences of living *in*, rather than
with, media, one indeed conceives of a life with and through,
rather than next to or beside technology. In an interview with
Wired magazine in 1997, David Cronenberg – director of several films in which technology and the human body fuse such
as *Videodrome* (1983) and *eXistenZ* (1999) – is asked whether
he embraces or abhors technology. Cronenberg answers that
"Technology is not the name-less other. Technology 'R' Us: to
embrace technology is to embrace, and face, ourselves. This
we must do, and fearlessly."[12]

The available evidence suggests that people generally
absorb technology rather fearlessly indeed, often passionately appropriating the hardware and software of media in
ways not necessarily intended by their designers and manu-
facturers. Surveys in the United States by the Pew Research
Center[13] and the Kaiser Family Foundation,[14] across Europe
by various Eurobarometer studies,[15] and on a global scale
by market research firms such as Nielsen and Comscore, as
well as through the United Nations and the Organization
for Economic Co-operation and Development (OECD), consistently report on ever-increasing and tremendous varieties
of uses of all kinds of media by people around the world.
Life without media seems impossible to fathom for many
– especially when it comes to children, adolescents and college students. Responding to such reports in the United
States, child and adolescent psychologist Dave Verhaagen told
national newspaper *USA Today* (on February 2, 2010) that
media technology is "simply a part of their DNA, it shapes
everything about them."[16] Similarly, Michael Rich, a pediatri-
cian and director of the Center on Media and Child Health
in Boston, is quoted by the *New York Times* (on January 20,
2010) as saying that, with media use so ubiquitous, it is time
to stop arguing over whether this is good or bad and accept it
as part of children's environments, "like the air they breathe,
the water they drink and the food they eat."[17]

Media as part of our genes, our food and every other "natural" element of life may seem like a far-fetched notion. This may be so – but it is an old one. In the earliest examples of currently ubiquitous genetically engineered life forms, computer-driven factory production, hand-sized video cameras and self-moving (auto-mobile) machines, biologist and feminist theorist Donna Haraway saw the rise of new, boundaryless forms of life and culture that ultimately force us to redefine what it means to be human: "By the late twentieth century, our time, a mythic time, we are all chimeras, theorized and fabricated hybrids of machine and organism; in short, we are cyborgs" (1990: 150).

Cyborgs, or cybernetic organisms, were originally concretely considered as people prepared for space travel and as a response to the need to adapt the human body to any potential environment. Discussing various options at a May 1960 conference on psychophysiological aspects of space flight, scientist/musician Manfred Clynes and psychiatrist Nathan Kline proposed the term *cyborg*, describing such an "exogenously extended organizational complex" as someone whose "robot-like problems are taken care of automatically and unconsciously, leaving man free to explore, to create, to think, and to feel" (1995[1960]: 30–1). This notion of cyborgs immediately led to excited headlines on page 31 of the *New York Times* (published May 22, 1960): "SPACEMAN IS SEEN AS MAN-MACHINE – scientists depict the human astronaut as component of a 'cyborg' system." Writing in *Playboy* magazine in July 1961 on the potential or perhaps even inevitable obsolescence of man due to increasingly versatile and intelligent machines, futurist Arthur C. Clarke took up Clynes and Kline's notion of the cyborg and extended it intentionally into the realm of media life: "One day we may be able to enter into temporary unions with any sufficiently sophisticated machines, thus being able not merely to control but to *become* . . . a TV network" (1964[1961]: 226; italics in original).

Cyborgs have been enthusiastically adopted by science-fiction writers and filmmakers, generally reducing the complexity of the cybernetic organism to a human body that includes some synthetic parts. We now know and sometimes fanatically support such infamous cyborgs as the Cylons (short for 'cybernetic lifeform nodes') in the *Battlestar Galactica* TV series and movies (in 1978, 1980 and 2004), the Terminators in the *Terminator* franchise of motion pictures and TV series (from 1984 to 2009) and the Borg collective as part of the *Star Trek* universe (originally appearing in 1989 in the second season of *Star Trek: The Next Generation*). Cyborgs such as Cylons, Terminators and the Borg are generally depicted as cold, heartless villains, murderers and assassins, reflecting some anxiety about human–machine convergence.

Like our general comfort with using all kinds of machines, a certain anxiety about man–machine hybrids is not new either, tapping into long-lasting worries about artificial and otherwise more or less lifeless humanoid beings such as, for example, those expressed in a satirical short story by Edgar Allan Poe titled "The man that was used up," first published in 1839 in *Burton's Gentleman's Magazine*.[18] In this story, Poe encounters a "singularly commanding" and "*remarkable* man – a *very* remarkable man" (1981[1839]: 364–5; italics in original): Brevet Brigadier-General John A.B.C. Smith. After thoroughly investigating the source of Smith's unrivalled perfection and enthusiasm for "the rapid march of mechanical invention" (366), he eventually is confronted in terror with Smith as nothing but "a large and exceedingly odd-looking bundle of something" (369) with arms, legs, shoulders, bosom, eyes, tongue and palate mechanically attached. Poe subtly exposes our unthinking fascination with technologies, while at the same time exploring the transformative capacity of human–machine hybridization.

Roughly two decades earlier, in 1816, German writer and composer Ernst Theodor Amadeus Hoffmann published a short story entitled "Der Sandmann"[19] that proved to be influential for many genres of art and scholarship dissecting the complex relationship between human and machine affinities, especially when it comes to the dearly affective nature thereof. Hoffmann's story centers on the rapturous love of the young poet Nathanael for Olimpia, the daughter of Spalanzani, a famous professor of physical sciences. Before falling in love with Olimpia, Nathanael was engaged to Clara, who "could by no means be called beautiful," and she "was no friend to muddle-headed enthusiasts" (1992[1816]: 99–100). Their happy engagement was roughly disturbed by the appearance of a figure of Nathanael's childhood nightmares: the Sandman, whom his parents invoked as a wicked man who steals the eyes of children who do not want to go to bed – but also a hideous figure Nathanael blames for causing his father's death.

After being confronted with this Sandman again as an adult, Nathanael turns inward, gradually becoming superstitious and paranoid – much to the frustration of the "cold, prosaic temperament" (101) of Clara. Eventually he runs away from Clara, accusing her of being an "accursed lifeless automaton!" (103). Soon thereafter he spots the "wondrously beautiful" (106) Olimpia – using a spyglass as an extension of his eyes to watch her as she sits at her bedroom window, day in and day out. He falls in love with her, especially after seeing her play the piano with great skill at a ball. After the ball, he gets a chance to dance with her, about which experience he notes that, though he considered himself a good dancer, "the peculiar rhythmic regularity with which Olimpia danced often disconcerted him and made him realize how badly he kept time" (109). Although other people warn him that Olimpia is nothing but a dummy, Nathanael proceeds to ask her hand in marriage. When he finally finds out – in a gruesome way – she is an automaton, Nathanael goes berserk. Luckily, he is captured and saved. He even gets back together with his beloved Clara. But in the end his past obsession catches up with him as he makes the dreadful mistake of looking at her through his old spyglass. Going mad, the "tormented, self-divided Nathanael" (118) jumps to his death from a tower on the town square.

The reason for this rather lengthy retelling of Hoffmann's horror story is not just because I am a fan of his work. As Steven Johnson (1997: 175) argues, "Der Sandmann" serves as the inspiration for such classics in the genre of mistaking machines for humans and the other way around, like the computer *Hal* in Arthur C. Clarke's 1968 novel *2001: A Space Odyssey* and Stanley Kubrick's film version of the same year, and the biologically engineered humanoids called replicants in Ridley Scott's film *Blade Runner* (1982; based on Philip Kindred Dick's 1968 short story "Do androids dream of electric sheep?"). At the heart of these stories is a recognition of the fact that man-machine hybrids are not just simply human bodies with synthetic elements attached, but rather should be seen as entities raising much more essential questions about what life is, and how we may never again be able to clearly distinguish between humans and machines once some kind of crossover is established. Hoffmann, who was not particularly fond of the established social order, or of the dominant intellectual elites of his time (neither those celebrating the rationalism of the Enlightenment nor the dreamers of the Romantics), favored a more hybrid and therefore rather unsettling reading of reality. Moving beyond all-too-easy categorizations of where media begins and life ends (and vice versa) opens the door for endless speculations about the validity of any and all categorizations of what is supposedly male or female, self and other, thing and not-thing . . . up to and including such metaphysical issues as truth or falsity, reality and unreality, and the taken-for-granted differences between media and life.

Taking issue with the terminology and all too often science-fiction-based vision of a "cyborged" humanity and focusing more on a lifelike interpretation of media, Italian philosopher Luciano Floridi wants us to talk about a future of *inforgs* instead, as "We are all becoming connected informational organisms (inforgs). This is happening not through some fanciful transformation in our body, but . . . through the reontologization of our environment and ourselves" (2007: 62). Instead of focusing on the either/or of cyborgs and inforgs, American cultural historian Mark Poster suggests we should rather talk about globally networked digital *humachines*, which represent "an intimate mixing of human and machine that constitutes an interface outside the subject/object binary" (2004: 318). Humachines are neither exclusively humans nor machines, Poster maintains, but rather must be seen as life forms for whom there is neither determinism by technology, nor freedom from machines.

Beyond the present-day specificities of cyborgs, inforgs and humachines, Katherine Hayles offers a bold suggestion: humans have always been posthuman. Her view of the posthuman takes as its point of departure the notion that the human body is "the original prosthesis we all learn to manipulate, so that extending or replacing the body with other prostheses becomes a continuation of a process that began before we were born" (1999: 3). For Hayles, the posthuman is a profoundly empowering concept, as it stretches human cognition across the man–machine divide, thereby profoundly extending one's range of understanding (and possibility of action). What is important about all these suggestions for the media-life argument is the deliberate consideration of both tangency and transitionality regarding the boundaries between the physical and non-physical, between machines and humans. Manovich's rule of the remix for the practice of everyday (media) life is reflective of Haraway's observations about the inexorably recombinant nature of human–machine relationships, as well as Hayles' explanation of how we became posthuman: media and life are interconnected and independent, and in the process transform and become each other.

Prosthetic gods

Haraway, Poster, Floridi and Hayles are not the only, nor the first, theorists to consider the radical potential of questioning the traditionally absolute difference between people and things. Consider the opening sentences in Marshall McLuhan's seminal work, *Understanding media*, published in 1964: "During the mechanical ages we had extended our bodies in space. Today, after more than a century of electric technology, we have extended our central nervous system itself in a global embrace, abolishing both space and time as far as our planet is concerned" (2004[1964]: 3).

In 1967 McLuhan followed up with *The medium is the massage*, a partly graphic novel co-designed with Quentin Fiore, in which he states "All media work us over completely . . . they leave no part of us untouched, unaffected, unaltered . . . All media are extensions of some human faculty – psychic or physical" (26). Cinema, for example, can be seen as an extension of our dreams; the phonograph, an extension of song and dance; and, as seen in Hoffmann's tale "Der Sandmann," a spyglass is an extension of our eyes. Nicholas Gane and David Beer (2008: 39) point out how McLuhan seems to be a little inconsistent in his approach to the impact media supposedly have on us, as media working us over completely sounds decidedly less harmless than media as extensions of man. Such inconsistency is not unusual for McLuhan's work, and its apparency should not detract from the underlying attempt by the Canadian philosopher to address and make explicit the articulations of media with life. What McLuhan concretely offers, in terms of considering media life, is first and foremost the recognition that the impact of media goes beyond the content of the media. In other words: we should be keenly aware of the material dimension and technical infrastructure of media, as these shape whatever information is sent or received in fundamental ways. A second contribution of McLuhan's to understanding media life is his suggestion that media are not different from life, but should be seen as extensions of it in the broadest sense of the word: media amplify, accelerate, supercharge, enlarge, zoom in (or out), redact and bring life into focus.

Architect and urbanist Witold Rybczynski (1983) introduces more rich historical perspective on the boundary-crossing properties of technology and the human condition. Rybczynski opens his account with a reference to the work of Sigmund Freud, who, in his essay "Das Unbehagen in der Kultur" (translated as "Civilization and its discontents" and originally published in 1930), calls attention to how we invent and deploy all kinds of tools and appliances to overcome the imperfections of our body and mind. In doing so, human beings surround themselves with technologies that put them at farther removes from direct, un-mediated experience. The lived experience of being what Freud calls both "a feeble animal organism" (1930: 38) and a "prosthetic God" (39) can therefore be seen as filled with ambivalence and uncertainty.

Freud suggests that even what seems comfortably familiar and thus known to us becomes (or can become) profoundly unfamiliar, unsatisfying and even eerie when we look at it differently. From a psycho-analytical point of view, media can thus be seen as both that which provides us with comfort and entertainment, and that which reminds us (at times) of what to feel guilty about – for example our outsourcing of pleasure to machines. Extending Freud's essay, the further our immersion in media goes, the more powerful media can be as a source of fantasy or fear. Media can be seen as Freud's prostheses – alluringly augmenting life, and at the same time always ready to make us look at our world and ourselves differently, exposing us to the uncanniness of everyday life. The effort to look awry is something Slovenian philosopher Slavoj Žižek passionately promotes towards everything in life in order to highlight that our common tendency to consider things good, evil, true or false is really just a temporary compromise each of us makes in the daily struggle between what is real and what is clearly the realm of fantasy – between what something is and what it means to us. Unfamiliarity is built into everything that seems familiar, waiting to be exposed by looking at it differently. In media life, such ways of *Looking awry* (the title of Žižek's 1992 introduction to the influential work of French psychoanalyst Jacques Lacan) are omnipresent and impossible to avoid. It could be argued that a media-life point of view comes retrofitted with ways of looking awry – of seeing things we take for granted in different (and often disturbing) ways. Living a life in media exposes us to the uncanny nature of what Henri Lefebvre describes as the necessary diversity of *everydayness* (1987). Where Lefebvre considered the dominant media of his time – cinema and television – as diverting our attention away from the everyday, I would suggest that our present-day media also allow the opposite. This exposing (or bringing forth) of reality in media precipitates an integration between humanity, nature and technologies.

The ongoing fusion of information and organisms, of man and machine, and of media and life amplifies and accelerates a distinct notion of uncanniness in our daily perception of the world around us. In a 1919 essay titled "Das Unheimliche" (translated as "The uncanny"), Sigmund Freud mentions as his inspiration for discussing uncanniness – the often rather frightening aspect of being confronted with some-thing completely unexpected and unknown – feelings of uncertainty evoked by his reading of Hoffmann's short story about Nathanael, the lifeless (yet lifelike) doll Olimpia, and the scary Sandman. This is an early example of how the con-frontation with human–machine hybridization is uncanny, as it leaves in doubt where life begins and ends, how to make sense of this new device (or lifeform), and how to give mean-ing to our feelings and relationships with it. As in Nathanael's case, our relationship with technology in general and media in particular is intensely emotional and at the same time pro-foundly problematic to us. Freud, according to Rybczynski, sees technology as "really a set of artificial organs, extensions of our natural ones. He understood . . . that the relationship between ourselves and our tools is often blurred, and fre-quently intimate" (1983: 4). In a story reviewing a decade's worth of reports covering new technologies for the *New York*

Times (published on November 24, 2010), David Pogue considers as one of the most important insights about the role
of technology in people's lives the fact that "Today's gadgets
are intensely personal."[20] Whether it is an innate aspect of the
man–machine relationship, or something that is more or less
particular to the digitally networked, mobile and screen-based
devices so many people carry around these days, the associations between humans and their media are personal, affective
and intimate.

Intimacy between technologies and humans – between
media and life – leads Sherry Turkle to ask a fundamental question: "What kinds of people are we becoming as
we develop more and more intimate relationships with
machines?" (2005[1984]: 294). Rybczynski's take on this
issue is a challenging counter-question, one that seems
similar to the remarks made by Rich and Verhaagen when
they responded in the Winter of 2010 to the news of youths
spending every waking moment with media, sustaining an
argument that effectively critiques cultural anxieties regarding man–machine intimacies: "We claim that we are afraid
of becoming machinelike, but what if technology is actually
humanlike?" (Rybczynski, 1983: 226).

It is possible to argue that at the start of the twenty-first
century an either/or debate about the digital and the physical
has become empirically, as well as theoretically, rather unsus-
tainable. Given the arguments outlined here, I propose that
American media anthropologist Eric Rothenbuhler summarizes what should be considered to be the starting point for a
grounded discussion on media life: "media are something *we
live inside* as much as they are technologies we use for expression, information, influence, and entertainment" (2009: 280;
italics added).

Divine beings in a post-metaphysical world

Media as the air we breathe, as part of our genetic code, as extensions of our bodily and sensory being, as the inter-changeable code of technology and biology – it certainly seems like we have arrived at a crucial point in time, where an unmediated life is inconceivable – even impossible. Media and life are mutually implicated. Any technological system is also a social system, as Austrian media academic Christian Fuchs notes throughout his work on social theory and (new) media, as technology enables and constrains human com-munication, while at the same time human actors re-create and shape technology by producing, communicating and consuming it (2008: 122). Any and all media must there-fore be seen as techno-social or sociotechnical systems – as determining what people can say and experience, while at the same time being subject to (often subtle) transforma-tions originating from the social process of their everyday use. Dutch philosopher Jos de Mul concurs, adding how media not only come between society and us, but also play a funda-mental role in how we come to understand ourselves. De Mul defines media as "interfaces that mediate not only between us and our world (designation), but also between us and our fellow man (communication), and between us and ourselves (self-understanding)" (2009: 95). A similar argument comes from Scott Lash, who asks what happens when forms of life go technological – answering that making sense of the world through technological systems does not mean we become cyborgs but rather *interfaces* of humans and machines, that "are conjunctions of organic and technological systems" (2001: 107). Lash emphasizes an awareness of the various meeting points between bodily and machinic systems as the best way to make sense of media life.

Steven Johnson (1997) goes as far to suggest society can be characterized as operating increasingly on the basis of an *interface culture* – a way of being that is premised on the

ways in which people understand information and communication as it comes to them (and how they participate in it)
using media. The best example of such a powerful interface
is the avatar – the virtual representation of you. The avatar is
a term derived from Hinduism, where it refers to the incar-
nation of a Supreme Being. In the online multiplayer game
Ultima (1997), the avatar is the embodiment of a set of ethical
guidelines and virtues. Particular to the avatar is a potential
for customization to suit individual preferences – an avatar
thus can be seen as a more completely malleable augmentation of someone's offline identity. It is quite normal to have
and maintain multiple avatars in everyday media life, where
one's mediated identity can consist of a buddy icon in Instant
Messaging, a profile picture used in company intranets, and
a character in three-dimensional (3D) computer role-playing
games like *World of Warcraft* or *Everquest*, or in non-gaming
environments such as *There* or *Second Life*. The keys to avatars
as technological forms of life are their divine qualities: avatars
are omnipotent, omnipresent and omniscient. Avatars, unlike
human beings, are special, because they can be anyone, go
anywhere, find out and know about anything – depending on
the parameters of hardware (technological infrastructure and
devices), software (code, protocols and programming) and
– as Richard Doyle (2003) articulates about a state of bioin-
formatic living – *wetware* (people as embodying both physical
and mental interactions in media).

Looking at the world through the interface of the avatar, it is
difficult to escape the conclusion that the premise of a media
life seems to turn people into gods. Returning back to the
work of Freud, one has to acknowledge that his recognition of
man as a prosthetic God foresaw this development. I want to
look more closely at what Freud said at the time, as it provides
profound insight into our identity in media life:

> If we go back far enough, we find that the first acts of civi-
> lization were the use of tools . . . With every tool man is
> perfecting his own organs, whether motor or sensory, or

is removing the limits to their functioning . . . by means of the telescope he sees into the far distance . . . With the help of the telephone he can hear at distances which would be respected as unattainable even in a fairy tale . . . these things do not only sound like a fairy tale, they are an actual fulfillment of every – or almost every – fairy-tale wish . . . Long ago he formed an ideal conception of omnipotence and omniscience which he embodied in his gods . . . To-day he has come very close to the attainment of this ideal, he has almost become a god himself . . . Future ages will bring with them new and probably unimaginably great advances in this field of civilization and will increase man's likeness to God even more. (1961[1930]: 37–9)

Perhaps being or feeling divine is not that far-fetched a premise in media life, considering the rather impressive array of powers we have at our disposal to manipulate and shape our own reality: the computer mouse, the remote control, the joystick and the smartphone are but some relatively simple examples of the magical instruments people wield on a day-to-day basis. Ours is a post-metaphysical and anthropo-technological time, argues Peter Sloterdijk, in which technologies (media) do not dominate man (life) – instead, biology and technology are fused in a symbiotic venture, and in this context people have to figure things out on their own, as groundless as their avatars, and similarly grounded by the constraints of hardware, software and wetware. In a fascinating concretization of this abstract premise, Prime Sense – an Israeli company responsible for developing the motion sensor chip for Microsoft's Xbox 360 Kinect game console, allowing hands-free gaming using your body movements to manipulate content on the screen – in 2008 advertised its technology with the slogan: "Be Your Avatar."[21]

Sloterdijk's observation about our near-complete self-reliance in this context must be taken seriously, for how do we know exactly what we are doing in media? This question could be framed as simply as, for example, asking yourself how you decide what information – pictures, statements, videos – you select for inclusion on your Facebook page, who to friend or defriend (a term that the *Oxford English Dictionary* first formally included in 2010). The study of media, self and society should be considered as the study of our *informational universe*, as Wolfgang Hofkirchner, Christian Fuchs and Bert Klauninger (2005) argue, where the questions we ask of life must include what we know of the world (ontology), how we know about the world (epistemology) and what the world should be like (praxeology). Their comprehensive appeal reminds me of an earlier essay by political scientist Langdon Winner who, while commenting in 1995 on debates in the US about the future of telecommunications technology, wrote: "it is evident that, for better or worse, the future of computing and the future of human relations – indeed, of human being itself – are now thoroughly intertwined . . . Choices about computer technology involve not only obvious questions about 'what to do,' but also less obvious ones about 'who to be.'"[22]

Winner identifies the responsibility for scholars in this context as "helping a democratic populace explore new identities and the horizons of a good society." Roger Silverstone passionately argues that, as people have become dependent on media for the conduct of everyday life, any consideration of media must also be a normative one – as "The mediapolis is both a reality and an ambition" (2007: 186). When considering all elements and aspects of media life, it feels important to follow Silverstone's advice. As mentioned before, people, media and the places and spaces they inhabit not only are "tightly and dialectically intertwined" (5), but also are anything but neutral agents in the process of co-constituting everyday life. The convergence of media and life is contested and ongoing, and therefore it is a moral process. Such a process includes descriptions and explanations of how people and things are, and also how they should become. Facing profound challenges in the fields of computational biology, bioinformatics, embodied cognition and artificial life, Luis Rocha, Director of the international Computational Biology Collaboratorium, states that:

In the context of life, we do not want to be tied uniquely to carbon-based life, or life-as-we-know-it, but we also do not want life-as-could-be to be anything at all. The challenge lies precisely in finding the right amounts of systemhood and thinghood, as well as the interactions between the two, necessary for a good theory of life, real or artificial.[23]

Media life is not a question of technology, oor of human beings. Chilean biologist Humberto Maturana perhaps put it best in a 1997 essay on the question of whether we should see human beings as opposed to machines, or consider machines as instruments of human design: "The question that we must face is not about the relation of biology with technology . . . nor about the relation between knowledge and reality . . . the question that we must face at this moment of our history is about our desires and about whether we want or not to be responsible of our desires."[24]

At the heart of the project in this book is the question of what a good, passionate, beautiful and responsible media life looks like.

CHAPTER TWO

Media Today

where media organize all aspects of our everyday lives and disappear

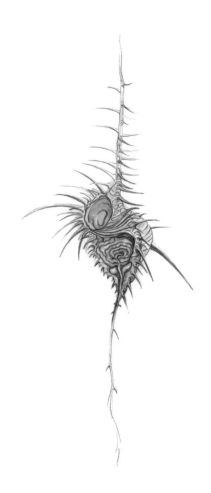

Writing in *Media Magazine* (published October 2005), market researcher Jim Spaeth claims that:

> Media has become the fabric of our lives. Once upon a time, our family and other social relations were the fabric of our lives, or at least that's the way the story goes. But in our postmodern era, nothing is real until it's on one of the major networks, cable news, the Internet, or another media feed. Proximity is nothing; connectivity is everything. We all know this to be true. Just look at that group of friends walking down the street "together": each one is on a cell phone with someone else. Or look at that individual walking alone, tethered to an iPod.[1]

In this description of what Spaeth calls "a day in the media life" media indeed seem to be everything and everywhere. In his account, media are first considered as the television, cell phones and personal computers. Second, media are the content and networked experiences one may find using such devices. Perhaps most significantly, media are seen as providing the fabric of people's lives – a claim echoed in Manuel Castells' account of the global network society we live in, in which media provide "the symbolic fabric of our life," working on our consciousness, providing "the raw material out of which our brain works" (2010[1996]: 365). The presumed role of media as part of our awareness of self and others, and thus providing the fabric of our lives, must be read in terms of what French sociologist Émile Durkheim originally coined as our collective consciousness: an awareness we share, which is "society living and acting within us" (1997[1893]: 84). Such an awareness is progressively produced by the various ways in which people interact, performing subtle yet pervasive routines and rituals that signal who we are and where we belong. Historically, the raw materials for providing the fabric of everyday life came from more or less formally organized groups in villages and townships across the countryside, and wards and parishes in the city, as well as by all kinds of guilds, clubs and trade unions. The design of living spaces – a market square as the heart of the city, the local pub and tea house as the pivotal places to socialize in public, a family room as the center of the homestead – additionally followed a logic of furthering social congregation, collective storytelling and shared narratives. The social and symbolic fabric of society or a particular group included all kinds of procedures and ceremonies intended to communicate to people what kind of community they were part of.

Community-confirming rituals not only include elections, carnivals and fairs, but also, and perhaps more significantly, consist of public torture and executions. The link between the death penalty, a society's social and symbolic fabric, and the premise of media life was established quite literally by Supreme Court Justice Samuel Alito in a public debate (on October 7, 2009) about whether videos depicting animal cruelty are protected as free speech under the US Constitution. As reported by numerous news organizations at the time, Justice Alito raised the issue of whether videos portraying humans being killed would be protected as well. In Alito's words: "People here would probably love to see it. Live, pay per view, you know, on the Human Sacrifice Channel."[2]

Alito's remarks have precedent. Well into the nineteenth century people accused of serious crimes were publicly punished; women would be burned at the stake, while men were hanged, drawn and quartered. Today, numerous countries and regions in the world continue this tradition – such as stoning in some parts of Africa and the Middle East, and capital punishment in over fifty countries worldwide (including the US and Japan). Although executions in most places are not public, they are usually attended by a small group of people and are reported on by local and national news organizations – in effect reminding people of the consequences of deviance from the group norm. In their research on crime, deviance, punishment and torture in the US in the seventeenth century and France in the eighteenth and nineteenth centuries, Kai Erikson (2004[1966]) and Michel Foucault (1995[1975]) show

how one of the functions of such often very public rituals was to convey what kind of people the audiences for such displays were supposed to be. With the advent of the industrial revolution and a corresponding process of worldwide urbanization, such stable markers of a society's fabric began to give way. Foucault suggests that, in the place of these powerful yet unreliable ceremonies – as the crowd might actually sympathize with the torture victim – came a strict regime of systematic (re-)training of communities by all kinds of social institutions: prisons, schools, universities, hospitals, the military, up to and including the highly formalized and neatly cubicled office space of today. Rather than being born into a community, people were now disciplined by institutions to become cogs in the machine of a collective consciousness-providing overarching social structure.

In more recent times, the consensus about social institutions and town squares providing the principal fabric of the communities we live in has given way to more critical analyses of how a sense of community in a post-industrial world is primarily established through our social imagination, fueled by and expressed symbolically in media. Greek philosopher Cornelis Castoriadis developed such a notion of a society's social imaginary in his *The imaginary constitution of society* (1975), emphasizing how our sense of self and society is subject to a process of permanent mediation. Eric Hobsbawn and Terence Ranger (1992[1983]) furthermore question what is considered traditional and rule-giving based on a presumably long historical trajectory, as these are often rather recent inventions by specific groups (such as political or religious organizations) to serve particular ends. Benedict Anderson (2006[1983]) similarly suggests that many, if not most, types of modern-day community with which people identify are wholly imagined, because these instances of shared identity and presumed social fabric are not based on everyday face-to-face interaction any more. All of this is not to say that the social fabric in media is just a figment of our imagination, governed by whim. The work of Canadian philosopher Charles Taylor (2002) points out that, while our conceptions of society may be imaginary, over the course of history such phantasmal perceptions come to be quite concrete – as, for example, embodied in our social institutions, and managed by the rule of law and common conventions (such as the market economy). What Taylor therefore introduces and makes relevant to concerns about media life is the realization that whatever goes for our social fabric is at once real *and* imaginary. In this sense, media enable our participation in the construction of reality, as they remind us of a social reality we are inevitably part of and give shape to (and, as Taylor would add, should be mindful and respectful of).

Throughout her work, Turkish political philosopher Seyla Benhabib adopts a parallel perspective on human cultures as intrinsically fluid and constantly changing, while at the same time reflective of particular places and peoples. What Benhabib (1992) signals is the continually constructed, permanently porous and hence always *unfinished* nature of the key elements that supposedly provide us with a coherent sense of who we are and where we belong. Taking the notion of society, tradition, community and culture as a social imaginary into the realm of the individual, British sociologist Anthony Giddens (1991) succinctly argues how, in our late modern times, identity itself has become a creative and reflexive project – something that is produced rather than given, continuously created by the individual instead of handed down through the generations. Much like that of culture and community, production of the self therefore takes on an ongoing, fragmented, always changing and, at the end of the day, precarious trajectory. Extending such insights to the everyday lived experience in today's *liquid modernity*, Polish social theorist Zygmunt Bauman considers how all of this produces "a permanently impermanent self, completely incomplete, definitely indefinite – and authentically inauthentic" (2005: 33).

Beyond the human realms of culture, community and identity lie the non-human underpinnings of our world: objects, organisms, technologies and the hardware and software of media. Just as the way society and identity are organized is at once real and imaginary, so is the matter that constitutes our universe. Political theorist Jane Bennett (2010) makes the case for a *vital materialism* in our consideration of contemporary society, forcefully arguing for a fused perspective on life and matter as both possessing agency and potential for action. For Bennett matter has a lively materiality that is "active and creative without needing to be experienced or conceived as partaking in divinity or purposiveness" (93). She counters claims that "only humans and God can bear any traces of creative agency" (120), pointing to the active role matter such as food, metals and electricity play in the transformation of the world and our experience of it. Feminist theorist and particle physicist Karen Barad offers an intriguing way past the life-and-matter dichotomy by proposing that the relationship between matter and culture is one of "agential intra-action" (2004: 814), as everything in the world acts upon everything else all the time, regardless of whether it is human or non-human (2007: 132ff.). She forcefully moves our thinking beyond the age-old distinction between reality (what something is) and representation (what it appears to be in media), remarking that there are only agential realist phenomena constituted out of dynamic relations between nature, the body and materiality. Barad's work shows that nothing is timeless or ahistorical, that everything is always iterative, performative and (thus) in a constant state of *becoming*.

With reference to media life, the work of Bennett and Barad falls within a cross-disciplinary tradition of theorizing about the relationships between nature and society, humans and things, or mind and matter towards a more messy, lively and altogether fused perspective. As Barad stipulates: "The point is not merely that there are important material factors in addition to discursive ones; rather, the issue is the conjoined material–discursive nature of constraints, conditions, and practices" (2004: 823). In a series of essays bundled in

We have never been modern (1993[1991]), French science and technology theorist Bruno Latour offers that our proclivity of neatly separating the natural, technological and social worlds is a particular feature of the modernist project, disempowering us from making sense of (or effectively dealing with) phenomena such as global warming and biotechnologies. Instead, Latour advocates a "nonmodern" constitution, premised on a "nonseparability of the common production of societies and natures" (141). A medial touchstone for this kind of symbiotic thinking about matter and life is provided by Friedrich Kittler. Like Latour, Bennett and Barad, Kittler is adamant about the agential potential of matter – which, in his argument, deliberately includes media. His media theory raises one's awareness about the fundamental force of media in shaping the social fabric and what we can say about it – power which only grows as we tend to ignore media when making sense of the world. To Kittler, "this crazy coincidence of forgetfulness with technological change" (2009: 26) that pervades the history of philosophy and social theory directly relates to "the exclusion of physical and technical media from questions of ontology" (23).

The deceptively simple statement that media provide the social fabric of everyday life therefore comes with a profound implication: it makes everything we associate with who we are, what we belong to and what our world is made of speculative. Given the ubiquity and pervasiveness of media, and considering their remixed and endlessly remixable qualities, American media literacy scholar Douglas Rushkoff finds it should come as no surprise that people increasingly see themselves not as consumers (or citizens), but rather as co-creators of society as "we begin to become aware of just how much of our reality is open source" (2003: 37).

An acute awareness of the permanent impermanence of our existence does not just belong to the realm of poets and philosophers. We are faced with the unsettling truth that none of us has a clear, stable and consensually certified grip on reality, and that this reality – while being most definitely real – in itself is quite lively indeed. This profound frustration is on brilliant display in the movie *A Few Good Men* (1992). Jack Nicholson's character – Colonel Nathan R. Jessup – is questioned in court by Lieutenant Daniel Kaffee (played by Tom Cruise). After a long drawn-out exchange, Kaffee finally exhorts "I want the truth!" – to which Jessup shouts "you can't handle the truth!" David Morley ties our failure to fully appreciate the complexities of daily life to technological forms, and suggests that in our daily efforts to naturalize and domesticate media we try to make life more manageable and therefore less threatening (2007: 212). Slavoj Žižek is among those who extend this argument to claim that it perfectly symbolizes our relationship with reality itself: we cannot handle its truth, it is always just beyond our grasp – so we unavoidably turn to media to take part in a social reality that approximates (but never completely resembles) the real. In other words: living in media turns reality into something we (think we) can *handle*.

A media archaeology of artifacts, activities and arrangements

What this chapter's opening quote about media life reflects is the intricacy and significance of adequately and inclusively defining what media are, as well as determining how we got to the media we have today. Considering how media can be viewed as being any (symbolical or technological) systems that enable, structure or amplify communication between people is but the first step. Mindful of the manifold meanings of media in life, new-media scholars Leah Lievrouw and Sonia Livingstone propose a comprehensive framework for operationalizing the role media play in society and everyday life, considering media as *infrastructures* that run underneath, through and in the background of social structures. As infrastructures, they argue, media incorporate "the artifacts or devices used to communicate or convey information, the

activities and practices in which people engage to communicate or share information, and the social arrangements or
organizational forms that develop around those devices and
practices" (2004: 23). Following Lievrouw and Livingstone's
approach, media become structuring in their omnipresence,
as they disappear from our direct awareness. As noted earlier (in 1984) by German cultural anthropologist Hermann
Bausinger:

> If one pursues the more recent transformations of technol-
> ogy, not in the sense of the history of technology, but in
> relation to the everyday, then what is most significant is a
> rise in the inconspicuous omnipresence of the technical
> . . . Today machines, technical instruments, are no longer
> things which give offence, no longer things which demon-
> strate processes – they have been ironed out, disguised with
> façades, technology is absorbed. (346)

Looking at media as infrastructures (or, in Bausinger's
terms, as an ensemble) puts media on the same level as
emotion and the human body: running in the background,
increasingly invisible and generally taken for granted.
Leopoldina Fortunati combines this infrastructural approach
with Kittler's appeal for an ontology of media to argue how
media both amplify and sacrifice affect in human interaction,
as emotions "must submit themselves to the technological
limits and languages of a machine" (2009: 13). Referring
specifically to today's technologies – the mobile phone and
internet – she works through the various ways in which
media *give life* to the material and immaterial structure of
the global socio-technical system that is our communicative
environment.

In order to understand our current media life, we need to
know how we got here. Consider for a moment to what extent
people (can) know about the various kinds of technologies
in today's average media-rich home. As Michael Noll writes
about the evolution of media, "A tremendous number and
variety of communication media are available for the home

– so many, that one wonders whether there is room for anything else" (2006: 6). In her comprehensive review of the *media home* throughout the twentieth century, Lynn Spigel (2001) considers how the "linked histories of domestic architecture and electronic communications" (386) reveal enduring fantasies and fears, regardless of the specific technologies involved – such as a nostalgia for traditional family roles, and utopian visions as well as anxieties about future gender and generational relations when negotiating access to media. Thorsten Quandt and Thilo von Pape take a biophilosophical route through the present-day media home, considering these common everyday living arrangements as *mediatopes*: the social, physical and technological living environments of media (2010: 332). For more than a year, Quandt and Von Pape followed 100 German households (through interviews, observations and surveys), showing how media move through the household in flocks, how the identities of various devices change over time, how younger and older media fight for survival in the home environment and therefore all have distinct and dynamic life cycles "connected to the life of the users themselves" (339). This intimate interrelationship between the lives of people and their media "paints a picture of an evolving, *living* media world within the domestic environment of the household" (343; italics added).

With all these technologies competing and evolving, it is crucial to note that newer media and their uses tend not to replace, but act as accelerators and amplifiers of long-term trends in the sociotechnical history of other media and their role in the arrangements of people's daily lives. In this development there is no necessary end-point, and different media are usually transformed through a complex interplay of perceived needs, competitive and political pressures, and continuous social and technological innovations – an altogether rather messy evolutionary development Roger Fidler calls the *mediamorphic* process (1997). In this process Fidler emphasizes that "media do not arise spontaneously and independently – they emerge gradually from the metamorphosis of old media . . . when newer forms of communication media emerge, the older forms usually do not die – they continue to evolve and adapt" (23). He warns against *techno-myopia*: the tendency of people to overestimate the short-term impact of technology, while simultaneously underestimating its long-term potential.

A second mistake when considering the social history of media artifacts is to fall into the trap of what Henry Jenkins calls a *black box fallacy*: the idea, that "Sooner or later . . . all media content is going to flow through a single black box into our living rooms (or in the mobile scenario, through black boxes we carry around with us everywhere we go)" (2006: 14). Jenkins realizes that every year he sees more, rather than fewer, black boxes in his living room. Although he rightly considers this kind of thinking – popular among media industry folks and technology fans – a fallacy, Jenkins commits one of his own by not pursuing his line of thought farther. As the Czech-born philosopher Vilém Flusser notes in his work *Towards a history of photography* of 1983, with the rise of omnipresent electronic and screen-based media people increasingly understand media devices, as well as the sensations such technologies produce, as *black boxes*: we know what goes into them (ideas, values, actions and experiences), and we can witness the impact of what comes out of the boxes – but we generally have no idea about what goes on inside. As people become habitually fused with their machines, Flusser argues, the interior of the black box of media and mediated culture remains obscure and indeterminate – with the end-result that "history will flow into the box, and . . . it will come out of it under the form of myth and magic" (2002[1993]: 67). Flusser's main concern dealt with our proclivity to take the images produced by technical media as reality – something Paul Taylor suggests we still do to this day: "in many ways we act as if they are real and we only pretend to pretend to believe that they are mere representations – despite what we might say, in terms of actual doing, we treat them as if they were real" (2010: 15).

Rather than stating the obvious about media – for instance that some particular functionality of a contemporary machine has antecedents in earlier devices and uses thereof, or that what is made in media seems increasingly naturalistic – media artifacts, activities and arrangements should be understood in the particular context they are part of (which zooms in on unique differences), while at the same time unearthing their constituent elements (a processual approach that usually emphasizes some kind of continuity), with respect to what people actually *do* with media. In this, one should follow the advice of media historian Mitchell Stephens (1998), who calls on us to be mindful of the magic and wonder of media as they rise and fall throughout history and society. It is important to – as Flusser demands we do – "demythify" (2002[1993]: 67) media. Yet one cannot help but recognize that media are also magical. The magical nature of media relates in part to Arthur C. Clarke's Third Law of Prediction, which states that "any sufficiently advanced technology is indistinguishable from magic."[3] Media are like magic because they seem to work and perform all kinds of functions in our daily lives that largely (and increasingly) escape our active awareness. Things just seem to happen – reality becomes a bit more bearable – when we wield media like magical wands, as, for example, Swedish semiotician Göran Sonesson writes: "The media habitat does indeed go out of existence, and transforms into a entirely new one, with the invocation, not of a spell, but of the remote control" (1997: 67). The space in-between demystification and magic – between grounding and groundlessness – provides the most fertile soil for an exploration of media life.

Most, if not all, contemporary aspects of media – such as wireless communications and mobility, multimedia and convergence culture, ongoing technological automation and augmentation of human affairs – have deep historical roots.

This means that a lot of the international social and cultural trends that can be associated with media are generally better understood in terms of a continuity of issues, rather than as sources of rapid, monumental change. The way people design, develop, adopt and eventually come to discard media does not necessarily follow a neat, linear or progressive trajectory. The people involved often develop machines (or parts thereof) independent of each other; cultural appropriation of technologies flows from unintended events and uses; not a single standard or protocol for communication is ever permanent or inevitable; and dead media live on embedded in updated devices and evolved practices. Newer media do not get better, nor do people's uses of media improve with each installment, upgrade or invention. Wiebe Bijker, Thomas Hughes and Trevor Pinch (1989) understand technological changes and developments as social constructs, whereby any particular technology gets shaped by the actions, ideas, biases and beliefs of the people involved in the entire process, from design to actual implementation. Just like our notions of self and our sense of belonging, media hardware and software are constantly changing projects. Janet Fulk (1993) adds that the adoption and perception of (new) media is at all times subsequent to social pressures – for example, people tend to be keener to embrace new technologies if people they like do it too. This does not necessarily mean that media, once part of people's everyday lives, are used the way they were originally intended to be by those who design or market them – in fact, more often than not the success of a media artifact is determined by activities never seriously considered by the network of people and institutions involved in its development.

Texting on the mobile phone is a great example of an unintended uptake and use of media. From its design and standardization in the mid-1980s, it was never expected to be used much outside of technology circles. Since the late 1990s it has become the most popular feature of the device worldwide. In other words: all aspects and elements of the material design, development, distribution, usage and eventual appropriation of media are subject to social production. Emphasizing the complex social and cultural forces influencing every step of the origins of technologies and, more specifically, the evolution of media (from inception to adoption) does not mean that people are in complete control of their technologies – it does suggest, however, that it is vital to consider media in context. And, generally speaking, such contexts tend to be messy. As precisely articulated by Derek Powazek in his "On The Network Manifesto" (published on June 11, 2011): "People are messy. The technology we invent is messy, too. Deal with it."[4] Such an appreciation of the overall rather unmoored, messy, complex, fluid and hybrid nature of relationships between media, society and everyday life is vital when thinking through the practical realities of our lives as lived immersed in digital media. As computer scientist Paul Dourish and cultural anthropologist Genevieve Bell advocate in *Divining a digital future* (2011), one has to recognize and embrace both the *myth* and the *mess* of technology.

Graham Thomas and Sally Wyatt show how the messiness of media developments features prominently in the history of internet, which "is not an instance of historical inevitability . . . At different moments during the history of the Internet, closure has been variously made and undone, with the involvement of new actors, the connection of networks using different protocols, and the development of new interfaces and applications" (1999: 696). If anything, argue Thomas and Wyatt, contestation, uncertainty and unpredictability about design and use are built into the history of media. British historians Asa Briggs and Peter Burke suggest, upon comprehensively reviewing the social history of media from the early days of the printing press up to today's "high-definition, inter-drive, mutually convergent technologies of communication" (2009: 12), the entire media system – including all of its relationships between what media are (artifacts), what people do with media (activities) and how this fits into their everyday lives (arrangements) – can best be understood as being in continuous flux.

Considering the almost constant reminders computer and internet users get to upgrade their software, and the persistent marketing of new versions, editions and formats of popular consumer electronics (such as mobile phones, computer operating systems and games consoles), it sometimes seems as if media artifacts advance more rapidly than our everyday practices and social arrangements can keep up with. This in turn continually confronts people with increasingly complex and swiftly liquefying technologies for which we have to come up with new languages, habits and routines – or at least, that is how the media in our life can make us feel. In 2009 the US-based satirical news site *The Onion* produced a fake news story entitled "Sony releases stupid piece of shit that doesn't fucking work" (released on February 9), making fun of the ways in which people are usually expected to cope with the continuing acceleration of media artifacts. The report covers the introduction of a new "stupid box thing" which is a "time vampire" so difficult or even impossible to use (according to a corporate spokesperson) that it would "make everyone in the modern home want to tear their fucking eyeballs out."[5] The point of the video is clear: those who design and market new media technologies force people to constantly upgrade their software or get completely new hardware that is difficult to use, largely because no one has enough time to get used to it. At the end of the story, the news anchor states that there are plans to release an upgraded version of the device "by the end of the year – just when you figured out the goddamn remote control for this one . . . it never ends, this shit."

Feeling deeply at breakneck speed

The transient nature of our selves, our technologies and even our ideas of community and society may be a particular feature of our time – as British social theorist Nikolas

Rose argues in *Inventing our selves* (1996) – and thus accompanies ways of making sense of, and being alive in, media life. Norwegian media sociologist Terje Rasmussen feels that an integrated perspective on media and society helps us to think of media as part of the whole fabric of routine everyday life and practice. Considering internet as a model for contemporary society, Rasmussen submits that we live in *"a distributed society"* (2003: 462; italics in original), because internet encourages people to create and maintain a sheer endless variety of personal and impersonal relationships and networks fulfilling all kinds of goals and functions, on both the micro-level of everydayness, and the macro-level of the organization of world society. As noted by Stiegler and Tomlinson, Rasmussen considers the seemingly blistering speed of social change as a correlate to technological trends. British geographer David Harvey signals the gradual change in the human experience of space–time relationships in the course of the twentieth century – exemplified by this increasing speed of travel and telecommunications – as a benchmark for a global change in people's sense of reality itself. Media become the playground for a search for meaning and belonging – not just by consumption or what Harvey calls "flexible accumulation" of artifacts and ideas that would make up one's sense of self, but also by producing, co-creating, assembling and remixing "a whole series of simulacra as milieux of escape, fantasy, and distraction" (1990: 302). The remixability of media life heralded by present-day observers like Lev Manovich is seen here as the primary perpetrator disrupting a socially responsible, coherent and otherwise meaningful existence.

Despite these observations, Harvey does not necessarily see people as hapless victims of the fragmented worldview engendered by media. American literary theorist Fredric Jameson (1991) on the other hand laments the impact of what he calls the *mediatic* system on people's sense of order and identity, implying that what all these media ultimately produce is a world where we incessantly look at ourselves and each other through media. For Jameson as well as his French counter-part Jean-François Lyotard (1984), a media life evokes a rather bleak world without history, where boundaries and categories we use to make sense of our everyday lived experience continually collapse. Most of these and other formidable theorists of our time directly or indirectly take their cue for thinking about media from influential German intellectual and cultural critic Walter Benjamin, who in 1936 proposed that modern media primarily act as a source of distraction (rather than concentration), producing "illusion-promoting spectacles and dubious speculations" requiring no attention on the part of the public.[6] Although all these prominent pundits consider media to some degree, they do tend to see media more or less exclusively as a disruptive and unsettling agent, perpetually pulling the rug out from under our lives. Although this certainly could happen, the same process works the other way around – media also provide us with ties that bind, with social glue, with common frames of reference: media perform and project the shag of the social. As we know from arguably the most memorable line of Jeff Bridges' character The Dude (in the hilarious 1998 movie *The Big Lebowski*), a rug really ties the room together. If media are the rugs of our lives, what do they tie together, and how might we be able to prevent them from making us blind to what they do?

Whatever the fabric is that media provide, it seems to be changing color and consistency at an accelerating pace. Social theorist Nicholas Gane considers the impact such technology-inspired speeding up may have on the potential for reflection, as "The information age is, above all, about instant living. It is about the intervention of ever-faster technologies into all spheres of 'human' life . . . It is also, perhaps, about the speed-up of social and cultural transformation in general" (2006: 21). Paul Virilio is among those who consider our immersion in an information- and communication-governed reality determined by the twin powers of immediacy and instantaneity as leading to inevitable disaster. Faced with the globalization of

telecommunications and a corresponding explosion of unlim-
ited information, people are disempowered from informing
themselves and thus unable to question the status quo or take
meaningful action against it. Virilio considers a worldwide
detonation of this *information bomb* (2006[1998]) inevitable, and Erik Davis equally epically refers to such a situation
of paralyzing massive information overload as the coming
datapocalypse (1999). Science-fiction writer Neal Stephenson
consonantly invokes an *infocalypse* (in his influential novel
Snow crash of 1992) as the name of a software program containing a vast multimedia library, featuring a rather cheerful
Librarian who provides its user with instant information on
anyone and anything. The informational universe as emblematic of lived experience in media would inevitably lead to forms
of instant living, the destruction of time (in terms of being
able to adequately assess one's future and past), and complete
social inertia, as Virilio concludes: "*Everything, right now!* Such
is the crazy catch-cry of hyper-modern times, of this hyper-
centre of temporal compression where everything crashes
together, telescoping endlessly under the fearful pressure of
telecommunications, into this 'teleobjective' proximity that
has nothing concrete about it except its infectious hysteria"
(2008 [2005]: 100; italics in original).

Whether providing us access to an informational universe
or destroying humanity by an overload of information without context or meaning, it seems clear that one should have,
as Gane proposes, "a heightened theoretical sensitivity to the
problems of analyzing real-time processes and occurrences,"
as well as keep an open mind towards the fact that "the social
itself [can be] seen to have technological underpinnings,"
which would mean that, in order to understand media life, one
should focus on "the interfaces between humans and technologies, and . . . the radical transformative powers of these
technologies" (2006: 32–3). In a similar vein, Paul Taylor
laments how "information theorists have taken the notion
of the all-at-once pace of change produced by information

technologies and failed to question fully its cultural costs" (2008: 785).

Beyond the problematization of speed all too common in the literature on media and life, Taylor emphasizes that thinking should move past the instantaneity implied in media to include how it *feels* to live a media life – how people are affected on a sensual and emotional level. Perhaps a completely mediated life reduces us to technical organisms, as French sociologist Jacques Ellul (1964[1954]) originally warned – in the process, not destroying but surely subordinating a spiritual and moral life to the technique of modern machines and their operations. In this context, Jameson considers a waning of affect emblematic of living in media. Sure, people still have emotions and indeed express them, but those feelings are performed for others in media and therefore are "free-floating and impersonal and tend to be dominated by a peculiar kind of euphoria" (1991: 72). It is possible to argue that the mediation of affect (in social media such as Twitter and Facebook, via personal media like video chat and text messaging) elevates emotional excess. In media life, our emotions, in whatever shape or form and in response to whatever mediated or quasi-mediated stimuli, are profoundly pointed and personal and pregnant. As an economist, Edward Castronova studies synthetic worlds – like Sony's *EverQuest* and Blizzard's *World of Warcraft* – precisely because his experiences in such universes are extraordinary, and their attraction for people seems to be derived from the sense that "they provide better emotional experiences than ordinary life does" (2005: 274). How intense and authentic such mediated feelings can be is shown by the example of the arrest (in October 2008) of a Japanese woman who killed her virtual husband in the online game *Maplestory*. After the man, who was married to her in the game but not outside of it, broke off the online relationship, she signed on to his profile with his username and password and terminated his avatar.

As longitudinal experimental studies show, people

generally respond to media in much the same way as they treat other people in everyday social interaction. Indeed, as virtual-reality scholars Jeremy Bailenson and Jim Blascovich show in *Infinite reality* (2011), human beings cannot help but feel that what they experience in media is real – even though the rules of grounded reality are suspended. The brain, the body and heart all participate in generating sensations and emotions when we engage with media. Their earlier experiments with human–media interaction lead Byron Reeves and Clifford Nass to conclude, that "Knowledge of how media work with people is knowledge of things social and natural" (1996: 256). British psychologist Michael Apter (1992) furthermore points out that people's emotional responses to mediated sensations are not just natural, but also functional: they allow us to exercise our emotional reflexes – such as fear, horror and grief, but also pleasure and delight – in a relatively safe environment. In fact, we need that sense of safety in order to experience excitement, which in turn helps us to cope with feelings of anxiety and fear in general.

Instead of a *waning* of affect in media life, Brian Massumi (2002) concludes that an *excess* of affect characterizes our contemporary condition – it is just that we lack an adequate vocabulary to describe and explain it in a completely mediated or virtual context. An in-between position is offered by media theorist Mark Hansen, who argues that our confrontations with increasingly true-to-life experiences in media not only lead us to feel more strongly about fully mediated people (such as avatars), but at the same time make us aware of our own "embodied human expressivity" (2003: 207). In her work with children and teenagers, Sherry Turkle (2011) even finds that they often express a preference for interacting with technological beings – such as robotic animals – rather than real ones. The next step in this process would be to consider the consequences of interacting with fully fledged emotional machines like Lieutenant Commander Data in the *Star Trek: The Next Generation* TV series (running from 1987 to 1994) and films (between 1994 and 2002). Data is a robot (although he would say "an android") that throughout the series strives to become more human. The character played by Brent Spiner almost achieves humanity by implanting an emotion chip (which occurs in the *Star Trek: Generations* motion picture of 1994), allowing him to experience the full range of human emotions. This is perhaps not necessarily a far-fetched scenario, because, as artificial intelligence expert Marvin Minsky (2006) notes, humans can be seen as *emotion machines* consisting of extremely complex but ultimately replicable neural associations and connections.

What Turkle and many other scholars of media and society suggest is that the integration of media and society has profound consequences for the way people relate to each other. At the same time I would argue that people lose themselves in media to find exactly what seems to be missing outside of media: a more or less coherent sense of self, belonging and community. And, in media, we now find all the institutions and organizations and rituals and displays telling us who we are (supposed to be) that used to only exist where people would physically meet. Beyond fretting over whether the machines of media turn people into technological animals or not, the media-life approach necessitates a perspective beyond good and evil (while acknowledging that a media life is not without its problems), sprinkled with a sizeable dose of messiness regarding its history, and a passionate respect for feeling and affect, interpreting the interface of people and media as "a kind of epitome of human life itself" (Briggs and Burke, 2009: 286).

The key to the success of a media artifact in people's lives lies in its ability to be lifelike – to be part of what humans as social animals do: trying to fit in (and stand out), expressing ourselves, figuring out what is going on around us and what we are supposed to do, validating our existence and sense of self, liking and loving ourselves and others. This discovery of sociability as the basis of media in people's lives runs throughout the history of media artifacts. American psychiatrists Thomas Lewis, Fari Amini and Richard Lannon poignantly note in their exploration of love in contemporary culture how "an ironic revelation of the television–computer age is that what people want from machines is humanity: stories, contact, and interaction" (2001: 198). Media producers, policymakers, pundits and professors alike often underestimate or just fail to consider, what media tend to be used for most in people's lives: sensitive, impassioned and movingly emotive communication and conversation. Leopoldina Fortunati (2009) wonders whether this oversight has made the ways we so often consider media and society seem without heart, advocating a strengthening of the investigation of electronic emotion. As communication theorist James Carey somewhat similarly lamented: "Because we have looked at each new advance in communications technology as an opportunity for politics and economics, we have devoted it, almost exclusively, to matters of government and trade. We have rarely seen these advances as opportunities to expand people's powers to learn and exchange ideas and experience" (1989: 27).

It is astounding how, time and time again, both the industry and the academy seem to forget that it is their sociability that explains (the ubiquitous adoption and pervasive use of) media. In many accounts of the history and adoption of media, one detects a thinly veiled seamlessness – a way of describing and analyzing the technology strictly in terms of its success as defined by market penetration, and its gradual reworking from a presumably lifeless machine into a generally reproductive yet potentially transformative social tool. Such a perspective reflects an underdeveloped emphasis on how media *become* life – where becoming refers to media extending the communication and conversation capabilities of their users, media embedding themselves physically with people through forms of wearable computing, and media finally becoming part and parcel of every aspect of daily life and their users' sense of self.

Charismatic technologies of love

There is an emerging consensus among researchers that the appropriation and use of media constitute a particular lifestyle. Summarizing the situation in the US in 2009, reseachers of the Pew Internet & American Life Project concluded that "Mobile connectivity is a powerful differentiator among technology users. Those who plug into the information and communications world while on-the-go are notably more active in many facets of digital life."[7] This *digital life* is to a large extent based on a mobile lifestyle, according to cross-national comparative reports on attitudes and behaviors related to wireless devices and communication. Studies combining qualitative and quantitative data from Asia, Europe and the US map a globally emerging mobile communication society in which what people do with mobile technology serves to reinforce, maintain and create collective identity, while at the same time functioning as an expression of a distinctly personal style and way of life.

How far and wide a mediated lifestyle plays out in our everydayness is evident in the work of media anthropologists such as Daniel Miller, studying the various roles social and mobile media play in the lives of a variety of groups in society: students, migrant workers and the homeless. Miller and his colleague Mirca Madianou conclude that people around the world, coming from a wide variety of social and economic backgrounds, increasingly live in a situation of *polymedia*: exposed to a plurality of media which change the relationships between communication technology and society by the mere fact of their omnipresence and seemingly effortless integration into the social and emotional realm of people's everyday existence.[8] As they state in their work on Filipino and Caribbean people living in the UK, and their left-behind families in the Philippines and Trinidad: media are our *Technologies of love* (2012). In his fieldwork, Miller (2011) finds that people spend so much time living with media that media become their life – in effect, they treat media as their home. This results in typical home idioms being translated into media contexts, for example by incessantly decorating one's online social network profile, or by constantly re-arranging and tidying up one's personal computer or smartphone. Just as the home gets infused with (and reshaped through) media – for instance, with a home cinema or media room – our media become domesticated spaces typified by a mass personalization effort: customized ringtones, individualized screensavers and wallpapers, fine-tuned arrangements of favorite websites (i.e. bookmarks) and television stations, tailor-made carrying pouches and various forms of wearable media, and so on.

The central role of media in general, and the mobile phone particularly, in processes of personal transformation towards greater individualization and transnational connectivity leads Fortunati (2001) to describe them as *charismatic technologies*. In this sense, media consist of artifacts with identities of their own, enabling and enticing their users to appropriate them progressively into more and more aspects of everyday life. In the process, the character of communication devices changes from objects of material culture to functional and symbolic artifacts, and onwards to fully integrated and highly dynamic social artifacts. Once inseparable from the domestic sphere of everyday operations, media become part of the day-to-day coordination of both family and personal life. In research done in the US by UCLA's Center on Everyday Lives of Families (CELF), and across Europe by the scholars involved in the European Media and Technology in Everyday Life (EMTEL) and the EU Kids Online networks, media feature prominently as sites of struggle and negotiation of power and authority in the family home. In doing so, media add a certain dynamism and mobility to the daily rhythm of life, while at the same time extending and amplifying existing networks and ways of doing things. As Kenichi Ishii (2006) concludes in his studies of mobile media use in Japan, the key to understanding the social consequences of the introduction of mobile media into society is their contextual mobility: the extent to which people using such technologies (think they) are in control of incoming communications. Such real or perceived control as media offer in turn contributes to a much less stable, more individualized and nuanced micro-coordination of social interactions in the context of households and life in general. Nick Couldry and Anna McCarthy see in the process a gradual co-creation of a *mediaspace*, "encompassing both the kind of spaces created by media, and the effects that existing spatial arrangements have on media forms as they materialize in everyday life" (2004: 1–2). The (illusion of) control that a mediaspace affords both makes it distinct from other spaces in life – for example those of the home and work – and at the same time explains its gradual colonization of other spheres of human existence.

The potential of media to organize social reality and public space adds a level of complexity to the daily rituals of communication that raises concerns regarding the extent of people's tetheredness to technologies, and how media can be seen as connecting devices, while at the same time allowing us to exclude people from communication and conversation. Media artifacts, their uses and how they fit into the daily lives of people around the world amplify media life's complexity in two directions at the same time. On the one hand, today's omnipresent, personalized and networked media can be seen as "intrinsically solipsistic" technologies (Morley, 2007: 211), enabling the ongoing retreat of people into quasi-autonomous personal information spaces that can be kept free from the noise of others. The point of building and maintaining social relationships in media is not, as Lev Manovich articulates in *The language of new media* (2001), the *telepresence* of others through media, but rather their absence (or *anti-presence*). We can affect a social reality without necessarily being there. On the other hand, such individualized immersion at-a-distance instantly and haptically (considering today's touch-screen technology) connects people with people anywhere else, thus stretching their very own social bubbles into a fully mediated space of global coexistence where we seek a common humanity (if only because we are biologically wired to do so). This space is what Peter Sloterdijk calls a *mediasphere* (2004), forming an invisible electronic shell around us whereby our entire experience of others becomes mediated. Sloterdijk seems convinced life in a bubble of media leaves people blind to coexistence.

In an attempt to bridge the false dichotomy between social isolation and connection as implied in media life, Indian cultural anthropologist Arjun Appadurai (1990) introduced the concept of a *mediascape*, based on a recognition of how media are central to shared imagined worlds co-created and maintained by persons and groups spread around the globe. Appadurai's analysis brings home the connection between media, everydayness, and global society – for example by stressing how an ongoing deterritorialization of people through global labor and family migration contributes to the production and maintenance of symbolic ties with more or less imagined socialities in media. At the same time, all this mediated global connectivity does not exclude or necessarily limit local interactions – in fact, numerous studies show that media above all contribute to a process of ongoing glocalization of communities, defined by Canadian social network analyst Barry Wellman as "the combination of intense local and extensive global interaction" (2002: 11). To some extent this explains the growth and success of diasporic media in general and 'new' or mobile media in particular, while this conclusion at the same time amplifies concerns about speed, scale and volume in the transnational circulation of images and ideas. A glocalized world society is provincial in the sense of Peter Sloterdijk's assumptions about people turning increasingly to the inner world of a "modern individuality, supported by a complex media environment that enables multiple and permanent auto-references" (Sloterdijk, quoted in Ohanian and Royoux, 2005: 235), while it is also markedly part of Appadurai's observations of an accelerating global flow of "people, machinery, money, images, and ideas" (1990: 11). The same media support and supercharge these seemingly different trajectories.

The unseen disappearance of invisible media

Combining Sloterdijk's *mediasphere* and Appadurai's *mediascape* with an appreciation of the infrastructural role of media in people's lives, it seems our media are gradually disappearing from view while at the same time influencing our lives more and more in terms of our (real or perceived) control over them and their control over us. Media, concludes Lisa Gitelman in her history of phonography and the World Wide Web, are located "at the intersection of authority and amnesia" (2006: 6), as people tend to ignore the role of media in their lives, and in the process forget how the kind of media they use format and shape their interactions with the world around them. Back in the 1980s Umberto Eco similarly observed the multiplication of media into every aspect of everyday life and suggested that our awareness of art, culture, and really any kind of information changes in the process: "media are genealogical because, in them, every new invention sets off a chain reaction of inventions, produces a sort of common language. They have no memory because, when the chain of imitations has been produced, no one can remember who started it, and the head of the clan is confused with the latest great grandson" (1998[1983]: 146).

Both Gitelman and Eco point to a profound paradox intrinsic to the findings of studies on the appropriation and use of media. The more people use media in the domains of everyday life, the more reflexive debates about the potential consequences of such media become. It certainly seems that people are not just aware of the media in their lives – our everyday interactions are often (and perhaps increasingly) shaped around this awareness. Media organize family life, act as the platforms for life's micro-coordination, and serve as the starting point for endless debates about their proposed effects on people: whether children become more violent because of playing video games, whether listening to the backmasked lyrics on the 1985 album "Hell Awaits" by Slayer turns fans into Satan-worshippers, whether spending a lot of time with media in general makes people impatient and forgetful,[9] and whether all media really just, well, fry our brains.[10]

At the same time as folks can be sincerely concerned about the role of media in everyday life, people's lived experience with media makes media disappear. In media usage studies, the differences in time reported as spent with media through, for example, phone surveys, personal written diaries and participant observation are stark.[11] In most countries around the world, reports and studies on the amount of time people use media are more or less similar: almost every waking moment is either directly (paging through a magazine, making a phone call, tuning in to a show on the radio, surfing to a particular website, and so on) or indirectly (having music, images and video in the background while traversing public spaces; a computer or mobile phone in always-on mode) spent with media. Yet when asked about it, people tend to forget most of their media use, mainly because they are concurrently exposed to multiple media at the same time, and most of their media use occurs in combination with other everyday activities such as working, hanging out and eating.

Jay Bolter and Richard Grusin signal "the ambivalent and contradictory ways in which new digital media function for our culture today . . . in which digital technologies are proliferating faster than our cultural, legal, or educational institutions can keep up with them" (1996: 312). They suggest this ambivalence stems from a double logic of *remediation* embedded in all media. On the one hand, media make themselves known to us by remixing and multiplying their properties: today's phones include music players, video screens and so on; any television show or advertisement uses conventions and formulas from previous genres, formulas and formats; and people are, in their daily activities, concurrently exposed to media. This has the potential to make us hyper-aware of media. Yet at the same time Bolter and Grusin argue that media work very hard to make themselves invisible through a logic of immediacy, which erases or automates their operations. Examples are increasing realism in sophisticated digital games, and numerous programs within the broad genre category of reality television. The immediacy of media, then, makes our ongoing negotiations between who we (think we) are and the broader social reality of which we consider ourselves part (but that remains largely invisible to us other than as experienced through media) subject to the mediation of media technologies that, more and more, endeavor to fade from our active awareness of them.

Although it is somewhat simplistic to discuss media in temporal terms, one way of considering new media *new* is to look at the extent that today's media make us forget that they are even there – when our use of them becomes seamless, when our disbelief in their limitations is suspended, when the horizon of our lived experience cannot be meaningfully separated from media any more. As Mark Weiser writes, "The most profound technologies are those that disappear. They weave themselves into the fabric of everyday life until they are indistinguishable from it" (1991: 94). Weiser's vision of computing as an integral, invisible part of people's lives so that the computers themselves vanish into the background inspired the paradigm of ubiquitous computing, based on a conviction that "people live through their practices and tacit knowledge so that the most powerful things are those that are effectively invisible in use," therefore the computer designers' "highest ideal is to make a computer so imbedded, so fitting, so natural, that we use it without even thinking about it."[12] Weiser formed his ideas about invisible media during the 1980s. At the start of the twenty-first century, scores of contemporary authors across different academic disciplines do not hesitate to point out that most of our current media are in fact so mundane, so thoroughly domesticated and ambient that, as British sociologist Trevor Pinch posits, "technologies become invisible, just part of the stuff of life" (2010: 409).

The invisibility of media as natural interfaces providing a more or less seamless experience of (mediated) reality is enhanced by our general blindness regarding the material dimension of media. We generally are not willing or able to look inside the media of our lives. Relatively few know how to reprogram the computer operating system, hack their smartphone, or bootstrap a home theater set-up. Douglas Rushkoff goes as far as suggesting that, in order to effectively take charge of their technologies in particular and media life in general, people have a choice to either *Program or be programmed* (2010). Moving beyond hardware skills, one must ask what exactly the formal rules underpinning the design and functioning of media – codes, protocols, programming languages, software and so on – do to the way we use media and to what extent the biases embedded in their materiality shape, limit and expand our worldview. Cannon Schmitt advocates awareness of a new materialism, as media and mediation are not insubstantial, innocent or merely passive relays between our senses and experiences, but generate a specific reality on (and of) their own. Schmitt coins such an approach as *materia media*, referring to "medial substances" or "the substances used in media practice" (2004: 11). In his work with Jay Bolter on the various ways in which media technologies and genres refashion, rival and pay homage to each other, Richard Grusin stresses "the inseparability of . . . the reality of media [and] their materiality as objects of circulation within the world of humans and nonhumans, of society and of things" (2004: 26). On the other hand, literature on the primacy of technology's social construction has a rich and well-established history, and popular culture consistently reminds us that, no matter how many times the crew of the starship *Enterprise* may get overrun by the avatars or malfunctioning computer programs of their famed holodeck, the humanoid lifeforms in the *Star Trek* universe ultimately prevail. Combining the *Star Trek* context with addressing our cultural blindspot regarding the material dimension of media, it could be argued that we wander around in the world as if it indeed resembles a holo-deck, whose invisible forms, formats and logic determine what we can and cannot do. This holodeck-based life, in what David Altheide and Robert Snow (1991) call our *media worlds*, forces us to adapt to its conventions, rules and rituals – much like the Liliputian, Brobdingnagian, Laputan and other worlds made the unfortunate surgeon Lemuel Gulliver fit their socie-ties in Jonathan Swift's famous novel of 1726.

Beyond pointing to the generally unreflective and therefore largely unseen ways in which media find a place in people's lives and considering their relative invisibility as technologi-cal infrastructures, it is vital to argue on a more fundamental level that people can never really see media, because "it is diffi-cult . . . to think outside of the media networks through which we express and communicate our thoughts" (Gane and Beer, 2008: 32). Friedrich Kittler builds his work around the realiza-tion that we have become blind to our media to the extent that, even when we try to say something meaningful about media, we need media to express it. Once we start articulating more precisely what media are and how they fit into our everyday lives, we come to the inevitable conclusion that they are not "external and extensive objects" that we can switch on or off and therefore control, but that "[media] on the one hand and man on the other are inseparably linked by an endless feed-back loop" (2009: 29). In Kittler's history of communication media, this feedback loop accelerates with each stepping stone – from writing and printing via telegraphy and analog media to digital media. He predicts that, ultimately, media technolo-gies will overhaul each other to evolve beyond the essential intervention of humans.

Linking the omnipresence of media in our everyday envi-ronments and their role as providing the fabric of our lives with our generally low (or indeed absent) awareness of the impact and existence – let alone the physical and social infra-structure – of these technologies, Shaun Moores (2005) considers media as disembedding mechanisms, borrowing a concept from Anthony Giddens' work on the consequences of modernity. Disembedding mechanisms are expert systems that organize large areas of the material and social environ-ment in which we live. One could think about the knowledge and expertise of the architect and builders in the design and construction of the home, which we tend to understand little of, yet completely rely on in everyday life. The same goes for the media we use on a daily basis – relatively few of us know or understand enough about media to effectively take them apart or program, hack or otherwise rework them. A notable excep-tion would be the wonderful work of the Amsterdam-based Gender Changers Academy – a social collective of female volunteers who "have a critical curiosity about technology," "know stuff" and "have attitude!"[13] They offer free workshops for women on how to take computer hardware and software apart, how to build and maintain a website (using free open source software), and in general on how to "break things, make jokes and ask so-called stupid questions."

Considering how deep the rabbit hole of media goes, nei-ther Kittler's analysis nor the holodeck-metaphor for media life seems so strained after all. Any day in our media life ties us in with a social and symbolic fabric that is pervasive and, largely because of its ubiquity, remains relatively invisible. It is the rare person who can call his or her subjectivity into question, as much as it is the exceptional human being who can bring forth the media in their experience of the world. The question perhaps is not how little or much we know about the technological infrastructure lying underneath our homes, streets and oceans, or what kind of programming languages we can or should master. The fundamental implication of the ways people currently and generally use media today is that media cannot be seen as mere extensions of us and therefore externalized to us. There is no outside to media that would allow for a comparison between media and life. We are not becoming more like media, nor will media sooner or later overtake us – we *are* media. A media life is therefore better understood as a deliberate attempt to become aware of how the relationships between media as artifacts, activities and social arrangements work in various ways to amplify and accelerate our everyday way of life, and empower us to take responsibility for our media, and for what we want and expect of ourselves and each other.

CHAPTER THREE

What Media Do

where media record and store everything and we lose ourselves in media

"[T]he dominant information technologies of the day control all understanding and its illusions," writes Friedrich Kittler in the foreword of his work on emerging media in the nineteenth century, and in the process "what remains of people is what media can store and communicate" (1999[1985]: xl). Media, in other words, make us lose ourselves. Quite literally sometimes, as Kittler remarks in a 1998 speech in honor of British music theorist and composer Brian Eno: "music shows us that a culture is only as popular as it can lose itself in its own technologies."[1] In his work, Eno often uses an approach he calls *generative music* – using a computer and synthesizer with software programmed to autogenerate music on the basis of a series of protocols. As Eno explains the process (in a talk on June 8, 1996): "the machine is going to improvise within a set of rules . . . They govern major considerations like the basic quality of the piece to quite minor ones like exactly how the note wobbles . . . This piece of music, which is quite unpredictable and sometimes has quite large gaps in it . . . this music is making itself now."[2]

When media become both ubiquitous and invisible, we may very well be losing ourselves in our technology, to the extent that it indeed generates our lives on the basis of a specific set of rules. As American economist Brian Arthur states in his take on the evolution of technology: "this thing that fades to the background of our world also creates that world" (2009: 10). Just before that happens, there is an opportunity to intervene in the inevitable. We can look under the hood, kick the tires, and check the oil – while driving. Media life does not necessarily entail surrender to the gods of technology – nor does it mean turning our backs on divine intervention. It just suggests that, in terms of what media do, the human–machine relationship is always already recombinant.

Media and life co-evolve in ways governed by the many mixed and altogether messy ways in which machines and humans co-create each other. Technologies multiply and converge, as do the various uses of technologies. The directions of these developments trend seldom as intended by either designers or distributors, nor do people completely control the dissemination and adoption of specific technologies. Humanity and nature are not necessarily technologizing along the lines of cybernetics as proposed (and carefully critiqued) by Norbert Wiener in his book *The human use of human beings* (1950). Nor should technology be exclusively considered as a universal biological phenomenon, as put forward by Georges Canguilhem in a 1947 lecture entitled "Machine and organism." The French philosopher stressed the need for a biological philosophy of technology, tentatively concluding that: "technology allows man to live in continuity with life, as opposed to a solution that would see humankind as living in a state of rupture for which we ourselves are responsible because of science" (1992[1947]: 64).[3] Sean Cubitt (2005) similarly calls for a nuanced appreciation of the less-than-clear and increasingly dissolving boundaries between *polis*, *physis* and *techne*: the human world, the green world (i.e. nature) and the technological world. Media in Cubitt's work are conceived more broadly as *ecomedia*: providing the essential communicative devices and interfaces for improved human–nature relationships. Katherine Hayles (2012) believes in the co-evolution of humanity and technics, a process which she sees in terms of a contemporary *technogenesis*. Although Cubitt and Hayles are expressively hopeful about the consequences of their analyses for our participation in the worlds we live in, it seems far from clear what media do during such processes of co-evolution, mutual shaping and co-creative communication. Whatever it is that media do, it seems to become increasingly pervasive while media are fading into the background of our lives.

> Every word one has ever read, whether in an e-mail, an electronic document or on a Web site, can be found again with just a few keystrokes. Computers can analyze digital memories to help with time management, pointing out when you are not spending enough time on your highest priorities. Your locations can be logged at regular intervals, producing

animated maps that trace your peregrinations. Perhaps most important, digital memories can enable all people to tell their life stories to their descendants in a compelling, detailed fashion.[4]

In this quote from their March 2007 article in *Scientific American* magazine, Microsoft Research Center's Gordon Bell and Jim Gemmell articulate the motivation for their ongoing MyLifeBits project: finding a way to record and store everything a person experiences in a lifelong digital archive, making all those memories searchable and accessible with an easy-to-use software tool. In a conference keynote address outlining his company's vision for the future, Google's co-founder Eric Schmidt (on September 7, 2010) similarly talked about an "age of augmented humanity" in which our memories and experiences are all part of a living archive:

> Ultimately, search is not just the web but literally all of your information – your email, the things you care about, with your permission – this is personal search, for you and only for you . . . We can suggest what you should do next, what you care about. Imagine: We know where you are, we know what you like . . . A near-term future in which you don't forget anything, because the computer remembers. You're never lost.[5]

The notion of media as a potentially perfect archival assistant harks back to Vannevar Bush's influential proposal for solving what many considered was the main problem exposed by World War II: how to gather, store and make easily available enormous amounts of data in an information-saturated world. Writing in the *Atlantic Monthly* magazine of July 1945, Bush refers to the typewriter, movie camera, and telephone to claim that "The world has arrived at an age of cheap complex devices of great reliability; and something is bound to come of it."[6] What should come of it, Bush argues, is a machine consisting of a desk, a couple of screens, a keyboard, and sets of buttons and levers he called the "memex": "a device in which an individual stores all his books, records, and communications, and which is mechanized so that it may be consulted with exceeding speed and flexibility. It is an enlarged intimate supplement to his memory." One of the wonders of this machine would be that it "will take instructions and data from a whole roomful of girls armed with simple keyboard punches, and will deliver sheets of computed results every few minutes."

At the time of writing his essay, Vannevar Bush was the director of the Manhattan Project, a network of American, Canadian and British scientists and engineers who, between 1942 and 1946, were charged with developing the atomic bomb. His proposed solution to the problem of military, political and economic information overload came down to doing away with the need to remember everything by surrendering to the fantasy of a *total archive* of life. Because, surely, "Having a surrogate memory creates a freeing, uplifting, and secure feeling," the MyLifeBits researchers claim, "similar to having an assistant with a perfect memory" (Bell and Gemmell, 2006: 93). Between the memex and the MyLifeBits project, many other types of hardware and software have been developed that are equally inspired by the premise of relieving people of the need to remember. The theory and design of internet and its protocols (such as hypertext) can be considered to be inspired by Bush's suggestions for a *hypermedia* artifact that establishes links between different types of information. The notion of media serving as one's personal assistant led Apple in 1987 to propose and showcase a so-called *Knowledge Navigator*: a tablet-style computer with a touchscreen interface featuring an animated butler-type software agent who would find and reproduce information, contacts and schedules for the user, and even make phone calls.[7] With the introduction of the *Apple iPhone 4S* in 2011, the notion of a mobile media device that talks back at its user in a human-like way, while acting as a personal assistant (using the learning-software-based application *Siri*), came to fruition.

Welcome to the unforgettable

Today, Vannevar Bush's apprehension about information archiving and retrieval is exclusive not to the military, government or businesses (most likely it never was), but to each and every individual. Both deliberately and unintentionally, people generate more information about themselves, what they do and what they care about than any social institution or agency at any time in history. In the process people collectively create a vast repository of their lives in media – a living archive that gets continuously updated and, unlike our brains, always remembers information in the same way it was originally recorded and stored. As American marketing guru Seth Godin writes in his 2006 mini-manifesto: "the internet doesn't forget. And sooner or later, the internet finds out."[8] Minnesota district judge James Rosenbaum in the same way calls attention to the elaborate deception of a computer's Delete key, as "once a computer file is generated – let alone disseminated – internal and external copies proliferate. And each is impervious to deletion" (2000: 393). What this recording of everything and delusion of deletion means, argues Jeffrey Rosen in the *New York Times* magazine (of July 21, 2010), is that we have arrived at the end of forgetting:

> We've known for years that the Web allows for unprecedented voyeurism, exhibitionism and inadvertent indiscretion, but we are only beginning to understand the costs of an age in which so much of what we say, and of what others say about us, goes into our permanent – and public – digital files. The fact that the Internet never seems to forget is threatening, at an almost existential level, our ability to control our identities; to preserve the option of reinventing ourselves and starting anew; to overcome our checkered pasts.[9]

Rosen hopes that face-to-face communication will restore our ability to judge each other's character, and advocates forgiveness and new forms of empathy in the process. In his book *Delete: the virtue of forgetting in the digital age* (2009),

Viktor Mayer-Schönberger recommends that digital archives should come with an expiration date like grocery items, after which the information would be permanently erased. To Mayer-Schönberger, perfect digital remembering will lead to shattered lives, threatening "us individually and as a society in our capacity to learn, to reason, and to act in time" (197–8).

Both advocates and critics of the media's uncanny capacity to record and store our lives stress the importance of being in control. But even such control comes with critical caveats. Writing in the Winter 2005 issue of the *New Atlantis* magazine, Christine Rosen sees in the way people use media to both consume and produce information (for and about themselves) evidence of an emerging age of *egocasting*, where sophisticated technologies give us "the illusion of perfect control," inescapably leading to a "thoroughly personalized and extremely narrow pursuit of one's personal taste" (2005: 52). For Rosen, hypothetical devices like the memex and *Knowledge Navigator*, or actual media artifacts such as the remote control, (digital) video recorder and portable music players do not just relieve us of the need to have a working memory of our experiences – these technologies and what we do with them in fact make us forget about our fellow human beings in general, as they allow people to focus only on things of interest to them. Her concerns mirror those voiced much earlier by Socrates, as told by Plato in his *Phaedrus* (360 BC). When discussing the value of different kinds of media, including the tools of speechmaking, musical instruments and writing, Socrates laments how the art of letters is sometimes suggested to make people "wiser and give them better memories; it is specific both for the memory and for the wit." The Greek philosopher, who in 399 BC was condemned to death by the men of Athens for questioning common sense and thus "corrupting the social fabric" (De Botton, 2001: 27), moves on to state that:

> [teaching people to write] will create forgetfulness in the learners' souls, because they will not use their memories; they will trust to the external written characters and not

remember of themselves. The specific which you have discovered is an aid not to memory, but to reminiscence, and you give your disciples not truth, but only the semblance of truth; they will be hearers of many things and will have learned nothing; they will appear to be omniscient and will generally know nothing; they will be tiresome company, having the show of wisdom without the reality.[10]

Following in Socrates' footsteps, Jesuit priest and historian Walter Ong (1982) argues in his history of the transition from orality to literacy, that the written word restructures consciousness in ways that make it more difficult to remember communication – as it is inevitably distanced from whomever expressed it. Paraphrasing Plato's account of Socrates and Ong's historical analysis in a media-life context, one could argue that when media are seen as alleviating us from the necessity of remembering, any and all information and associations after that moment can only remind us of people and things, yet put direct experiences of the world (and the people in it) at a distance from us. Peter Sloterdijk (2004) performs a contemporary iteration of Socrates' critique, questioning blindness to the experience (of others) of a life inside one's own mediasphere – a bubble of lived experience that simultaneously stretches the globe as it envelops the lifeworld of the individual. Sloterdijk's mediasphere is an abstraction of the *telecocoon* Japanese anthropologist Ichiyo Habuchi (2005) finds in his research into the role mobile media play in everyday life, noting how we seem to be increasingly preferring to communicate (and commune) with others without having physical interaction. People's witnessing of others (and experiencing alterity altogether) thus becomes once removed from reality when outsourced to media – and in the process, argues Leopoldina Fortunati (2005), body-to-body communication becomes an increasingly evanescent prototype for the quality of human interaction.

In an assessment of the personal consequences of the changing nature of work under conditions of electronic globalization, Richard Sennett (1998: 21) likewise laments how no one becomes a long-term witness to another person's life any more. Finnish media archaeologist Erkki Huhtamo (1997) shows how, throughout history, media have been seen as removing people from their surroundings and others, whether through excessive use of nineteenth-century kaleidoscopes – turning us into *kaleidoscomaniacs* – or because of a late twentieth-century infatuation with virtual worlds – giving rise to a race of *cybernerds*. Christine Rosen returns to these recurring worries by pointing out that our blindness to others is premised on our capability to exercise an unparalleled degree of control over our media exposure to people, spaces, ideas and experiences. She concludes her assessment of egocasting by emphasizing an anthropotechnological anxiety similar to Sloterdijk's: "We haven't become more like machines. We've made the machines more like us. In the process we are encouraging the flourishing of some of our less attractive human tendencies: for passive spectacle; for constant, escapist fantasy; for excesses of consumption" (2005: 72).

It is in this context that the MyLifeBits approach to personal lifetime storage becomes relevant to everyday life. Overall, the combined dilemmas of too much information, continuous immersion in all kinds of media, and the twin illusions of control and deletion that those media offer seem to suggest that what media ultimately do is allow us to forget the past, including the people and experiences we would rather ignore. Outsourcing our memory to media thus shapes a life continuously lived in the here and now, as well as giving rise to a life where every past act and occurrence remains permanently in view.

The old meme of media's ability to record and thereby steal the authentic nature and direct experience of life can also be found in what conceivably contains its most ominous interpretation: a short story entitled "The Aleph" by Argentinean author Jorge Luis Borges, originally published in 1944 in literary magazine *Sur*. In this story, a writer regularly visits the father of the recently deceased Beatriz Viterbo – someone the writer desperately loved. The visits take place in the 1930s, and describe how the author "came to receive the gradual confidences of Carlos Argentino Daneri" (1998[1944]: 119). Daneri is a budding writer himself, staying inside all the time to work on an epic poem with the goal of lyrically describing the earth in its entirety. He does not feel the need to travel anywhere in order to write about the earth, as at home he is "surrounded by telephones, telegraphs, phonographs, the latest in radio-telephone and motion-picture and magic-lantern equipment" (120), media which amplify and extend his senses, assisting him in universally experiencing the world. After his house is threatened with demolition to make way for a fancy café, Daneri confides in the author the crucial nature of staying in the house to work on his poem, as it contains an immovable Aleph. In the words of the Daneri character, Borges defines an Aleph as "one of the points in space that contain all points" (126), "the place where, without admixture or confusion, all the places of the world, seen from every angle, coexist" (127), and as "The microcosm of the alchemists and Kabbalists, our proverbial friend the *multum in parvo* [translation: much information condensed in a small device], made flesh!" (128; italics in original). Although the author is convinced Daneri is a madman, he rushes over to see the Aleph. Describing his experience with this "small iridescent sphere of almost unbearable brightness" (129), Borges writes how, when looking at/into the Aleph, he has the simultaneous experience of infinite things in universal space – including all the mirrors on the planet while none of them reflect him as he looks into the device. A direct result of this instantaneous confrontation with all the knowledge of the universe was the fact, that once he was back outside, walking down the street, "there was nothing that had the power to surprise or astonish . . . anymore" (131).

Borges' amazing tale in turn inspired William Gibson to include a similar device, also called an Aleph, in his first set of novels, referred to as the Sprawl trilogy: *Neuromancer* (1984; the book which introduced the term "cyberspace"), *Count Zero* (1986), and *Mona Lisa Overdrive* (1988). In Gibson's world, an Aleph is an expensive biochip with almost limitless storage capacity, containing an approximation of the entire world (referred to as a matrix). The chip allows people to plug into it and live on in cyberspace while leaving the body behind. The memex, the *Aleph*, the *Knowledge Navigator*, as well as the goals of Google "to organize the world's information and make it universally accessible and useful,"[11] should be seen as part of a long history of fantasizing about absolute libraries, starting perhaps with the famed Library of Alexandria (constructed in the third century BC). The problem of such archives – including the real-time, redactable, participatory digital archive that is emerging around us – is not so much the making available of what Italian author Italo Calvino in 1993 satirically described as our *world memory* (in a short story with that title, describing the project of building "a centralized archive of human kind," "a general and simultaneous history of everything . . . moment by moment"[12]), but its underlying system of categorization. This is the essence of the MyLifeBits project: the challenge is not so much the capturing of all the data of life, but rather finding ways to meaningfully organize and access this information. This inevitably entails a structural forgetting in the way we organize data: various ways in which we make it easier or harder to find certain types of information, about certain things, people or activities. This is where Calvino and Borges warn us about the dangers of living with (or in) a total archive, as Calvino writes: "if there is nothing that needs correcting in the world memory, the only thing left to do is to correct reality where it doesn't agree with that memory." Google, as the ambitious collector of all our data, provides the paradigmatic media-life solution to this problem: it ignores or erases sensemaking categories from the wealth of information, and in the process provides privileged access to some (but never all) information.

A retelling of the Aleph story serves as a powerful reminder of what happens when we take the qualities of media to their logical end-point, well beyond Google's ambitions.[13] If we potentially can always see everything at once – or operate under the illusion we do – and therefore have to remember nothing, what kind of world do we experience? This would be an immediate world without history or future, considering the implications of Spanish philosopher George Santayana's 1905 maxim, "those who cannot remember the past are condemned to repeat it."[14] A lack of historical sensibility would thus reduce us to perpetual infancy. In an alarmist book and testimony for the British House of Lords in 2009, Baroness and neuroscientist Susan Greenfield similarly asserts how our immersion in media resembles "the 'booming, buzzing confusion' of the infant brain," reducing us to a "state of sensory oblivion, stripped of all cognitive content and bereft of self-consciousness" (Greenfield, 2009: 259). It may be convenient to dismiss such rhetoric for its a-historicity and the construction of a false before/after media dichotomy, but it is nonetheless important to consider how both utopian and dystopian views have been and will be an essential (if unfortunate) part of the conversation society has with itself regarding its technologies, machines and media.

Mindless Martini media

Outlining the future of the British Broadcasting Corporation (BBC) in May 2005, its Director of New Media and Technology, Ashley Highfield, argued that the company's approach would be based on the assumption that people want to access media "on their terms – anytime, any place, any how – Martini Media. We'll see what programmes appeal in this new world and how people search, sort, snack and savour our content."[15] This vision of media available any time, any place and anywhere included possibilities for users to create and share their own content on BBC websites, which company spokespeople claimed is a typical feature of today's *Martini generation*. The Martini concept refers to a series of 1970s television and radio commercials for Martini, a popular brand of Italian vermouth. The adverts featured a jingle that in 1977 became the hit song "Dancing easy" by South African singer Danny Williams, featuring these memorable words: "capture a moment – that Martini moment – anytime, anyplace, anywhere – there is a wonderful place you can share – and the right one, the right one – that's Martini . . ."[16]

Richard Harper and colleagues remark that in the decades after this advertising campaign the term "Martini solution" has been used with specific reference to (mobile) media, whereby claims are made "that they allow people to do things in time and space that they could never do before" (2004: 536). As the authors suggest, it sometimes seems that, when faced with media's omnipresence, people – professionals and professors alike – cannot help but forget that media tend to be used in specific situations and in particular places. Beyond media's particularities, media in general can be considered to be both ubiquitous and pervasive: they are impossible to (completely) escape from, and cannot be (completely) switched off. With respect to the situated use of media, a third property of media is their remixed nature: all media are reworkings of previous versions, in terms of both their material dimension (e.g. design, infrastructure and functionalities) and their immaterial aspects, such as the various ways in which media are appropriated and used. Beyond these three fundamental properties, what media tend to do primarily in our present-day context is: disappear.

One way of looking at the vanishing spectacle of media is to see how their materials, bit by bit, blend with our living environments. In the field of architectural design, a heightened sensibility about both the material and immaterial dimensions of our mediated living spaces finds expression in the development of so-called *transmaterials*: components used in the construction of buildings that blend all kinds of properties, often including media. Combinations of materials include hardware, software, concrete, wood, masonry, metals, plastic, mechanical and electrical elements, and particular finishes (on walls, doors and windows). Composite transmaterials include concrete walls that combine with optical fiber to enable them to transmit light or project images of the outside world (a Hungarian product called Litracon); a transparent metallic mesh called Mediamesh (developed by German company GKD) that functions to *medialize* building façades by integrating light-emitting diodes that one generally finds in television and computer screens with woven steel; and Sonomorph: a building system consisting of aluminium- and glass-reinforced plastic panels responding to light, the proximity of people, and touch (a product of Norwegian architectural, art and research office Bifokal). According to architect Blaine Brownell, transmaterials share properties in that they are ultraperforming, multidimensional, repurposed and recombinant, intelligent, transformational and interfacial. In his subsequent work on trends in materials innovation, Brownell (2011) signals that one of the most significant trends is dematerialization and an increased ephemerality of materials, as architectural design meets the demands of environmental sustainability and rapidly changing cultural patterns and behaviors.

In the world of computer and video games, the pioneering work of Nintendo can be seen as yet another example of the way media endeavor to drop out of our sight. In 2005 Nintendo introduced a wireless controller interface (nicknamed Wiimote) for its Wii games console, intended to make the player's interaction with the device "intuitive."[17] In 2009 Microsoft followed suit by presenting its Project Natal device, combining a miniature camera, a movement sensor, microphone and computer processor running proprietary motion-capture, facial-recognition and voice-recognition software, allowing for controller-free gaming. In 2010 the project was renamed Kinect (from the Greek word *kinēsis*, meaning movement), deliberately indicating how the human body *becomes* the controller interface of the Xbox game console.

Wiimote and Kinect are steps in what computer designers and developers consider a gradual transition in the way people interact with media devices, from command-line interfaces (typing a limited range of commands on a computer screen) via graphic user interfaces (allowing people to use media via images rather than text, as in the desktop metaphor of personal computers) to a natural user interface (NUI) that is supposedly invisible to its users. Developments in the realm of NUI are moving fast, and signal how design and engineering communities follow cultural trends closely. Colleagues at Indiana University's School of Informatics and School of Fine Arts, for example, developed what they call a Surface Kinetics INterface (SKIN): an interdisciplinary design approach for sophisticated interactive surfaces. For Heekyoung Jung, Youngsuk Altieri and Jeffrey Bardzell, such a design approach emphasizes the affective, experiential and cultural values of digital objects, next to their more mundane functions, and thus recognizes how the multiple media in our lives are not just relatively simple things that we need to perform straightforward tasks with, but rather should be seen as technologies that we interact with in a more or less seamless, mindless, yet profoundly emotional and intimate way:

> As digital technology is applied to everyday objects, interaction design is increasingly polyvalent in its aesthetics; that is, digital artifacts, instead of striving for closed meanings, are now striving for open meaning . . . in a significant conceptual shift, surfaces are no longer about mere decoration of a functional system, but can now embody aesthetic qualities of interaction, both in terms of experiential qualities and the construction of meaning. (2010: 85)

Jung, Altieri and Bardzell started their SKIN design process by considering living creatures – including hedgehogs, starfish and carnivorous plants – as metaphors for objects with surface-changing properties (87). In doing so, they apply organic concepts to the design properties of digital objects, ending up with design concepts such as a cup that would inflate itself when hot liquid is poured in, a tactile computer mouse that changes its surface to make the user aware that she is spending an awful long time clicking and moving it, and an interactive lampshade that changes it shape – like the opening and closing of a flower – depending on the sound level in its immediate surroundings. The work on SKIN is part of a larger project toward "more influential, affective and intimate human–object relationships" (91), premised on a realization that people's relationships with the physical world are dynamic, polyvalent and intuitive. The surface is not necessarily a surface, Jung and his colleagues write, but "it can be essential to the generation of different meanings and experiences" (91).

One does not have to look at the animal world for metaphors to understand and design a physical and technological place – the human body can also be seen as analogous to our physical environment – especially when it comes to media. As museum curator and graphic designer Ellen Lupton (2002) writes, contemporary designers approach the surfaces of products and buildings increasingly in terms of the human skin:

> The rise of digital media over the past decade has changed the practice of design, providing tools for making objects and buildings that resemble living creatures – modeled with complex curves and forms – while remaining distinctly artificial ... Surfaces have acquired depth, becoming dense, complex substances equipped with their own identities and behaviors ... Translucency and mutability have replaced transparency and permanence. The outer envelope has detached from the interior volume. Flexible membranes are embedded with digital and mechanical networks ... Industrial skins have assumed a life of their own.[18]

Two concrete examples of appropriating the human skin not just as a metaphor but as a media artifact are the Skinput sensor device and Bare Conductive ink. Invented by Becky

Pilditch, Matt Johnson, Isabel Lizardi and Bibi Nelson from the Department of Industrial Design Engineering at the Royal College of Art in London, *Bare Conductive* is promoted as a union of the organic and the electronic: a nontoxic, water-soluble ink that can be used to "create custom electronic circuitry on the skin as well as any surface where water-based paints would be appropriate." Among its applications is a project with British DJ Calvin Harris and Sony Music called the *humantheziser*, where people painted with Bare Conductive are played like musical instruments.[19] Skinput is another instance of a similar skin-based natural user interface, applying a method that allows the body to be appropriated for manual input using a wearable bio-acoustic sensor.[20] The design consists of an armband equipped with various vibration sensors, which pick up frequencies that occur when someone taps on the arm with their finger. By projecting an image of, for example, a computer menu onto the lower arm, the body effectively becomes a media input device: the wearer taps a specific part of his or her arm, the signal gets 'sensed' by the armband, and sent as a command to a computer (for example, a portable music player or games console). The designers and researchers involved explain their inspiration for appropriating the human body as an input device by "our sense of how our body is configured in three-dimensional space – [that] allows us to accurately interact with our bodies in an eyes-free manner," thus emphasizing invisibility as a requirement for more effective media-and-life integration. Looking at these and other trends in (contemplating and doing) architectural and interface design corresponds with a general trend in the way we use and think about media in everyday life: they tend to gradually disappear from our active awareness and consideration and thus become profoundly powerful in shaping our actions.

Considering a decade-long series of experiments on how people interact with computers, Clifford Nass and Youngme Moon conclude that individuals mindlessly apply social rules and expectations to computers, ignoring cues that reveal what

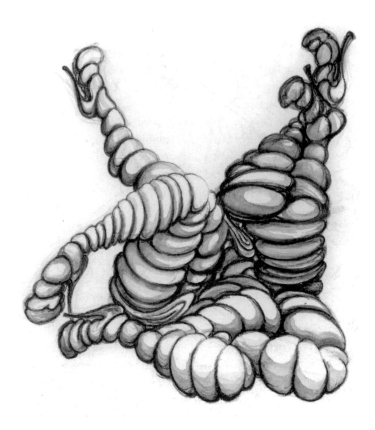

they consider the essential asocial nature of technologies, so that "the treatment of computers as human is ubiquitous" (2000: 84). In later work, Nass and colleagues consider the ubiquity of media multitasking in conjunction with people's generally mindless response to media, suggesting that individuals who use a lot of media at the same time "have a greater tendency for bottom-up attentional control and a bias toward exploratory, rather than exploitative, information processing" (2009: 15585). Although there is not a neat causal relationship between using a lot of media and being distracted all the time (something often suggested in both popular and scholarly publications), Nass points to a phenomenon observed throughout the history of humans and their technologies: that it requires painstaking (mental) work for anyone to be actively aware of the tools they are using when performing daily tasks and rituals. Especially when we consider technology as somehow neutral, Martin Heidegger argues in his essay "On the question of technology" (originally presented as a lecture in 1949), we become blind to the ways in which it structures and shapes our interaction with (and perception of) the world and our role in it: "we shall never experience our relationship to the essence of technology so long as we merely conceive and push forward the technological, put up with it, or evade it. Everywhere we remain unfree and chained to technology, whether we passionately affirm or deny it."[21]

When considering the ubiquity of contemporary media in terms of artifacts, as well as what people generally do with their devices, the emphasis increasingly seems to be on a certain fluidity of content and experiences across multiple media platforms, and a general logic of immediacy governing our daily interactions with media, all coupled with an ongoing drive among those who conceptualize and design media to make our interactions with media effectively invisible. In the movement from bulky, expensive and difficult to handle machines to tiny interactive gadgets, transmaterial-based living spaces and lifelike interfaces that the Martini generation can use any time, any place and anywhere, media today become quite literally, concretely and experientially lifelike.

The key to understanding what the multiple media in our lives do is to move beyond the question of whether they are good or bad for us – and consider their essence as tools, practices and meanings shaping (and being shaped by) the way we are in the world – not just their tendency to become like us, but how media are us. Considering the key qualities of media in terms of their lifelike ubiquity, pervasiveness and remixability brings us a bit closer to a mindset of – as Heidegger would say – turning any media device from a thing we just use (which thus is 'ready-to-hand') into an artifact that is open to questions about what is the matter with it. However, as Marianne van den Boomen notes, we tend to only question media when they stop working or do not work the way they are supposed to – when the "extraordinary apparatus" that is a computer "suddenly becomes a black box" (2009: 253). Your laptop only becomes a machine you think about when it fails to boot up, a mobile phone ceases to be an extension of your lifestyle when you forgot to pay the monthly bill, and a book only becomes a book when its missing a page at a crucial part of the story. Often we only think about media when they break down, or when we attribute some social problem to media. Such an argument obscures a perhaps more accurate observation about what contemporary media tend to do: as commonly invisible interlocutors of our lives, wherever, whenever and whoever we are, they record, store, access and ultimately redact life.

Yes we can (record, store, access and redact life)!

Today's media record, store, access and control your life. Regarding the media's qualities of recording and storing data, the promise of providing a lifetime store of everything inspires a consideration of the social implications of a life lived vicariously through media, where (potentially) everything gets stored and therefore nothing needs to be remembered. Increasingly, our current media devices record everything we do – whether we like it or not: internet service providers and other telecommunications companies (sometimes pressured by security firms, police organizations, and government agencies) keep logs of our phone calls placed, e-mails sent, applications downloaded, videos watched and websites visited. Much of the recording is done by machines – dataveillance which enables highly automated and systematic observation of data.[22] This machine-to-machine (M2M) communication about what we are generally up to is the second leading source of accelerating internet traffic (after mobile data), according to a 2012 analysis by Cisco Systems.[23] This would seem to suggest that it is not only optional, but also advisable to find ways to circumvent or outrightly reject the recording of our lives through the media we use. Yet most of this archiving of life is done not by machines, nor by ominous government agencies or impenetrable corporate strongholds, but by individuals and peer groups among themselves. Most significantly, the key to understanding the archive in media life is to look at how people document, maintain, share and publicize their own existence in media – a practice called *life caching* by consumer trends firm Trendwatching (in 2005): "collecting, storing and displaying one's entire life, for private use, or for friends, family, even the entire world to peruse," using omnipresent digital tools and technologies such as free blogging software, memory sticks, high-definition cameras and all other kinds of "life capturing and storing devices."[24] Beyond life caching, several emerging practices refer to the potential of a media life completely recorded and archived on a permanent basis, including the making public (and indeed publicizing) of life in media:

- lifestreaming: a precursor to Gordon Bell's MyLifeBits project, originally defined in 1997 by Eric Freeman as "a time-ordered stream of documents that functions as a diary of your electronic life; every document you create or other people send you is stored in your lifestream" (1997: 14);
- lifecasting: live broadcasting of your everyday experiences using wearable media or a webcam via social media platforms such as Ustream or Stickam.[25]
- lifelogging: Canadian computer scientist Steve Mann in 2002 experimented with *cyborglogs* or glogs, in which individuals are supposed to record and publish their everyday experiences "while walking around, often without any conscious thought and effort, as stream-of-(de)consciousness

glogging."[26] The goal of lifelogging, as *Wired* magazine's Kevin Kelly stipulates, is to record, archive and share all information in one's life.[27]

Considering the fact that the vast majority of people's time online (in media) is spent at social networks like Facebook, the many variations of recording, storing and publishing one's life are not only a mainstream pursuit, but altogether more vast and powerful than any top-down registry or archive of citizens or consumers can be. Archives in the past could be associated with a kind of dark, gothic and labyrinthine library, as for example featured in the 1986 film *The Name Of The Rose* (featuring Sean Connery, directed by Jean-Jacques Annaud), based on Umberto Eco's 1980 novel *Il nome della rosa*, in which access to the archive and control over its contents is a privilege – an elitist enterprise. In the book and film, people are murdered as punishment for accessing and reading what were considered subversive books in the tightly controlled and rather ominous library of a fourteenth-century monastery. In today's media life, archives are predominantly created, curated and collectively shared in real time among individuals and institutions alike. Access to subversive material is not only paramount, the information itself is generated and made available by the individual users of the archive.

The notion of recording, storing and sharing access and curation of your life in media may not be equally appealing to everyone. Beyond such apprehension, it may not even be such a good idea to willingly submit to the essentially self-revealing nature of contemporary media life. Asked for advice on what it takes to become president when speaking with a group of 14- and 15-year-olds on September 8, 2009, US President Barack Obama answered: "I want everybody here to be careful about what you post on Facebook, because in the YouTube age, whatever you do, it will be pulled up again later somewhere in your life. And when you're young, you make mistakes and you do some stupid stuff."[28]

Such advice seems to make sense – as employers reportedly check social network sites to research job candidates. Countries such as Germany and Spain attempt to curtail such practices, seeking to make it illegal for prospective employers to check up on applicants' private postings – clearly assuming that as we live through networks of mass self-communication sometimes we need to be protected from ourselves.[29] Although such efforts may be noble, there is perhaps something to be said for not opting out, for enthusiastically embracing the recording, storing and sharing potential of present-day media. Ironically, this insight is also shared by President Obama, if one considers his statement (on January 28, 2011) in response to the mass demonstrations across Egypt, referring directly to the Egyptian government's attempts to shut down the country's internet and mobile communication services: "I also call upon the Egyptian government to reverse the actions that they've taken to interfere with access to the internet, to cell phone service and to social networks that do so much to connect people in the 21st century."[30]

Considering the amplifying and accelerating role mobile phones (especially texting) and online social networks play in current processes of social change – such as in Ukraine in 2004, Iran in 2009, Egypt in 2011, and Syria in 2012 – it seems as if the future belongs to those clearly not shying away from sharing their life and passions with the world in media. Sherry Beck Paprocki, one of the authors of *The complete idiot's guide to branding yourself* (2009) states in the *New York Times* (of March 27, 2009), "If you don't brand yourself, Google will brand you," referring to a perceived need to control the kind of information people find about you when they type your name into a search engine. *New York Times* reporter Alina Tugend motivates her story on the challenge of presenting yourself online as "Not being online today is akin to not existing."[31] Apparently, it is not enough to have a profile on Facebook – you need a Twitter account and a YouTube channel, you should be uploading your own video mash-ups, design custom levels in your favorite computer game, and on the whole use any kind of media to tell everyone about everything.

American comedian and satirist Stephen Colbert – host of the popular TV show *The Colbert Report* on the Comedy Central cable television channel – uses the examples of Blippy.com (where people list all their credit card purchases) and IJustMadeLove.com (where you can publicly register every time you have had sex) to propose a new service integrating all the online places where "ordinary people . . . publicize their lives in minute detail."[32] In a segment aired on February 2, 2010, Colbert christens such a site as Knowny: "which records every interaction, every movement of every person on earth and posts them online like a storm of random data points that shouts out to the blind, indifferent universe: 'we exist! we exist! please, please, let this mean something!'" His explanation for our seemingly insatiable appetite (and the increased social pressure) to mediate almost everything about our lives is the human desire to be known: "cognoscor ergo sum [translation: I am known, therefore I am]". Albeit indirectly, Colbert seems to refer to the assumption rooted in the ancient Greek philosophy and literature of Plato and Homer – namely, that at the heart of human being lies the desire to be recognized (in Greek: *thumos* or *thymos*). Francis Fukuyama uses this concept of "thymotic self-assertion" (1966: 173) to articulate how, historically, increasing freedom of expression can be coupled with people's rising expectations and demands regarding their sense of identity and self. Zygmunt Bauman adds that a media life is not just about being known but, perhaps more importantly, about being seen – suggesting that René Descartes' famous proof of existence "I think therefore I am" (originally published in 1637), in a fully mediated mode of being has been elbowed out by "I am seen, therefore I am" (2010: 20). To put it somewhat differently, in the context of this book: people want to be known and seen, and a media life can (finally) fulfill that desire. Colbert raises a profoundly significant question at the end of his show: whether what we are mediating (making us "fully known") is the same as who we really are (as that is "kinda personal").

During the 1990s numerous authors suggested that the main motivations for collectively recording and sharing our lives in media are identity play, such as gender bending (trying out a different gender by choosing and outfitting avatars in particular ways), and creating a *second self* that lives in the virtual world of computer screens and internet. Perhaps unsurprisingly, researchers at the time generally found confirmation of the hypothesis that intensive media use in general, and being online in particular, contribute to social isolation. Most of these studies were carried out well before the start of social media like Friendster (2002), MySpace (2003), Facebook (2004), YouTube (2005) and Twitter (2006). As communication scholars Patti Valkenburg and Jochen Peter conclude based on a review of the literature, in the years since such services launched the exact opposite conclusion tends to be drawn in studies on mediated modes of social cohesion and community formation, leading them to hypothesize "that online self-disclosure accounts for the positive relationship between online communication and social connectedness" (2009: 4). Similar assessments by sociologists (DiMaggio et al., 2001) as well as psychologists (Bargh and McKenna, 2004) confirm that the way media work on issues such as cultural participation, community and social capital, psychological well-being, and the formation and maintenance of personal relationships enhances rather than ejects existing patterns of behavior. A general conclusion seems to be that the "unique, even transformational qualities," of internet in particular and, considering the internet's assimilation into other media, media in general, "encourage self-expression [which] facilitates the formation of relationships on other, deeper bases such as shared values and beliefs" (586).

A nuanced appraisal of what media do either overlooks, ignores or takes for granted the intrinsically interwoven character of human–machine relationships. An important dimension in all of this, as Stephen Colbert so eloquently noted, is the real or perceived need for an audience. "In Space No One Can Hear You Scream" reads the tagline with which the science-fiction horror film *Alien* (1979) was promoted. In cyberspace, everyone screams – and it is difficult, if not impossible, to tell whether anyone is listening. All of this mediated screaming is part of a shift "where *social* life has already turned into an *electronic* life or *cyber*life" according to Zygmunt Bauman (2007: 2; italics in original). For Bauman, today's media are "electronic confessionals" that turn people into "apprentices training and trained in the art of living in a confessional society" (2–3).

Bauman's cyberlife is primarily a consuming life, as he sees people in media turning into commodities requiring constant updating, remaking, marketing and promoting. Our social network profiles are like the pictures of food next to a fast-food chain restaurant's drive-through lane: overemphasizing the attractiveness and juiciness of what is on display, downplaying or altogether erasing the generally bland and definitely not-always-good-for-you-substance that will be yours once purchase is made. It is a compelling perspective, particularly when set against the often less than thoughtful ways in which people connect (and disconnect), friend (or defriend), log on (and log off). Bauman accentuates his apprehension about what he considers as a built-in "possibility of instant, trouble-free and (hopefully) painless disconnection" (2007: 107) of media life. For the philosopher, this is a life lived literally on *surfaces* (cf. screens), and figuratively on the *surface* – a "perception of current social bonds and commitments as momentary snapshots in the ongoing process of renegotiation, rather than as steady states bound to last indefinitely" (2010: 17). On the other hand, people's interactions online and confessional behavior in media generally are quite meaningful – just as such actions offline are, leading scholars of interpersonal communication in media, such as Nancy Baym, to conclude that "new media do not offer inauthentic simulations that detract from or substitute for real engagement" (2010: 98). In other words: there is nothing necessarily superficial (or deep) about media life.

The key here would be not to draw distinctions between what people do and what media do, but to focus on what the qualities of living in media are. What happens in a media life remixes the permanence of sheer limitless recording and storage of every single aspect of our lives with the relative impermanence of continuously communicating all that detailed information to the world. Mass self-communication consists of self-monitoring, self-branding and self–other interaction, concurrently using a dynamically changing array of technologies and services. The media we use for these practices technically structure the way our activities are recorded and stored, softly determine how we (and others) access the data, and offer affordances to redact, edit and revise information about ourselves and others. In the process, media subtly augment and extend life as we wield them through increasingly natural user interfaces (such as touchscreens and motion sensors). Media disappear, only to re-appear as atmospheres, moods, abilities and personalities. It should therefore come as no surprise that people truly care about their media – and this emotional engagement with our *devices of wonder* (the title of a 2001 exhibition on the history of sense-enhancing and image-making technologies at the Getty Museum in Los Angeles[33]) accelerates what media do: recording, storing and sharing our lives. Yet this archival quality of media is as plastic as our sense of identity and community, as the link between a memory and its recording gets lost in the process of electronically filing just about everything about ourselves while opening up these private folders to public perusal and redaction. The disconnect starts when people construct and (through constant editing of their archive) reconstruct their identities and life narratives in their online archive, is further complicated by the ability of others to participate in these collections (e.g. cutting and pasting, tagging, annotating, forwarding and reposting), and becomes permanent through the highly idiosyncratic organization and practical day-to-day uses of the archive by individual users, their circle of friends and contacts, commercial companies, government agencies and the general public. This shift from the archive as a relatively closed, top-down, and institutionally controlled system to a more or less open, participatory and user-generated organism, when coupled with the ubiquity of recording practices particular to both the material and immaterial dimensions of media, leads Nicholas Gane and David Beer to argue that "life today is increasingly being played out *through* the archive than simply stored within it" (2008: 82; italics in original). In the foreword to their aptly titled *Information is alive* collection of essays (published in 2003), Joke Brouwer and Arjen Mulder similarly consider the sweeping ramifications of a persistently recorded, archived and redacted life: "In an information society there is no position outside of the [storing, linking, reprocessing, transforming and complexification of data] flows, an external position from which you can criticize or transcend the flows . . . We do not live in a society that uses digital archiving, we live in an information society that is a digital archive."[34]

The permanently impermanent archive

A recorded life in digital participatory culture presupposes a living archive. Considering qualities of media makes them come alive and be part of everything we do. German philosopher Sybille Krämer unequivocally states that "Everything we can say, find out and know about the world is being said, found out and known with the help of media" (1998: 73). In her edited volume *Performativität und Medialität* (2004), Krämer engages media life using the concept of *mediality* – suggesting that people perform themselves in terms of media. Consider, for example, how media can both benchmark and routinize observations about our environment, while at the same time disappearing from direct awareness.

Mediality operates between performativity and textuality, according to Krämer – between who we (think) we are, and what we do (from one moment to the next) – and thus introduces an inherently interactive and liquid dimension to life. What the process of publicly and privately, voluntarily and unintentionally recording, storing and redacting everything about our lives tells us about what media do is that today each of us has, as Vannevar Bush originally described, "a roomful of girls" continuously filing away our memories and experiences using increasingly invisible "motion-picture and magic-lantern equipment."

Whether we like it or not, whether we opt in or out, whether we choose to drop anchor or just surf the waves in a sea of information, what seems to be paramount is an overall tendency to accept (or expect) an almost organic archiving and redaction as the principal components of media life. Writer and artist Eugene Thacker defines this process as one of humanity and technology co-evolving as *biomedia*, explaining how contemporary biology and computing – such as, for example, in the mapping and manipulation of DNA – are based on a common assumption: "that there exists some fundamental equivalency between genetic 'codes' and computer 'codes,' or between the biological and digital domains, such that they can be rendered interchangeable" (2004: 5). For Thacker, the ongoing public and popular debate about the ways in "which a medium associated with immateriality and disembodiment will affect our views of having bodies and being bodies" (2003: 47) misses the point of what biomedia do: they turn the human body into a "body-to-come" (78). Media life as embodied experience comes with the caveat of permanent pliability – the expectation of auto-becoming and self-creation.

As more and more aspects of our personality and identity are mediated, our lives begin to mimic and express the qualities of media. In a telling example of this process, Nick Yee, Jeremy Bailenson and Nicolas Ducheneaut (2009) demonstrate how people interact with their avatars in collaborative

virtual environments (such as online games, discussion platforms, company intranets and so on): they adapt their behavior
based on what they look like online. This *Proteus effect* reveals
a subtle and pervasive process whereby media users make
inferences about their expected dispositions from their avatar's appearance and then conform to the expected attitudes
and behavior. What is fascinating about such a protean effect
– found for example in people who become friendlier towards
others online when their avatar seems attractive – is what is
notable about such mediated identities and lifestyles in general: they are endlessly flexible, versatile and adaptable. The
Greek myth of Proteus – as documented in the eighth-century
BC poem *The Odyssey* (attributed to Homer) – describes the
capability of the divine creature Proteus to rapidly change his
appearance in order to avoid capture. The protean quality to
endlessly mutate and elude permanent form can be ascribed
to his primary identity as a sea-god: a creature of the water. In
media, being liquid is not beholden to the gods (any more);
real, perceived or projected malleability transcends virtual
worlds or online games, and increasingly includes any engagement with media: from user profiles on social networks,
personalized menus and log-in settings on computers and
digital video recorders, to customized ringtones on mobile
phones. Makeovers, upgrades and adaptations are never complete, and, with Proteus in mind, must always be considered a
permanently unfinished, ever-flowing, liquid project.

The recording and storage qualities of media in life are thus
not necessarily capturing our essence, but give us (and others)
access to multiple versions of ourselves. How we manage all
these archived versions comes to be a crucial competence, to
be mastered over the course of a media life. As we co-construct
all these self-presentations, some of their characteristics are
reflections of who we (think we) are: our preferences, our
preferred memories. Some aspects of our attitude and behavior are distinctly protean, in that we to some extent become
the version(s) of us that is flexibly shaped in media. Imagine

collecting all the data about you that are recorded and stored
in digital archives – an elaborated project that would start with
a couple of hours of *egosurfing*: Googling yourself. Is every
version of you that lives in media the same – can we recognize and thus know ourselves and others in media, or do we
have to skillfully navigate and negotiate all the different bits
and pieces? A follow-up question would be whether the information about you (or anyone else) serves as an instrument
of prediction, or what Richard Grusin calls a logic of *premediation*, which "insists that the future itself is also already
mediated, and that with the right technologies . . . the future
can be remediated before it happens. This remediation is not
only formal but reformative" (2004: 19).

Grusin compares the way premediation works with the
Precrime division in the Philip K. Dick short story "The
minority report" (1956). In Dick's narrative, three "deformed
and retarded" (1987: 325) individuals work as precogs: they
can see into the future and predict who will commit a crime,
allowing the police to arrest them before the crime takes
place. On their own, these people are useless, but "impressive
banks of equipment" including "data-receptors" and "computing mechanisms" study and translate their prophecies into
actionable information. While Grusin chooses to focus on
the media's knack of premediating the future (and thereby
succeeding in removing the elements of surprise and seren-
dipity from our experience of what will happen), I am more
interested in a central point of Dick's story: the fact that the
precogs always produce multiple versions of the future, and
it is up to media and their users to figure out which report
is the one to go with. This choice in turn creates other time-
paths, bifurcating possibilities of different futures, and so on.
The role of media in this context is to record and store potential prospects and assist in the translation and projection of
possible time-paths. In addition to *Minority Report* (2002),
several of Philip K. Dick's stories have been made into popular motion pictures, famously including "Do androids dream

of electric sheep?" (1968; into *Blade Runner* in 1982) and "We can remember it for you wholesale" (1966; into *Total Recall* in 1990). Beyond the compelling science-fiction and technology-inspired visionry, Dick's work calls attention to the profoundly permeable perimeters between different types or versions of reality, between humans and machines, and ultimately between any kind of categories people use to make sense of the world. What makes his work so appropriate for a consideration of media life is its early signaling of malleability as the governing principle that underlies a life lived in media.

The future as thought of in media life is malleable, a quality which is intrinsic to the media people use on a daily basis, and therefore can be seen as in part made by the materiality of media. The fusion of human and non-human in direct reference to machines owes tribute to the emerging mechanistic worldview of the seventeenth century, according to evolutionary anthropologist Matt Cartmill, who outlines how from the 1600s "the natural world came to be seen as a vast machine, in which human beings were the only conscious entities and animals were nothing but robots made of meat" (1993: 93). This opened the door for philosophers and scientists alike to start looking for the machine in everything – including the body. Cartmill quotes English philosopher Thomas Hobbes, who in 1651 asked "why may we not say, that all *Automata* . . . have an artificial life? For what is the *Heart*, but a *Spring*? and the *Nerves*, but so many *Strings*?" (94; italics in original). While René Descartes may have been careful to separate the human mind from what Cartmill calls "the world machine," at some point bridging the man–machine gap would become inevitable. French physician Julien Offray de La Mettrie – in his 1748 essay "L'homme machine" [translated as "Man A Machine" or "Machine Man"] – argued against Descartes' distinction between matter and soul, instead suggesting that who we are, how we think and what we do are all mutually implicated. In his essay, De La Mettrie suggests that our expressions in (and use of) machines, technology, and media necessarily introduce an element of plasticity into our lives – removing a notion of predetermination or even predictability about what it means to be human:

> Words, languages, laws, sciences, and the fine arts have come, and by them finally the rough diamond of our mind has been polished. Man . . . has become an author . . . All has been accomplished through signs . . . and in this way men have acquired symbolic knowledge . . . Who invented the means of utilizing the plasticity of our organism? I cannot answer . . . I think that everything is the work of imagination, and that all the faculties of the soul can be correctly reduced to pure imagination in which they all consist. Thus judgment, reason, and memory are not absolute parts of the soul, but merely modifications of this kind of medullary screen upon which images of the objects painted in the eye are projected as by a magic lantern.[35]

De La Mettrie's words allow us to consider what media do on a symbolical as well as biological level. Symbolically, they introduce, amplify and extend a distinct sense of malleability into our lives: we become, and are considered or expected to be, authors of ourselves. Biologically, media produce and are produced by their materiality: the codes, protocols, conventions, wiring, programs and constituent parts that make up our media allow us to tell specific stories about ourselves. Perhaps it is possible to argue that all media together simulate our collective Aleph: in theory, we could see anything, everyone, anywhere, instantaneously. But our design and use of media imply that they do not really exist – we are wired to respond to media mindlessly. *We see everything without witnessing anything.* What gives media power, in other words, is their invisibility. If we side with Socrates for a moment, perhaps we could turn the tables on our media: if they put our experience of the world at a distance (and thus turn every single encounter with people and things into just another story to be recorded, stored and endlessly redacted), we should use media to put media at a distance – and quite possibly discover ourselves in the process.

CHAPTER FOUR

No Life Outside Media

where we become profiling machines

"If you put intimacy into a system, what kind of intimacy do you get back?" This is the question at the heart of the work of American media artist Jill Magid.[1] One of her installations, "Lincoln Ocean Vector Eddy" (L.O.V.E., 2007), takes on this question by logging encounters with a New York transit officer, who rides the subway all night long randomly searching some of its passengers (such warrantless police searches were introduced after the World Trade Center attacks of September 11, 2001).[2] Magid asks the officer to search her – deliberately interpreting the new rules literally – and he refuses, after which they start a testy relationship in which she explores to what extent she can feel secure (or not) with him in private or in public. In earlier work, Magid designed and developed a "Surveillance Shoe" (2000): complete with high heels and a built-in surveillance camera pointing upwards, and a battery pack and wireless transmitter embedded in the sole. The video footage of the project gives the viewer a voyeuristic peek up her skirt as she walks across town, while at the same time recording video of the city around her. As she explains, "Due to the fixed position of the camera to the shoe, that leg remains bound within the frame. While this leg appears stable like architecture, the actual architecture becomes mobile."[3] By stretching one's subjective experience of (and intimate relationship with) the lived environment to the objects it consists of – such as buildings, fashion and, most deliberately, media – Magid indirectly embraces a media-life point of view in her work.

Other examples of projects trying to bring forth intimacy and agency in omnipresent media can be found in the work of the US-based Surveillance Camera Players and the British Guerrilla Geographers. The Surveillance Camera Players (SCP) formed in New York in November 1996, and consist of a small group of people deliberately performing adaptations of contemporary plays in front of publicly installed surveillance cameras, thus providing the security officers the opportunity to watch some entertainment while they are scrutinizing the environment.[4] The group performed pieces in several cities around the US as well as in cities in Europe (including Amsterdam, Munich and Barcelona), and published a book entitled *We know you are watching* (2006), documenting its work, position papers, exhibits and other exploits. Similar groups in France and Australia use omnipresent media to disrupt rather than circumvent society's surveillance systems, generally to – as the Surveillance Camera Players' website states – unconditionally oppose the installation and use of video surveillance cameras in public places. The Guerilla Geographers direct their actions at people rather than those who watch them, as they are "engaged in engaging the public in small bands or groups . . . to cause thought, connected thinking, and stimulate the public and to wear down public resistance to geography, usually carried on by a number of small groups behind public(s) lines."[5] When moving about in public spaces, the artists wear clearly visible surveillance cameras (for example, mounted on helmets) and confront the people and place around them to raise awareness of the pervasive and invasive nature of closed-circuit television (CCTV) in everyday life.

The omnipresent and pervasive nature of media raises the specter of a globally emerging surveillance society, in which (in the words of media scholar and activist Felix Stalder) the "creation, collection and processing of personal data is nearly a ubiquitous phenomenon."[6] Benchmarking the field of surveillance studies, David Lyon remarks that "All societies that are dependent on communication and information technologies for administrative and control processes are surveillance societies. The effects of this are felt in ordinary everyday life, which is closely monitored as never before in history" (2001: 1). In later work, Lyon defines surveillance as "the focused, systematic and routine attention to personal details for purposes of influence, management, protection or direction" (2007: 14). Beyond noting that surveillance is, at the very least, an ambiguous concept carrying benevolent as well as clandestine connotations, Lyon calls attention to what surveillance does to people – how we act or feel differently in a given situation or place knowing (or assuming) that our behavior may be monitored, tracked, recorded and watched. This does not necessarily mean people feel more or less secure this way, nor does it fundamentally constitute an invasion of privacy. Even before the rapid proliferation of CCTV worldwide, and well in advance of sophisticated user profiling enabled through commercial Internet Service Providers, David Altheide observed in the 1980s how people, in the real or perceived presence of photo and video cameras, increasingly behaved in terms of what he labeled a *media self* (1984), always aware of at least the possibility of being captured in media. According to Altheide, such a persona is deeply performative, and learns (or is forced to learn) to constantly adapt to changing mediated circumstances. Lawrence Grossberg similarly foresaw an emerging "everyday world of media life" (1988: 389; italics added) experienced everyday in terms of our overwhelming orientation to omnipresent media. We are all surveillance camera players, and have been for quite a while.

Discipline, control and suspicion

Being seen changes our behavior. Monitoring, in this context, comes in many forms – and gets exploited for a variety of purposes. In his influential book *Discipline and punish* (1995[1975]), Michel Foucault extends this fundamental aspect of our biological wiring to the way society organizes itself around practices and expectations of surveillance. Foucault makes a powerful argument for looking at all social institutions – including schools, the military, factories, the office workplace, hospitals, as well as the modern family – as disciplinary mechanisms for monitoring and supervising people intended to instill docility and a consensual, one-size-fits-all morality. One would assume only prisons fulfill such a specific function, but Foucault challenges that conjecture, instead arguing that the prison is just the special-ized and preeminent locus of the realization of a disciplined and orderly society, embodying the ideals of "surveillance and observation, security and knowledge, individualization and totalization, isolation and transparency" (249).

Foucault's work is relevant for concerns regarding media life for two reasons. First, because he relates the emergence of a disciplinary society, as based on continuous surveillance and examination of its participants, to the rapid rise of technolo-gies and corresponding bureaucracies during the eighteenth and nineteenth centuries. Second, his genealogical trajectory mirrors media history insofar as today's concerns about ubiq-uitous and pervasive media can be seen as a logical extension of a development that has its roots not in omnipresent cam-eras or sophisticated digital tracking technologies, but in the self-organization of society as a whole. Gilles Deleuze extends Foucault's predictions by suggesting that a successfully dis-ciplined society based on our willing participation in vast spaces of enclosure (i.e. schools, factories, hospitals, prisons) ultimately would fade to the background, giving way to more subtle and therefore much more powerful ways of controlling the movements and actions of people.[7] With Deleuze, Richard Sennett (2006) discusses how, in the current culture of capi-talism, the factory as a model and concrete embodiment of control is replaced by the corporation, exerting influence not through constituting (and monitoring) its employees as a par-ticular group working together at a specific place, but rather by having temporarily assembled teams of individuals who compete with each other and among themselves for a chance to work and be recognized for working. Such temporary alliances are, furthermore, increasingly stretched across geo-graphical and temporal boundaries, as corporate holdings and their associated production networks span the globe.

If today's work environment increasingly embodies a social system governed by individually internalized modes of control, so is the contemporary family, as the supposed cornerstone of society or even civilization (as politicians and the clergy often like to state), turning into a dispersed and continually reassembling network. As in the contemporary workplace, the ties that bind the family as a more or less cohesive social unit are primarily sustained through monitoring at-a-distance, rather than through direct supervision. Family surveillance in the media-life context often works quite literally, as evidenced by trending styles of helicopter parenting experienced by children well into early adulthood. Considering the philosophy of *frictionless sharing*[8] informing the functionalities of social media such as Facebook and Spotify, Mary Gray reminds us of the way surveillance technologies mediatized the lives of teenagers in general and college students in particular, from the start: "While many members of earlier generations may find this level of self-disclosure and showcasing a tad creepy, remember: this is the nannycam generation. These students have been closely monitored and on display since they were in diapers. Is their comfort with online exposition (or exhibitionism) so surprising?" (2007: 74).

Canadian journalist Carl Honoré (2008) describes in-vogue mediated styles of parenting as *hyperparenting*, exemplified by the tendency of parents to closely monitor and track (and, when perceived necessary, like a helicopter swooping down, to intervene in) the lives of their children. According to Honoré this parenting style is a global phenomenon, fueled in part by a consumer culture's expectations of the possibility of a perfect life, with corresponding pressures to create the perfect childhood. In the context of today's work-centered lifestyles among middle-class families, much of this fretting over whether the kids are all right takes place in media. David Morley brings to mind the British example of the KidsOK service (operating from 2004 onwards), whereby a charity-supported commercial company provides parents with a mobile mapping service that automatically sends information on the location of their child's mobile – equipped with a global positioning system (GPS) receiver – to their cell phones. Referring to these and other cases of parental surveillance internationally, Morley concludes that "This is a world in which virtual parenting now has to carry some part of the burden of childcare and where being in electronic contact with a child . . . may come to play an increasing role in patterns of childcare" (2007: 208).

The combination of parenting, surveillance and media life – Morley uses the term *teleparenting* – can further manifest itself through installing technology in cars that allows at-a-distance monitoring of location and speed (and in the case of the Teensurance program of the Safeco Insurance company in Seattle, it can also remotely unlock car doors, call for roadside assistance, and shut off the ignition when parents want to control the automobile movements of their teenage child).[9] Communication researchers James Hay and Jeremy Packer contextualize the gradual move of sophisticated media and communications technologies from the office and home into the car in terms of how the supposedly liberating potential of auto-mobility and mobile communication gets deployed to enable finer forms of surveillance, social scrutiny and control. Referring to the work of Belgian sociologist Armand Mattelart, Hay and Packer argue that "movement and connectivity, particularly as they have been bound up with a concern about freedoms, are profoundly matters of governance – of governing oneself, of being governed through technologies, rules, routes and also (though not primarily) by political government" (2004: 218). In his book *The globalization of surveillance* (2010[2007]), Mattelart signals the emergence of a global *suspicion society* emerging from and existing next to discipline and control societies, based on a "mode of governing society by tracking" (of bodies and goods), whereby a preferred and ostensibly propagandized lifestyle of self-constraint and constant vigilance fuses with "new systems of full-time remote surveillance based on the inquisitional power of information technology" (198).

Although discipline, control and suspicion, according to Foucault, Deleuze and Mattelart, seem absolute, the essence of such analyses of the human condition is the way they reveal power to command, to cultivate and to catechize concern as distributed across all elements and aspects of society (and not just resting in the hands of a secret or discreet elite), being part and parcel of even the most mundane and intimate experiences of everyday life. Discipline, therefore, is enforced as well as (potentially) subverted by all individuals in everything they do. A second marker of these three thinkers' work in the story of media life follows directly from this observation, as power is not something that is essentially embodied by a select few, but rather must be considered as something always felt and acted upon, but never seen. Like media, power is everywhere yet nowhere – as it generally seems invisible or hardly noticeable to us. And much like media, such power is omnipresent, always watching (and recording) us in everything we do. As our lives move into media, monitoring has become a mundane, perhaps even *desirable*, part of social subjectivity.[10]

O Big Brother, wherefore art thou?

The various takes on the ubiquity of power through the practice of monitoring take their original cue from the writings of Jeremy Bentham, an English jurist and philosopher, who in the late seventeenth century proposed a model of a disciplined and orderly society based on being able to see everything and everyone all the time. Bentham called his principle of construction and plan of management a "Panopticon" (translation: all-observing).

In 1786 Bentham visited Russia to see his brother Samuel, who was charged with supervising a large number of workers and businesses in operation on the estate of Prince Potemkin.[11] In a series of letters to his father back home in London, Jeremy reflected on this experience, particularly regarding the intricate solutions his brother came up with to keep order among all the people under his supervision. These letters were eventually published in 1791, featuring his proposal for a plan of management "containing the idea of a new principle of construction applicable to any sort of establishment, in which persons of any description are to be kept under inspection."[12] This "inspection principle" would govern all orderly interactions between people in a space larger than just a block of buildings, according to Bentham, and its purpose was that of *"punishing the incorrigible, guarding the insane, reforming the vicious, confining the suspected, employing the idle, maintaining the helpless, curing the sick, instructing the willing* in any branch of industry, or *training the rising race* in the path of *education"* (italics in original). For Bentham, people working, learning, shopping, or doing just about anything else under constant surveillance would guarantee they would always be doing what they were expected to do.

Bentham's optimistic suggestions for a near-perfect society operating under conditions of invariable inspection clearly resonate in contemporary scholarship and literature, featuring prominently in George Orwell's book *Nineteen eighty-four* (1949). In this work, Orwell describes a totalitarian society whose citizens live under constant surveillance via omnipresent telescreens, which are monitored by the Thought Police.[13] People are reminded of this surveillance through televised advertisements and posters with the slogan "Big Brother is watching you" – but no one really knows who Big Brother is, or whether he is in fact a real person. Orwell clearly puts a more pessimistic spin on Bentham's utopian vision, raising doubts about the supposed benevolence of a centrally organized apparatus of inspection. His dystopian depiction of the consequences of a conformity-demanding all-pervasive surveillance system has been cleverly adopted by the advertising industry to rally consumers behind the banner of supposedly different, edgy or otherwise non-conformist products and services. The key example would be Apple's "1984" advertisement, which was directed by Ridley Scott and broadcast only once on American television on January 22, 1984. In the video a young woman dressed in Apple colors to represent Apple's

Macintosh personal computer destroys a giant telescreen featuring *Big Brother* (representing Apple's rival, IBM) as a means of saving humanity from conformity.[14] In 2004 the commercial was remixed and rebroadcast to introduce the iPod, and it has been parodied many times, including on March 5, 2007 by a supporter of at-that-time US Senator Barack Obama, inserting images and sound bites of Hillary Clinton (as Big Brother) and the logo of the Obama election campaign (on the shirt of the young woman) into Apple's 2004 remake of its original 1984 ad.

The juxtaposition of conformity against originality as an expression of concerns over omnipresent surveillance provides a seductive platform – not just for intellectual exploration, but also for compelling entertainment. In 1999 the reality television show *Big Brother* premiered on Dutch television as the brainchild of John De Mol Produkties (today part of Endemol Holdings, owned by Spanish telecommunications company Telefónica). The show featured 12 people living in a house outfitted with cameras everywhere, initially streaming their video recordings live on the Web. The day's footage was presented in a rigorously edited format for a daily primetime television broadcast. The show became massively popular, and local or regional editions and adaptations can be seen on television stations all over the world. Its central premise – an audience watching people coexist in a confined space with the power to vote individuals off the show (and thus out of their community of choice) – resembles Bentham's intentions for a panoptic plan of people management, as it is based on one's ability to see without being seen, to give "transient and incidental directions" determining what happens to those under surveillance.[15] There is something to be said for a view on life in our immersively mediated society as resembling, at least in part, the lived experience of a contestant in a massive reality television show, where you seem to have little or no control over the decision to vote you off – as in when or how you will lose your job, your partner, and even your home. All seem to be contingent upon the whimsical and intangible move-ments of global capital, markets, information and ideas, and your best bet is to be on public display (and on best behavior) at all times. As social network scholar danah boyd suggests about people's tendency to overshare personal information online, "in many situations, there is more to be gained by accepting the public default than by going out of one's way to keep things private. And here's where we see the shift. It used to take effort to be public. Today, it often takes effort to be private."[16]

Orwell's book and the *Big Brother* television format only pick up the pragmatic parts of Bentham's work. More signifi-cant than Bentham's proposals for building and managing a specific inspection infrastructure are his philosophical ideas about the purported consequences of surveillance for the way people work, live and play. As he writes in his first letter:

> Ideal perfection, if that were the object, would require that each person should actually be in that predicament [of being under constant surveillance], during every instant of time. This being impossible, the next thing to be wished for is, that, at every instant, seeing reason to believe as much, and not being able to satisfy himself to the contrary, he should *conceive* himself to be so. (italics in original)

In the fifth letter to his father, Bentham adds that "the per-sons to be inspected should always feel themselves as if under inspection, at least as standing a great chance of being so." What Bentham suggests – and what Foucault uses to ground his powerful theory of panopticism – is that surveil-lance in itself is not all-important. In fact, for a Benthamian ideal society to exist, only the *illusion* of surveillance is neces-sary: people need to think (at least most of the time, and in all things they do) that they are watched, tracked and moni-tored. Such an illusion is produced by people as individuals: we behave differently in situations where we think we are being watched. This can work quite literally, as studies show how people behave more cooperatively in places where there are subtle cues of observation – such as posters on the wall featuring close-ups of human eyes (as reported in a 2010 British experimental study by psychologists Max Ernest-Jones, Daniel Nettle and Melissa Bateson). Social scrutiny, enhanced and amplified by media, induces an evolved psychology of cooperation.

People-profiling service 123people used international Data Privacy Day (January 28) in 2011 to release the results of an online survey with 1,700 respondents (located mainly in Europe and North America), reporting that the vast majority of study participants felt that their personal information was at risk on the internet.[17] Most people also mentioned that individuals, not institutions, are responsible for safeguarding people online. Although few reported ever experiencing anything problematic because of free-floating mediated personal information, people are still convinced it is a tremendously powerful source for unarticulated threats, and refer to self-censorship as a preferred disciplining mechanism. One is reminded that thinking carefully about the role media play in everyday life should refer not only to the artifacts we use and see, nor just to what people generally do with them. Media fit into daily life in all kinds of complicated ways, and contribute to shaping our lives especially by their invisibility: we stop to think about media deliberately, and therefore assume their omnipresence (unless they break down). It is exactly at that moment, following Bentham, that media become all-powerful.

Panopticism revisited

Instead of using a notion of panoptic surveillance as a metaphor for the general control apparatuses of state and corporate institutions, or more concretely as an instance of the supposedly efficient administration of people and therefore of bureaucratic social control (as originally envisioned by Max Weber), in a media life it is necessary to theorize the process of universal inspection as a rather mundane function of everyday life. This would include, as Stephen Green advocates, "a sensitivity . . . to the fact that surveillance – intensified, diversified and empowered by information technologies – contains both urges for control and facilitation, for social management and social empowerment" (1999: 27). As a first step to that effect, Mark Poster considers people's total immersion in digital communication networks as a unitary discipline mechanism, all the more powerful because "the population participates in its own self-constitution as subjects in the normalizing gaze of the Superpanopticon" (1990: 97). Poster's *superpanopticon* as a model of society awash with electronic eyes has no technical limitations as it moves beyond a top-down regime of corporations and governments to include each and every individual (as long as he or she is a consumer – that is, someone with a social security number, a bank account or credit card). Simply by moving in public space, communicating electronically or making a purchase, we silently agree to be part of a panoptic society.

At the heart of panoptic surveillance operating in society, argues Greg Elmer in *Profiling machines* (2004), is its complete reliance on the collection of personal information bundled with the storage and cross-referencing of such data. Elmer emphasizes the automatic nature of such panoptic processes, as we are generally not (made) aware of the fact that our information is collected – for example when we use a cash machine, when we visit a website, when we program something on a digital video recorder. Ours is a personal information economy, concludes Elmer, governed and structured by profiling machines: media that hunt, gather, sort and archive data in order to discriminate individuals into previously categorized consumer lifestyle groups. On the one hand, this potentially makes media life easier: sophisticated systems that can predict what we want (and when we want it) remove uncertainty from the dilemma of choice, "and by extension the need to make conscious decisions is replaced by an uncannily familiar world of images, goods, and services" (2004: 244). Elmer makes a point similar to that in the work of Richard Grusin on the premediating logic of contemporary media, claiming that the functioning of digital media is premised on this ability to expose people's private lives to the world (more specifically to companies and markets), and to aggregate past behaviors in order to predict future ones. Tackling the same process from the other side, cultural theorist Eva Illouz shows throughout her work how our current confessional culture relies on emotional self-surveillance in service of largely economic and political expectations of a *perfect self*. In the process of publicly performing identities, Illouz argues, people narrate and come to experience their lives as "media-like lifestyles" (1997: 182).

By narrating our existence, we see ourselves and each other live. Importantly, this kind of mediated panopticism does not just rely on self-disciplining in order to fulfill real or perceived expectations, but in fact can offer quite significant rewards: bargains at stores or perks with airlines for participating in customer loyalty programs, special status conferred based on recurring visits to an online service, discounts for following the advice of automated product recommendation systems (such as at Amazon and other online retailers), and so on. Apparently it is in our best interest to cooperate, making the panoptic surveillance system seem benevolent and participatory in nature – even though it punishes for opting out: limiting choice, denying discounts, downgrading creditworthiness, barring access altogether. Participating in surveillance processes is not without consequences for users, as Mark Andrejevic (2009) reminds us. According to Andrejevic, the emerging online economy exploits the work of being watched. As users of all kinds of cards, as people under constant surveillance while being in public, and as online shoppers, we provide value-generating labor for the business and corporations that collect, record, mine or sell data about us. In doing so, we extend the work we were already doing for companies simply by watching television or listening to the radio: we were making ourselves available to be sold as audiences to advertisers. Media in this context provide the accelerant the global economy needs to sustain itself: providing access to potential markets and target demographics while at the same time opening up options and opportunities for consumers. While free software like iTunes makes available seemingly limitless libraries of artists and songs, these programs at the same time document, map and record the entire music inventory of their users. While a digital video recorder facilitates the simultaneous watching and recording of content across a bewildering range of TV channels, it offers up a lifetime of viewing behaviors for the companies involved. Combining different genres and forms of media in his analysis of surveillance in everyday life, Andrejevic documents how: "the elaboration and proliferation of desire is achieved through subjection to a discursive regime of self-disclosure whose contemporary cultural manifestations include not just the mania for interactivity, but the confessional culture of a talk show nation, and, most recently, the ethos of willing submission to comprehensive surveillance associated with the booming reality TV trend" (2002: 234).

Investigating how people perceive and understand surveillance in their daily lives, Kirsty Best finds that her study participants either think that there is a legitimate case to be made for surveillance, or more generally feel that "stopping participating in digital life [is not just] unpalatable . . . it is in fact impossible" (2010: 19). For Best, the fact that people tend to see surveillance as expedient at best, or as inevitable at worst, raises the question of whether consent can truly be said to exist. A key issue in this context must be the level of transparency about surveillance practices and their potential consequences available to those scrutinized. Given the pervasive and largely automated nature of surveillance mechanisms, it is perhaps safe to say that a clear and complete picture of the entire surveillance ecosystem remains elusive to all involved – including the very organizations implementing or commissioning surveillance in the first place.

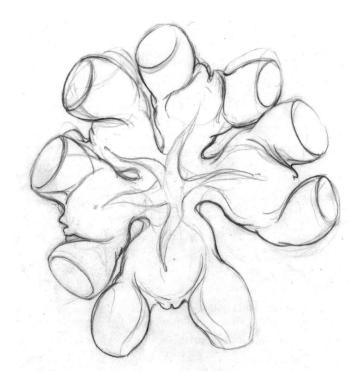

In their 2006 report for the British Information
Commissioner featuring detailed case studies of the consequences of surveillance in people's everyday lives, researchers
from the Surveillance Studies Network confirm that it affects
the entirety of the family's life chances, decision-making and
relationships.[18] Consider, for instance, the ways in which all
kinds of databases are linked by private companies, as well as
government agencies to deny or allow people access to specific
social services (and even countries), to support or withdraw
investments in particular areas or townships, and even to connect or bypass people in their search for a romantic partner
at an online dating service. Elmer concludes his analysis of
our personal information economy – an economy dominantly
driven by detailed, historical information about individuals

– expressing a grave concern: "Thus, as we watch and monitor others and are ourselves monitored, our preferences are fed back to us, producing an all-too-familiar environment . . . As a consequence, we may soon find it compellingly easy and convenient to consume 'more of the same', or conversely, increasingly more difficult to find something different" (2004: 245).

Beyond the economy and marketplace, similar panoptic processes are at work in the realms of education, labor and politics. The administration of increasingly complicated, customized and individually fine-tuned pathways through the maze of contemporary educational institutions demands considerable surveillance capabilities. As systems of higher education worldwide expand rapidly – in the process innovating and further developing existing programs, adding all kinds of new courses, curricula or even disciplines – the need for constant monitoring and tracking the progress of students, faculty and staff increases exponentially. The internationalization of higher education, furthermore, increases the level of student surveillance as it functions across different institutions, countries and regional systems.

Sometimes, a real or perceived need to keep track of students, coupled with the pervasive nature of universal convergence technologies in all aspects of everyday life, has institutions scrambling for surveillance mechanisms in ways that expose the general lack of reflective awareness people tend to have regarding their media. Consider, for example, the Lower Merion School District of Ardmore, Pennsylvania. With several other high schools around the US it participated (during the 2009–10 academic year) in a state-funded program that provided all of its students with a laptop computer. As a security measure, the school opted to install software for activating the built-in webcam of these laptops remotely. None of the students (nor their parents) were informed of this decision. In fact, people only found out about the arguably rather intrusive surveillance system after school officials sent a letter to one of the students reprimanding him for "improper behavior," an accusation which was supported by pictures taken of the student while he was alone in his bedroom at home – images silently recorded and sent back to the school's IT department by the free laptop's camera. One of these pictures showed him sleeping, and another one eating candy – which officials apparently considered to be "pill-popping" (as reported in *Wired* magazine of April 16, 2010). After concerned parents filed a lawsuit, thousands of webcam pictures and screen shots featuring many students were discovered on the school's computer servers. As a consequence, the school suspended its surveillance program – pending further investigation. As is common with media in general and surveillance systems in particular, we tend to only become acutely aware of them when they break down.

Like the fields of work and education, national governments and multilateral organizations (such as the European Union) are systematically increasing their surveillance of people and places, for example by passing legislation that requires telecommunications companies to store and make readily available source, destination and other data on any kind of mediated communication. All kinds of electronic gateways and technologies monitoring and screening access to public areas, such as airports, bus and train stations, sports facilities, parks and shopping malls, have become commonplace. Through such ubiquitous surveillance of public space, writes Finnish geographer Hille Koskela, "the panoptic technology of power has been electronically extended, making our cities like enormous panopticons" (2000: 243). Koskela argues that the rapid increase of surveillance technologies in city centers and other urban areas is intended to extend the sense of safety and security provided in out-of-town shopping malls and office parks into public space. In other words: through omnipresent media (operating as technologies of panoptic surveillance) public space becomes subject to the same rules and expectations of exclusivity (and corresponding perceptions of security) as the private places where we live.

The ensemble of surveilling mechanisms available to the state – including but not limited to national DNA databases, closed circuit television cameras in public places, identity documents outfitted with digital biometrics, and the ability to link and cross-reference across any and all computerized catalogs – is rather daunting. A particularly intimidating example of such tools affecting everyday life on the streets of neighborhoods is the ongoing development of talking CCTV cameras. Fitted with speaker facilities, such cameras allow human monitors to directly address people under surveillance in public spaces. In the UK such cameras are, for example, used in Middlesbrough, "where people seen misbehaving can be told to stop via a loudspeaker, controlled by control centre staff."[19] In the US, a similar instance can be found in a low-income housing complex in Washington, DC, whereby "residents and guests alike who have violated the stringent apartment rules have been singled out over the intercoms and given orders such as 'get off the steps,' 'no chairs allowed in the playground area' or, perhaps most common, 'no loitering.'"[20] The systems are put in place by commercial companies and tend to be funded through government grants and subsidies.

David Lyon cautions against an undifferentiated view of power, as prisons are not the same as schools, and the kind of power enforced by the state is markedly different from that wielded by commercial enterprises. On the other hand, one has to consider that new-technology contexts do blur the boundaries between society's institutions, their processes, and thus their practices of power. To treat surveillance mechanisms separately, in terms of the economy, education, the military and the state, ignores the many ways in which these institutions and their panoptic processes are linked. Government agencies enforce the copyright protections claimed by corporations. Internet Service Providers provide the police protocols for (and access to) people's online communications and browsing histories. Companies sell and exchange consumer profiles that can be matched with public records (such as real-estate ownership, property tax databases, professional and business licenses and court files).

A final dimension to the issue of panoptic surveillance is distinctly technological, as it refers to machines keeping track of (and communicating exclusively with) other machines. Here, the twin forces of media's increasing ubiquity and invisibility collude to produce an environment of context-aware computing, next-generation networks, and intermedia communications – in other words, an *internet of things*, heralded in a 2005 report by the International Telecommunications Union as a new dimension to be added to "the world of information and communication technologies (ICTs): from *anytime, any place* connectivity for *anyone*, we will now have connectivity for *anything*" (italics in original).[21] The internet of things, defined as a global internet-based information architecture facilitating the exchange of goods and services, according to some, will come to dominate mediated interactions. Benchmarked by the ability to tag objects with information that can be read at-a-distance by other objects, the internet of things provides ways to identify and coordinate flows of information, products and services between different technological systems. A constituent system for the internet of things is Radio Frequency Identification (RFID) technology, allowing any kind of object to be tagged with an electronic label that can be read at a short distance (up to several meters) for the purpose of identification and tracking using radio waves. RFID technology is used in a wide variety of everyday situations around the world: from electronically collecting fees for toll roads and facilitating entering and exiting buildings or public transit systems, to scanning products in grocery stores, passports at airports, books in public libraries, and student IDs at schools – up to and including implanting RFID tags in animals and humans.[22]

A specific example of a contemporary surveillance option at work in the private sphere comes to mind when considering the way overdeveloped societies tend to their elderly citizens. American researchers Sheri Reder and colleagues (2010), for example, fitted a range of objects in the homes of 12 elderly people with RFID tags – including the senior citizens themselves, with labels embedded in wristbands. The purpose of the system was to remotely monitor four activities: meal preparation, physical activity, vitamin use and personal care, and to convey this information in real time to the elder's family and caregivers. The researchers found that people used the technology as a passive alert system and communication tool. The trial participants – specifically the senior citizens and their children – reported an increase in perceived safety and peace of mind. The system, called Technology for Long Term Care (TLTC), correspondingly claims to help people keep an eye on their elderly parents without the need to visit them every day. Without a hint of irony, the government-funded project describes the key RFID element of TLTC, Sysgen TracPoint, on its website:

> Sysgen TracPoint utilizes state of the art, RTLS (Real Time Location System), RFID wireless monitoring technology that enhances effective management of long term care provider's greatest assets: its residents . . . TracPoint allows staff to quickly find the location of a resident, staff member or a critical piece of equipment quickly . . . Wireless RTLS resident tracking and elopement prevention functions allow for a more home-like, less restrictive environment while increasing effective behavior and wandering management . . . The wireless system permits resident monitoring in outside areas for increased resident freedom.[23]

The US-based PositiveID Corporation is one of the few international companies that produces and markets human-implantable microchips – under the VeriChip brand – and remote bio-sensor systems that can be used for building access control and patient identification purposes, but that, as PR stunts, have also been deployed to allow night clubs in Barcelona, Rotterdam and Glasgow to remotely identify their most important clients. As reported in UK newspaper the *Guardian* (on January 16, 2005), club owners like the advantages of such a surveillance system, as it allows bartenders and other club personnel to greet special customers by name, and pour their favorite drink without them having to ask for it in person.[24] In a story for the Associated Press (on July 23, 2007), Todd Lewan summarizes the debate about implantable microchips with specific reference to Big Brother:

> To some, the microchip [is] a wondrous invention – a high-tech helper that could increase security at nuclear plants and military bases, help authorities identify wandering . . . patients, allow consumers to buy their groceries, literally, with the wave of a chipped hand. To others, the notion of tagging people [is] Orwellian, a departure from centuries of history and tradition in which people had the right to go and do as they pleased without being tracked, unless they were harming someone else.[25]

Beyond the debate whether machinic surveillance is a good or bad thing, the developments in technology and media seem to go on unfettered, slowly but surely moving in (and in-between) all aspects of everyday life. The previously mentioned 2005 ITU report extols the virtues of this internet of things saying that it "will radically transform our corporate, community, and personal spheres" – for example by creating "smart homes for smart people," as well as a wide array of "smart things" that would be beneficial not just to commercial ventures, but also for "healthcare, defense or education" (2005: 2, 4, 6). Katherine Hayles raises perhaps the most profound stake when it comes to media-life-inspired concerns about surveillance in general, the internet of things, and the role of RFID technology in particular. To her, the key to our consideration of RFID as one addition to an increasingly sophisticated array of panoptic surveillance mechanisms is the suggestion that the world of objects around us ceases to be one that is passive and inert. Instead, we are now moving – whether we want to or not – through an altogether animate environment:

"Combined with embedded sensors, mobile technologies and relational databases, RFID destabilizes traditional ideas about the relation of humans to the built world . . . The challenge RFID presents is how to use it to re-think human subjectivity in constructive and life-enhancing ways without capitulating to its coercive and exploitive aspects" (2009: 48).

Consider for a moment moving through a world of objects that not only become meaningful through our handling of *them* (i.e. switching them on or off, throwing or pushing them, and so on), but are powerful as they handle *us* – by communicating with each other on the basis of data gathered in real time. Hayles considers RFID technologies in everyday life as distributed cognitive systems – like human beings are – making sense of the world by virtue of their (mediated) connections. All of a sudden our access to a specific place can be granted – or denied. A particular product is to be had – or seems unavailable. Someone responds, ready and willing to speak with us and address our query – or the device we used to access a service (for example, a phone or intercom system) remains eerily silent. Such decisions are made on the basis of things interacting with other things, relating information about people and products and past behaviors stored in different databases. The objects in our environment – the groceries in our shopping bags, the devices in our pockets, the doors through which we enter or exit man-made structures – are, in some way, alive. In the end, Hayles calls not (only) for strategies and tactics vis-à-vis surveillance, but critically considers how our engagement with media is "primarily and fundamentally an ethical struggle that continues as long as life in any form exists" (64–5). It is not just about how to interact with technology, but rather (or at the very least also) about what kind of technologies to design that truly allow us to take responsibility for what we want of this world.

Reverse engineering the panopticon

A second step towards considering the full potential and implications of surveillance in media life must also move beyond exclusively top-down principles of inspection (where the few scrutinize the many), and consider the same process in reverse. This yields a context of synoptic surveillance, where the many watch the few. Norwegian sociologist Thomas Mathiesen introduced the notion of a synopticon in the context of the relationship between (mass) media and society – something, he argued, Foucault originally overlooked. For Mathiesen, magazines, radio and especially television open up the world of celebrities and politicians to the surveillance of mass audiences – not that dissimilar from ancient spectacles such as the performance of actors in theatres where the many watched the few. What is furthermore significant about this history, argues Mathiesen, is that "panopticism and synopticism *have developed in intimate interaction, even fusion, with each other*" (1997: 223; italics in original). In doing so, he emphasizes a key point about the contemporary technologies that provide the artifactual backdrop to media life: the same hardware and software that makes total top-down surveillance of individuals possible enables those same individuals to "look back" relatively unseen at those who survey them. John Thompson's take on synopticism and media life extends this capacity of making visible and seeing without being seen as "not just the outcome of leakage in systems of communication and information flow that are increasingly difficult to control: it is also an explicit strategy of individuals who know very well that mediated visibility can be a weapon in the struggles they wage in their day-to-day lives" (2005: 31).

In a review of how terrorist groups and extremist movements use media, and outlining the response of mainly US security organizations, Gus Martin (2010) similarly alludes to the fact that people on both sides of the spectrum use digital technology and media extensively to find and produce information to further their aims. Using examples such as videos of hostage beheadings posted online and the pictures of torture victims at the Abu Ghraib prison in Iraq (in late 2004), Thompson considers how the new visibility of people and events is stretched out in time and space – as we can watch events happening in real time (through streaming video online and live television) and at the same time endlessly revisit digital recordings – while most of these acts of seeing are not reciprocal: the people watched generally cannot see us in return. This consequence of the mediatization of society clearly raises the stakes for those who want or need to be seen.

An important nuance in our take on society as established through mediated visibility and systems of surveillance is an awareness of how the presentation and representation of people, possessions and practices seems to be beyond any kind of centralized control – whether that would be a national government, a corporate entity or a single public relations manager. Mathiesen has his doubts about the empowering potential of the synopticon, considering its function to be largely that of silencing critical debate as it reduces public debate to whatever is deemed worthy to be shown on television, a media system which is (like all others) overdetermined by commercial interests. Although the current media ecology is perhaps more diverse and unruly than the one in Mathiesen's original account of synopticism, one has to consider the fact that much of people's mass self-communication takes place within the carefully policed boundaries of corporate networks and services. The terms of service of these and other media access providers tend to include warnings about posting or sharing information that is believed to be in violation of vaguely worded policies.

The freedom of (networks of) mass self-communication is not free at all. However, it can be productive, in that it produces alternate ways of seeing people, products and events. Concrete examples of productive synopticism – beyond the consumptive realms of political news reports, celebrity shows or even reality television – are websites such as local business review site Yelp, or social reputation systems such as auction site eBay. People reviewing anything from products and travel destinations to all kinds of services offered by commercial and public institutions collectively provide a comprehensive look at what otherwise would constitute a rather overwhelming and impenetrable corporate or governmental arena. The reliability of such reviews as one's reputation score on eBay and other more or less similar services is produced by the sheer size and relative permanence of such websites. As reputation systems researcher Paul Resnick and his colleagues summarize, "Systems that rely on the participation of large numbers of individuals accumulate trust simply by operating effectively over time" (2000: 48). Individuals who thus, collectively and anonymously, look back indeed have power, in part evidenced in the eagerness of marketers to cater to those who actively engage in reviewing products and services online and offline – as in the case of carrotmobs, where people mob businesses that make the largest pledge towards sustainable practices and in doing so inspire media attention to be directed to the companies involved.[26] Synopticism can be a collaborative exercise in exerting power insofar as it signals the universal human capacity for moral norms. Through synoptic surveillance, communities of anonymous strangers not only can form long-lasting and well-functioning relationships, they also participate in the forming and policing of moral norms. Research in the field of computer-mediated communication indeed suggests that, when people are part of a company of strangers, they tend to orient themselves quite acutely to the social and situational norms of the group. In other words: both in and out of media life, people in crowds do not necessarily lose their identity – they tend to mutually construct, adopt and maintain a collective identity.

In the context of synopticism considered as a powerful tool for the collaborative policing of moral norms, and an overall expectation for surveillance to act as a crime deterrent, it is important to note how since the 1990s the state has gradually ceded control of its surveillance mechanisms to private firms – in the United States as well as South Africa, China and the UK. In fact, many Western countries use private security contractors in international interventions – for example, in Afghanistan and Iraq. At the same time, residential areas in general, and gated communities in particular, outsource the policing of their enclaves to 'armed response units' and other security firms that monitor both private and public buildings, communities, shopping malls, public transport hubs (such as airports), and even military garrisons from afar generally using proprietary hardware and software. As Elke Krahmann (2010) carefully documents, the emergence of a global privatized security industry occurs largely beyond the scope of specific national or international rules and policies, and the number of people employed by such firms exceeds that of local, regional or national police officers by a ratio of at least two to one. In *Torture and democracy* (2009), Darius Rejali discusses how one of the consequences of this worldwide privatization of policing seems to be a form of more or less consensual use of torture, as generally unaccountable and unseen private security guards stand relatively unopposed when accosting, harassing and otherwise violently handling ordinary citizens. According to Rejali, this situation is not the result of war or a permissive legal environment, but rather gets produced by "informal arrangements among police, residents, and businesses to shape the urban landscape" (60). In other words, surveillance has been slowly but surely moving away from the all-seeing eye of the state and the police to the much more widespread and distributed gaze of the (private) many.

In a 2006 report based on consumer surveys and expert interviews worldwide, accounting and consultancy firm PriceWaterhouseCoopers (PWC) projects a vision of *Lifestyle Media* as the benchmark for lived experience in media. The company's report defines lifestyle media as "the combination of a personalized media experience with a social context for participation," requiring "two fundamental components: new content distribution models that put consumers in control, and more accurate and scalable data about what they are watching, doing, and creating."[27] The PWC report is just one among countless others from competing consumer research and consultancy firms, most – if not all – of which tend to be premised on the potential of near-perfect tracking and profiling of people through their media use. Instead of reading this trend as the final nail in the coffin of advertising, marketing communications and public relations, such industry observers see all kinds of opportunities for new practices: ads-on-demand, personalized and targeted ads, consumer activity ads, viral ads – all of which presuppose that consumers want to be involved in the advertising process, whether through voluntarily submitting their personal information to a company in order to receive customized communications and services or by actively participating in the content of the ads.

The media industry's framing of a supposedly empowered (because co-creative) consumer is not without problems. Joseph Turow, for example, considers the construction of media users as chaotic, self-concerned and willingly contributing to a pervasive personal information economy as serving a strategic logic of marketing and advertising organizations "to present their activities not as privacy invasion but as two-way customer relationships, not as commercial intrusion but as pinpoint selling help for frenetic consumers in a troubling world" (2005: 120). Framing people as unruly and participatory media users furthermore allows industry professionals to aim at 'taming' the masses into statistically significant segments, lifestyle groups or subcultures. The primary function of advertising and marketing in this context would be to reduce their clients' anxieties and lack of knowledge and imagination regarding the consumer. Perhaps all of us, in (social) media, ultimately act out those same deep anxieties, by mediating ourselves in an attempt to reduce our uncertainty about who we are, what roles we are supposed to play, and how to engage the largely unknown and unseen people around us in a completely mediated runaway world. At the same time, much like the way the advertising industry necessitates its own existence, the notion of a more or less uncertain and unruly world 'out there' can be seen as a personalized construct providing each individual a motive to constantly monitor themselves and others in media – thus validating mutual surveillance and taking self-monitoring to a whole new level.

Beyond the panopticon

What must be clear is that different systems of surveillance in media life do not only impact the lives of people who are suspected of committing (or who are likely to commit) crime, or just those who have a political agenda or want to be represented in certain ways, or merely folks who shop a lot. In a media life, everyone is both subject and object of surveillance. It is in the ways we choose to act under such conditions of many and multiplying all-seeing mediated eyes that we can take responsibility for our actions and thus for the kind of society we want to live in. It is therefore striking that the overwhelming majority choose to actively participate in surveillance – everyone is spying on everyone else. Massive mutual monitoring is the backbone of social media, and consumes the majority of time people spend with media, informs the fundamental strategies of businesses across industry sectors, and inspires the management of many (if not most) relationships in contemporary society: between the state and its citizens, organized religion and its faithful, employers and employees, lovers and loved ones. Such intense mediated observation and, perhaps more importantly, the expectation thereof seems befitting an increasingly stretched sense of community – with family members and friends scattered around the world, with colleagues and competitors next door as well as on the other side of the planet, with relationships and communal commitments engaged until further notice. As the principal components of contemporary lived experience – including but not limited to identity, space and place – are socially produced in media, it should come as no surprise that people use media to seek the counsel of others by observing how they live and, in a fascinating act of what biomathematicians Martin Nowak and Karl Sigmund label as "indirect reciprocity" and "third party altruism" (2005: 1291), massively put their own lives on display in return. As Danish digital media scholar Jakob Linaa Jensen expresses it, "In a complicated society, everyone watches everyone and accountability and the monitoring of performance become important aspects of the policy-making process. We are already part of a mediated, political Omnopticon" (2007: 380). Jensen's notion of *omnopticism* – where people live in a state of constant mutual surveillance – is considered by some a social system that democratizes the panopticon, and can thus neutralize centralized, top-down hierarchical forms of authority. Individuals are thus seen as empowered by the use of surveillance devices, such as wearable computers, personal cameras and cell phones, as people are now surveilling the surveillers, as well as surveilling each other.

On the other hand, one should be mindful of Jeremy Bentham's original insight, that it is the *illusion of surveillance* that holds the key to managing an orderly society. Perhaps many of us do not necessarily share everything about ourselves. Research clearly shows that both young and old media users deploy increasingly sophisticated tactics to manage their privacy online, and that the vast majority of media users are at the very least aware of potential problems with living in public. But all of us expect or suspect we are being watched – by the state every time we enter a public space, by corporations whenever we shop, by employers at each instance of using the company's networked technologies, and by the person or persons next to us as they most likely wield the same kind of surveillance devices as we do.

We have to recognize how in a media life every single individual is implicated in the maintenance of social order – but not exclusively nor necessarily in the service of consensual or otherwise communally governed relations of discipline. Today's perfect disciplinary institution does not run uninterrupted through society in some kind of generalized way, as Foucault suggested would be the case in the fulfillment of Bentham's original panoptic design. In a media life, the profiling machines Elmer signaled are not just the ubiquitous technologies of either panoptic or synoptic surveillance structuring the everyday experiences of citizen-consumers. In fact, each of us can be considered to be a profiling machine as we collectively hunt, gather, sort and archive data in order to expose our life and that of others to the world. Certainly, this way of living in media has profound productive potential for (self-)discipline, control and suspicion. On the other hand, the devices, messages, practices and values espoused in media are anything but uniform or uncontested. If one even moves a little bit beyond the relatively safe algorithmic waters of Google, Facebook and Wikipedia, the messiness of contemporary media is awe-inspiring. If we spend only a fraction of our time in mobile media linking up with the hundreds of people in our extended social networks, we would still be overwhelmed with the richness and diversity of human contact and communication. Perhaps Lars Qvortrup is right in assuming that hypercomplexity is not a problem, but rather a solution for the times we live in, and omnoptic surveillance is both the tool and collective practice we need ready-to-hand to see the world (and ourselves in it) the way people and things really are. Media *make* us real, because we *create* ourselves in media.

CHAPTER FIVE

Society in Media

where we live in media forever

People use a lot of media more or less simultaneously a lot of the time – most of the time generally unaware of the fact that they are concurrently exposed to media, a multiplication of mediated experiences which in turn contributes not only to the overall lack of awareness of media in our lives, but also amplifies and accelerates an ongoing fusion of all domains of life (such as home, work, school, love and play) with media. Research into how people use media runs paramount throughout both the industry and academy, crossing numerous sectors and disciplines, all contributing to an overwhelming array of stories, studies, reports, journal articles and books documenting how, generally, people around the world use more and more media all the time. The numbers that map people's media use at times have a certain intimidating, even invasive quality: we live our lives in a context of more, faster, all-encompassing, profoundly pervasive and therefore omnipresent media. Anthropologist Keith Hart uses these kinds of statistics to propose his take on our lives in media:

> We are living through the first stages of a world revolution . . . It is a machine revolution, of course: the convergence of telephones, television and computers in a digital system whose most visible symbol is the internet. It is a social revolution, the formation of a world society with means of communication adequate at last to expressing universal ideas . . . It is an existential revolution, transforming what it means to be human and how each of us relates to the rest of humanity. (2009: 24)

Sometimes, the statistics documenting media use indeed seem to signal a revolution, and force us to reconsider the basic foundations of our common humanity. A December 2010 survey across 22 countries by the Pew Global Attitudes Project documents steady growth in computer and cell phone use everywhere, concluding that "In regions around the world – and in countries with varying levels of economic development – people who use the internet are using it for social networking."[1] Reports on people's media use by Comscore (such as its 2011 year-in-review) emphasize the global nature of such trends, showing how social networking sites are used worldwide by over 80 percent of all people online.[2] In the 2010 overview of the World Internet Project (documenting computer and internet use in close to 20 countries), researchers come to the conclusion that, in what they label "a new digital media ecology," people do not just spend much more time communicating than consuming – their communicative behavior takes place primarily within the context of *peer-to-peer sociality* (Cardoso, Cheong and Cole, 2010: 7–8).

The 2011 GlobalWebIndex report by British consultancy Trendstream[3] – based on aggregated market research from 23 countries – suggests people's media use on a global scale moves towards what it calls real-time and social technologies. The global uptake of online social networks is part of a larger trend in the dance between media and everyday life towards a predominance of always-on, interconnected artifacts and activities that become the foundation for the arrangement of human sociality. *Wired* magazine's contributing editor Gary Wolf accelerates such assertions in his take on what famed media philosopher Marshall McLuhan would have made of our time of ubiquitous portable and networked communication technologies, deliberately invoking media life in the headline of his argument ("The medium is life," published on March 22, 2010):

> Humanism temporarily survived the era of electronic media only through the act of turning on a device . . . But when a medium is coincident with life, the last refuge for humanism is gone. . . . The long story of humanism – by which I mean the emergence of individual consciousness as a byproduct of our language and literature – comes to an end when we return, futuristically, to doing everything by hand.[4]

Wolf may not be that far off the mark, as numerous studies in different parts of the world show how media artifacts in general and mobile devices in particular have become inseparable parts of their users. As Finnish sociologist Ilkka

Arminen summarizes: "They are media, but they are also emotionally invested objects that are imaginative representations of their users" (2007: 433), which in turn suggests they directly affect the organization of social action and societies. Considering the complete convergence of the internet and the mobile phone, Arminen suggests that anyone interested in studying the social should engage with this "vastly expanding technological potential" (436). This insight is inversely shared by political philosophers Michael Hardt and Antonio Negri, who earlier argued that "the anthropology of cyberspace is really a recognition of the new human condition" (2000: 291). Mary Chayko (2008) takes up this challenge and goes as far as outlining the emergence of portable and networked communities as constitutive of contemporary society, where interpersonal relationships are built and sustained asynchronously and at a distance. She maintains that mediated bonds are not necessarily more or less reliable or meaningful than face-to-face relationships. Early empirical evidence regarding both the experimental and experiential fusion of social and computer networks in local communities – as, for example, compiled by Irish social computing scholar Patrick Purcell (2006) – suggests how different forms of computer-mediated communication usually have quite positive effects on community interaction, involvement and social capital, enabling people to keep in touch with old friends, colleagues and acquaintances, with media deployed largely in the service of connections. Such mediated connections produce cultural diversity and particularity as much as they foster allegiance and traditionalism. Despite finding that most of people's personal interactions using mobile media involve those they know from earlier or ongoing face-to-face contact, Kakuko Miyata, Barry Wellman and Jeffrey Boase (2005) see a *mobilization* of society, in which mobile connectivity increases both the volume and velocity of communication. This in turn accelerates a process pre-dating internet, as more people are "maneuvering through multiple communities of choice," which "should reduce informal social control and increase autonomy" (445–6). The question is what the exponentially increasing adoption and societal diffusion rates of our charismatic technologies tell us about the kind of society we are co-producing in media. In other words, what are we exactly, as people, when we live in media?

We're all fucking zombies

Writing about yet another among countless polls, surveys and reviews of people's media use, Hamilton Nolan of the *Gawker* blog expresses exasperation how all the breathless rhetoric in such reports boils down to one conclusion: "we're all fucking zombies" (posted on March 27, 2009).[5] Such reference to the living dead in the context of a complete mediatization of everyday life is not entirely without merit, as Finnish media archaeologist Jussi Parikka notes about one of the slightly more unsettling consequences of a media life: living with "the return of dangerous toxins and other residue from supposedly immaterial information technologies – hundreds of millions of electronic devices discarded annually, most of which are still working" (posted on July 8, 2010).[6] A media life comes with endless graveyards of often still-working mobile phones, personal computers, chips and circuits, wires and controllers. Recognizing the severity of this (un) dead media issue, in 2008 the United Nations, together with a host of other organizations (including the US Environmental Protection Agency), started the Solving The E-waste Problem (STEP) initiative.[7] This program considers e-waste (any kind of electronic equipment, including TVs, computers, mobile phones, home entertainment and stereo systems) a global problem, growing more rapidly every year because of the relentless pace of product innovations and replacement in electronics, in conjunction with ever-increasing worldwide demand for media. It is furthermore a global (and not a municipal or otherwise local) problem because of the complexity and cost involved in safely disposing of the many hazardous, yet also valuable – often precious – materials that make up media artifacts. The value of e-waste is partly determined by the fact that many of the parts are still working or can be made to work. Our devices, how we use them, and the organization of everyday life such activities engender are, by virtue of the technologies and techniques involved, intrinsically temporary and short-lived. At the same time, our life in media forever summons a past that can never be regained, as well as a past that never goes away – our media are always already *zombie media*.

Nolan and Parikka suggest with their ironic use of zombies that people's lives as lived in media come with a price: we apparently have to learn to live with a host of undead devices scattered all around us, media which at the same time turn us into (in the words of Nolan) "drooling brainwashed playthings." The use of zombies in an understanding of society and media life may in fact be quite appropriate, as *Time*'s Lev Grossman notes (on April 9, 2009): "[zombies] seem to be telling us something about the zeitgeist . . . If there's something new about today's zombie, it's his relatability . . . They're monsters of the people."[8] British literary scholar Nick Pearce concurs, signaling an ongoing *zombification* of society based on people's feelings of powerlessness in the face of boundary-erasing threats (such as stock fluctuations and crashes, terrorism and global warming).[9] The contemporary zombie, argues Pearce, has no real motivation, and no hope for the future.

In a talk given at a symposium on zombies at Winchester University (on October 28, 2011), British Romanticist Gary Farnell endorses the zombie as "the official monster of the moment," suggesting that the zombie "signifies an image of the truth of the current conjunctural crisis of global capitalism."[10] Relating zombies to the Occupy Together protests across the United States (and elsewhere) of 2011, the riots in the UK earlier that year, and ongoing protests in Arab countries, scholars like Pearce and Farnell feel zombies put a particular kind of human face on a widespread sense of crisis. At the same time, news reporters, technology pundits and other observers baptised such major upheavals at the start of the twenty-first century as a "Twitter Revolution" (referring to Iran in the *Atlantic* on June 18, 2010[11]), "Facebook Revolution" (referring to Egypt in *Time* magazine on January 24, 2011[12]), "The YouTube Revolutions" (in a headline about the entire Arab world in *Foreign Policy* magazine on March 30, 2011[13]) or, better yet, the "Facebook-Twitter-YouTube Revolution" (referring to the entire region in the Huffington Post on February 1, 2011[14]). This in turn prompted numerous commentators to dispute social media's role in causing the widespread protests and calls for change in the Arab world. Yet the protests and riots (and clean-ups) around the world do have certain properties that remind one of zombies: first, they tend to be based on social movements without leaders, lacking clear hierarchical structures and generally having no clear goals. If anything, the sheer diversity of goals makes them seem to cancel each other out. Second, they involve people from all walks of life: from East to West, North to South, black and white, men and women, old and young – again negating distinct classifications. Finally, not only does the social arrangement of these protests rely heavily on the use of media (which in turn enable the active involvement of people not necessarily present) – they seem infectious and viral, similar to how media can be. As Steve Anderson, director of non-profit organization OpenMedia, writes in a column for the Canadian weblog *Rabble* (on November 1, 2011): "[the Occupy movement] feels like an ongoing space infused with web values and practices. Their structure of participation mirrors that of the online encyclopedia Wikipedia . . . Will it last? I have no idea, but I think these social practices are addictive and contagious."[15] Sarah Juliet Lauro (excerpting her work for the *io9* weblog on January 13, 2012) links the Occupy movement back to zombies by suggesting that the collective disruption of public spaces takes its cues from zombies – more specifically, *zombie walks* occurring more or less regularly around the world: "These events seem to me to incarnate the youth culture's lament for its lack of real social power, and perhaps signal a willingness to change this."[16]

Combining observations about a zombification of society with the way people around the world not only live their lives in media, but behave *as* media in public (which, given media life, increasingly also means: in private), the zombie contagiously moves beyond metaphor. Theoretically, the possibility of a world turning into a zombie society in media forces us to rethink the kind of traditional categorizations so readily applied. The prime examples of such all-too-easy labeling are media and life. What if we can, through the idea of (media) zombies, move beyond physicalist readings of (media) life – which emphasize a more or less immutable thingness of media and disempower us from doing anything about our lives and the world we live in – instead deliberately opting for a vitalist position?

Everything (and everyone) zombie

The possibility of zombies makes for endless debates among philosophers, who find in what American philosopher Daniel Dennett calls the *zombic hunch* fertile ground to question whether there is more to mankind than the sum of its parts.[17] Dennett in particular regularly revisits this debate in an attempt to show that his competitor-colleagues who hold on to some kind of distinction between mind and matter (or between body and soul) do not seem to have empirical evidence for their claims. At the risk of oversimplifying an important and complex issue, the key to the ongoing zombic debate is our investment in separating or parsing out the phenomenal and the physical. This is where Nolan's use of the zombie concept comes in: when we live in media, one way or another, we become less aware of our surroundings, less tuned in to our senses, and thus, more like lifeless automatons.

The centrality of consciousness as a feature of humanity implicated in media use is delicately noted by David Buckingham in his assessment of the vast literature on media and society: "If these writers do not see all *technologies* as determining consciousness, they nevertheless seem to believe that *media* do" (2000: 42; italics in original). Michael Newman similarly outlines a long history of scholarship and lay theoretization on the perceived dangers of television, internet and mobile telephony – all media that at one point or another were (and still are) seen as suppressing active attention and turning media users into zombies (2010: 589). Such squaring of media with moral and intellectual decline serves to maintain social order, especially when it comes to the expert elite and anyone who may come to challenge their position in society. As Newman points out, there does not seem to be much evidence to suggest a causal connection between a culture's media and social devolution. Similarly, Katelyn McKenna and John Bargh argue, in a review of the implications of the internet for personality and social psychology, that "the internet does not, contrary to current popular opinion, have by itself the power or ability to control people, to turn them into addicted zombies, or make them dispositionally sad or lonely (or, for that matter, happy or popular), and neither does the telephone, or television, or movies" (2000: 72).

It is generally assumed that the ultimate human part determining consciousness is the brain. It is perhaps no surprise that Max Brooks' propitious book *The zombie survival guide* (2003) promises that, in order to commit suicide as a zombie or to efficiently remove a zombie threat, all one has to do is eliminate the brain. As Seth Grahame-Smith elegantly states in the opening of his remix of Jane Austen and zombies (titled *Pride and prejudice and zombies*): "It is a truth universally acknowledged that a zombie in possession of brains must be in want of more brains" (2009: 7).

Decapitation seems the preferred method for zombie disposal if one follows the films by specialist George A. Romero (creator of a series of instructional fare starting with *Night of the Living Dead* in 1968, via his most successful *Dawn of the Dead* in 1978, leading up to *Survival of the Dead* in 2009). Yet, as many would argue, there is more to the brain than information processing. And if that is true, whatever the extra piece of the puzzle of life is, it apparently makes the difference between being a zombie and not being a zombie. More to the point: you are a zombie when no one is home inside your head. This puts a premium on one's own individual experience and making sense of the world as the determining quality of existence – which is a rather problematic assumption.

If our entire experience of the world is indefinitely unique to our own understanding of it, we can never know whether we are the only real human beings on a planet otherwise populated by zombies. On the other hand, such a philosophical stance makes each and every one of us quite special. As Dennett writes in a 1993 reply to *zombie philosophers* such as David Chalmers, Noam Chomsky and others about their often-stated reverence for the mysterious pathways and processes in the individual brain as the ultimate "*Medium*" producing consciousness: "the message is: there is no medium."[18] Here, Dennett invokes Marshall McLuhan's 1964 expression "the medium is the message" to question whether the brain is extraordinary, and more ominously to challenge whether each of us is indeed really so special. People are indeed not special – if they are media zombies. We certainly seem to be. Consider, for example, the rationale for the founding of a Zombie Research Society (ZRS) in 2007, dedicated to raising the level of zombie scholarship because: "The zombie pandemic is coming. It's not a matter of if, but a matter of when. Enthusiastic debate about zombies is essential to the survival of the human race."[19]

Inspired by a similar awareness, Assistant Surgeon General Ali Khan of the American Centers for Disease Control and Prevention (CDC) on May 16, 2011 posted a "Zombie Apocalypse Preparedness Guide" on its website, drily informing people about what services it offers in case of these (and other) emergencies:

> If zombies did start roaming the streets, CDC would conduct an investigation much like any other disease outbreak. CDC would provide technical assistance to cities, states, or international partners dealing with a zombie infestation. This assistance might include consultation, lab testing and analysis, patient management and care, tracking of contacts, and infection control (including isolation and quarantine).[20]

This tongue-in-cheek reference to a potential zombie apocalypse made waves in media as word of the announcement spread virally across social networking sites and got picked up by major news organizations. Banking on this success, the CDC's newly formed Zombie Task Force followed up by announcing an online user-generated video contest. Blogger and professor of international politics Daniel Drezner applauded the CDC's efforts but lamented that he was not interviewed as an expert, as he had just published his book *Theories of international politics and zombies* (2011). In this work he imagines a world overrun with zombies, and considers the likely responses of national governments, international institutions such as the United Nations, and non-government organizations. The significance of Drezner's work lies in his conclusion that standard theories of how to organize and conduct international relations would not stand a chance against the undead. The point is: zombies do not care about international protocols, institutional conventions or bilateral negotiations. As the "Zombiephile" blog states eloquently (in its helpful list of the worst things to do during a zombie outbreak, published July 5, 2007): "don't get sentimental – zombies won't."[21] In Chris Harman's *Zombie capitalism* (2009), the zombie metaphor is deployed to signal how living-dead banks and nation-states keep the global capitalist project going, even though it produces disparate masses of people around the world. Harman invokes Karl Marx to argue how a renewed sense of class may mobilize people again to take collective action – in effect, pitting zombies against zombies.

Most directly related to media, in August 2010 the British Automobile Association (AA) issued a formal warning to the general public about the dangers of *road zombies*: people sharing the road while listening to music on headphones or using a mobile phone:

> Road zombies are isolated from all that happens around them . . . People go into their own private cocoon and their thoughts wander. They do things they wouldn't outside the cocoon. While we worry about people insulated from reality by the comforts of a modern car we don't worry as much about the far more vulnerable road users plugged in and isolated from the real world . . . Other common "zombies" are those pacing backwards and forwards while using a mobile phone.[22]

The AA clearly sees a problem with living life in media, and seeks recourse in zombies to raise awareness about it. Yet those very same media that turn people into road zombies infecting everyone around them can be seen as devices capable of resurrection. In this particular context, "the dead" refers to any amount of dead time people spend doing nothing: waiting, traveling, hanging around, walking to or from something (or someone), even driving a car. In their study among mobile workers in the UK, Mark Perry and Jackie Brodie (2005) found that people often refer to their media as in terms of killing time, but rather as reviving time, leading them to label personal communication technologies as *zombie devices* because of their ability to reanimate dead time. Sometimes our media can be temporarily turned into zombies by a computer virus designed to take over a networked personal computer, which then involuntarily infects other machines, creating and sustaining a large network of zombie computers. Such zombie networks can then be used to flood websites with information requests (often crashing servers and shutting sites down), send spam messages, and even access people's personal information. All the time a computer acts like a zombie, its owner would not even be aware of it (which, according to the philosophers, would mean the computer user might just be a zombie as well). There is a zombie in all of us – and in all of our media.

In the most complete sense of living a media life, our devices are (or can be) zombies; the way we use media turns us into zombies, and the way media organize our everyday lives mimics the workings of a zombie society (or, if one is less optimistically inclined, zombie apocalypse), as we roam the streets oblivious to our immediate reality pressing buttons and touching screens in order to immerse ourselves in a social space made out of technologies that do not care.

You are not special

Pertinent to my concerns about media life is the powerful para-digmatic potential of the zombie to provide a point of view that moves beyond all-too-easy categorizations (such as maintaining a futile discongruity between media and life). Sarah Juliet Lauro and Karen Embry explore a theory of zombies as the harbingers of a truly posthuman condition in their "A zombie manifesto" (2008). The zombie embodies an immanent state not governed by traditional dichotomies or dialectics, such as that between subject and object generally, or media and life more particularly, because the zombie's "irreconcilable body" (87) is neither living nor dead – it can only be understood as inseparable into distinct terms (95). In this respect, their embrace of the zombie to break through widespread ways of classifying and understanding social reality is reminiscent of Ulrich Beck's challenge to *zombie sociology* (originally voiced in the early 1990s), using as examples the categories of the national and the local:

> If it is true that the meaning of the national and the local is changing through internalized globalization, then the most important methodological implication for all social

sciences is that normal social sciences categories are becoming zombie categories . . . Zombie categories are living dead categories, which blind the social sciences to the rapidly changing realities inside the nation-state containers, and outside as well. (2002: 24)

In his 2010 book *Zombie economics*, Australian economist John Quiggin uses a similar framework for critically discussing what he considers living-dead ideas in macroeconomics. According to Quiggin, ideas such as a free-market ideology and trickle-down economics have already shown themselves to be less than useful – and therefore can be considered killed off. Yet they keep coming back: in the rhetoric of politicians, in the research programs of economists. It reminds one of Holocaust-deniers, global warming skeptics, creationists, and birthers who question the citizenship status of President Barack Obama in the US: in media, these more or less ridiculous ideas not only live forever, but periodically get amplified to temporary *truthiness*.[23]

It is in this spirit that Lauro and Embry zombify categories such as mind and matter, reducing them to zombie concepts that live on in name but have died in terms of their usefulness. As a life-form, the zombie is not some kind of remix between the empty containers of dead and (a)live life – as it is both, it is neither. For Lauro and Embry, thinking through the zombie idea reveals how it disrupts, unsettles and ultimately destroys the models people have carefully built to maintain the status quo – in society as well as in the academy:

> The terror that comes from an identification of oneself with the zombie is, therefore, primarily a fear of the loss of consciousness. As unconscious but animate flesh, the zombie emphasizes that humanity is defined by its cognizance. The lumbering, decaying specter of the zombie also affirms the inherent disability of human embodiment – our mortality. Thus, in some sense, we are all already zombies . . . for they represent the inanimate end to which we each are destined. (2008: 89–90)

The "Zombie manifesto" highlights global capitalism's reliance on people seeing themselves as unique individuals who, through conspicuous consumption, need to express that individuality in perpetuity. The zombie erases such a sense of personality – replacing it with what Shaka Paul McGlotten (2011) describes as an *impersonal sociality* – and thus calls into question "which is more terrifying: our ultimate separation from our fellow humans, or the dystopic fantasy of a swarm organism" (Lauro and Embry, 2008: 101). This provocation is picked up in Jussi Parikka's *Insect media* (2010), in which he discusses the widespread use of entomological concepts to describe, analyze and understand people's behaviors in media life in such terms as "collective intelligence," "hive minds" and "swarming." Parikka invokes zombies to propose a more inclusive way to understand forms of life:

> the biophilosophy of the twenty-first century should contextualize itself on such forms of the headless animality of insect societies or the new intensive meaning in states bordering life – the lifelike death of zombies. This biophilosophical moment . . . is characterized by a logic alternative to that of the prior approaches to thinking of life, namely the three modes of soul, meat, and pattern. Hence, such a biophilosophy also suggests a new way of understanding materiality not based on a substance or a form but as a temporal variation of affective assemblages. (47)

From a relatively benign and sometimes ironic use of zombies, one can move to an emerging field of zombie studies attempting to go beyond previously partitioned paradigms – dividing the world between nature, humanity and technology, parsing people into body and soul, dichotomizing development into nature and nurture, structure and agency, or product and process. Either way, it is perhaps safe (and at the very least uncannily inspiring) to say that the social order of our lives lived in media has all the hallmarks of a zombie society, as borne out by the research on how people around the world generally use media. The new human condition is fused with the material conditions of its immediate environment – both biological and technological. The question is what this altogether human yet zombified society in media life looks like, and what it feels like.

Aliens in mediaspace

If this indeed is a zombie society, what would the mediated equivalent be of chopping people's heads off? To answer this question, it would be valid to explore the contours of such a society – to see what kind of society people are co-creating in media. When we use media, we create different versions of the world. Media are not a window on reality – media make reality. As Jos de Mul writes, "Technology is an *ontological machine* that carries away the human world and mankind itself in a never-ending transformation" (2010: 7; italics in original). Considering people's omnipresence in media and the omnoptic surveillance mechanisms at work in everyday life, British sociologist Frank Webster (2011: 23) poignantly asks how else a society might know itself – if not through the infinite production and dissemination of information about what it is in media.

When it comes to documenting and making sense of our activities in media, there is a distinct tendency among scholars, government agencies and market researchers alike to draw some kind of distinction between specific generations in society. Young people presumably experience and therefore co-create a different kind of mediated world from that of adults; senior citizens and poor people tend to live through this transitional phase largely voiceless and powerless as they exist on the other side of a digital divide. On the other hand, none of these divides are static, all kinds of inequalities are at play, and there seems to be little or no clarity as to the precise consequences of differences in access found between particular groups of people in society. Nevertheless, it must be clear that, while close to 80 percent of the world population are mobile subscribers,[24] 20 percent of people in the world do not have access to electricity;[25] it is too easy to categorize people and even entire regions along lines of media use. If anything, what cuts across all people across all societies is an ongoing and accelerating immersion in all kinds of media, whereby media come to mean much more than their underlying technologies or what people do with them.

Since 2006, the Educause Center for Applied Research (ECAR) has conducted annual surveys and interviews with thousands of undergraduates at US colleges and universities about the role of information technologies in their lives. In its 2008 report, a quote from one of their teenage respondents is used to illustrate the broader trends borne out by the data: "I don't look at it as 'getting on the Internet.' The Internet is a part of life. It's a lifestyle."[26] The 2010 report opens with another student's sentiment expressed in that year's study: "My laptop is my life."[27] A combined telephone and face-to-face survey of more than 27,000 adults across 26 countries (commissioned by the BBC and conducted by international polling firm GlobeScan) in 2010 found that four out of five adults regard internet access as a fundamental human right.[28] A 2002 ethnographic report on people's use of media in general and mobile communication in particular by consumer research agency Context, describes the emergence of a *mobile life* thus: "Constant awareness of wireless finally wanes when people are truly living a mobile lifestyle," ultimately seamlessly integrating wireless in everyday life, "where people find it difficult to live a life without wireless."[29] Other reports on media life by scholarly groups, media companies and market research firms consistently claim how many, if not most users cannot imagine a life without media in general and mobile devices in particular, often feeling naked without them.

In this abundantly mediated and progressively more mobile lifestyle, media are such an augmented, automated, indispensable and altogether inalienable part of one's activities, attitudes and social arrangements that they disappear – they essentially *become* the life that people are experiencing on a day-to-day basis. Most authors of reports about people and their media scramble for concepts to label, classify, claim and tame them into segments – such as the Digital Generation, iGeneration, the Internet Generation, Net Geners, Generation Upload (as coined by a 2009 Vodafone marketing campaign in Germany[30]) and Generation C (where C stands for Content; coined by *trendwatching.com* in 2004[31]). Such terms are generally used for Generation Z (regrettably not short for Zombie): people born after the early 1990s – growing up after the fall of the Berlin Wall (1989) and the proclaimed end of the Cold War (1991), after the Tiananmen Square protests and subsequent massacre in China (1989), after the release of Nelson Mandela (1990) and the end of apartheid in South Africa (1994), after the end of military regimes and dictatorships across Latin America (Argentina in 1983, Brazil in 1985, and Chile in 1990), as well as after the introduction of the World Wide Web and the digital mobile phone (both in 1990).

Assuming that today's young people are indeed of a particular variety – if not zombies, they must be aliens – some scholars and market researchers no longer even bother interviewing or surveying anyone else when it comes to media. And, in a way, one cannot blame them – as young people themselves often seem adamant in claiming a unique profile for themselves, ostensibly set against whatever adults would want of them. This perception of feeling different is expressed in young people's media use. Studies among teenagers in a variety of countries document how the use of media for the majority has become a praxis of remixing, bricolage and participation, sometimes dubbed as a more or less unique 'media-meshing' lifestyle, whereby different parts of everyday life converge in the way people use multiple media more or less simultaneously throughout the day. As summarized in a 2005 study commissioned by *Yahoo!* among teenagers in Chicago, Mexico City, London, Berlin, Seoul and Shanghai: "Multitasking and simultaneous media usage are as normal as breathing for today's young people. This is a behavioral phenomenon known as Media Meshing. Media Meshing occurs when people begin an experience in one medium, then shift to another – and maybe even a third – to complement information, perspective, and emotional fulfillment."[32]

In their review of trends and data about young people and media life, John Palfrey and Urs Gasser (2008) depict those they call *digital natives* as an alien species who live in a completely mediated environment estranged from their parents, other adults and professionals. The authors suggest an approach of engaged parenting and a good education, insinuating that living a media life is a problem that needs to be solved. Don Tapscott's *Grown up digital* (2008) argues a similar case, suggesting the *net generation* is different from previous generations in that they do not view technology as technology, but rather as air, because they grew up with it as just another part of the environment. Both books move rapidly between locating the dangers of media-immersed kids and teenagers, and extolling positive attributes of these youngsters and their media by describing them as smarter, quicker and more tolerant of diversity, replacing a culture of control with a culture of enablement.

Such benevolent perspectives are in stark contrast with Mark Bauerlein's *The dumbest generation: how the digital age stupefies young Americans and jeopardizes our future* (2008).[33] In this bleak book Bauerlein laments just about everything teenagers do with media, suggesting that the only thing these kids are good at is: each other (in media such as Facebook and MySpace, that is). Similarly, Michael Bugeja's *Interpersonal divide: the search for community in a technological age* (2005) puts forward the argument that the digital revolution is in fact eroding interpersonal relationships and harming a sense of community. Bauerlein and Bugeja are some of the more high-profile pundits in a global field of experts who collectively seem to fall victim to *ephebiphobia*: the irrational fear of young people as expressed by adults throughout history. Here, media

life is deployed as a layer of augmented reality to voice much deeper concerns about the role children and youths have, or may come to play, in near-future scenarios of society.

In *Generation digital* (2007), co-founder of the US Center for Media Education Kathryn Montgomery is more nuanced in her appraisal of children and their media, suggesting that they are increasingly valuable target demographics (for commercial companies as well as political organizations) whose core developmental wants and needs – community, self-expression and personalization – are ready to be exploited and commoditized by marketers. Montgomery considers the engagement of young people with media as benchmarking the expectations and values of others. She highlights kids' critical appropriation of digital tools to challenge the entire music industry, to autonomously mobilize politically, and to integrate digital tools into their lifestyles in a wide variety of ways that often challenge or subvert the intentions of authorities (whether those authorities are parents, professors, politicians or business professionals). In a grounded assessment of the literature on digital natives versus the rest of the world's population, Australian educators Sue Bennett, Karl Maton and Lisa Kervin (2008) use caution. Although they recognize that young people "live their lives completely immersed in technology," where they "do not even consider computers 'technology' anymore" (777), research on what people actually do with their media simply suggests that "there is as much variation *within* the digital native generation as *between* the generations" (779; italics in original). In conclusion, Bennett, Maton and Kervin note, with specific reference to the zombies versus aliens debate: "We may live in a highly technologised world, but it is conceivable that it has become so through evolution, rather than revolution. Young people may do things differently, but there are no grounds to consider them alien to us" (783).

Rather than being exclusive to the young or only to those living in WEIRD (Western, Educated, Industrialized, Rich and Democratic) societies, media are constituent of each and every individual, as well as the wider social space people are part of (even though people use media differently, and digital divides as well as participation gaps persist).

Digital masters and *femmes digitales*

Whether utopian or dystopian, benevolent or malevolent, consumptive or productive, alien or zombie-based, people's lives are inseparably and inevitably lived in media. A society in media is similarly stratified along social fault lines, as status is conferred on the basis of whether people can be considered to be so-called *power* media users. Throughout both scholarly and market research reports on media usage patterns, hierarchies are constructed based on the extent to which people directly engage with the creative, participatory and otherwise more or less quasi-interactive options that media provide. Those at the top are inevitably people spending most of their time creating and editing their own media, which earns them labels such as *Creator* (from US-based Forrester Research[34]), *Digital Extrovert* (from British telecom TalkTalk[35]), *Digital Collaborator* (from the US Pew Internet & American Life Project[36]) and the fabulous *Digital Masters* and *Femmes Digitales* (as Dutch media agency Kobalt proclaims them[37]). In each instance, the research involved suggests that this group is relatively small, comprising less than a quarter of all media users. On the bottom side of such hierarchies lurk those who are not really into the spectacle of most media, and these poor folks tend to be dismissed as either *Tech Indifferent* (Pew), *Digital Refuseniks* (TalkTalk), mere *Spectators* or altogether *Inactives* (Forrester). This is not a large group either. The bulk of media users can be found somewhere in-between: watching a lot of television, listening to the odd radio station (mostly in the car, otherwise online), sending e-mails, texting on their cell phone, only now and then actually surfing the Web – as they are generally quite skeptical of the (quality of) information they find there. The elevated status of those who create, edit and distribute enables claims by or about such media omnivores to determine what is appropriate or expected for the rest.

The bottom line is that just about everyone – even those not necessarily online or plugged in – is drawn into media at one point or another. In the process, more or less new forms of being together, forming groups and alliances, hanging out with others, or otherwise maintaining some sense of belonging emerge. The various ways in which ever-growing numbers of people, both young and old, engage with each other through media are sometimes taken as stimulating a new form of community – one that is completely virtualized, solely existing online. The promise of online communities tends to be seen as either that of bridging existing social divides, or of bonding people with already-similar beliefs. Drawing data from various international research projects, Pippa Norris (2002) asserts that most online groups serve both functions at the same time. Although it is too early to draw definitive conclusions, the results from these and other studies suggest people who use the internet regularly feel it both widens and deepens their experience of community. This sense of community may not be so different from older, pre-modern types of social networks – as these were also largely based on relations based on kinship, proximity, peer status and interdependency as defined through the immediate extended family, work or school environment. Claims about the virtualization of communities as they are more or less exclusively created and maintained in online social networks run the risk of ignoring historical precedent, as earlier studies about community formation and preservation, by geographers such as Doreen Massey (2005 and 2007), suggest how, in the world's cities as well as the smallest rural towns, the boundaries of what constitutes spatial community tend to be relational, temporal and symbolic, rather than existing on a grid of absolute space. Any more or less stable notion of community must be seen as fundamentally contingent, exclusive and subject to anything but consensus.

Linking emerging forms (and social norms of) community with media life, cultural anthropologist Mizuko (Mimi) Ito finds that, especially among young people, "sociality gets augmented by a dense set of technologies, signifiers, and systems of exchange" (2005: 32). She describes this phenomenon as an emerging *hypersociality*, as people develop and perform identities in everyday life in relation to customizable, interactive media forms (such as videogames and television series in combination with websites). According to Ito, "This digitally-augmented sociality is an unremarkable fact of life now" (32). A sociological take on the same phenomenon by Ito's German colleague Andreas Wittel proposes that we conceptualize the way people relate in a media society as driven by a *network sociality*, where "social relations are . . . not based on mutual experience or common history, but primarily on an exchange of data and on 'catching up' . . . Network sociality consists of fleeting and transient, yet iterative social relations; of ephemeral but intense encounters" (2001: 51). Facilitated by media, this kind of sociality blurs the boundaries between work and play, and it opens up social relations to dynamic expansion (and contraction) as people can connect with or disconnect from each other through always-on networked technologies. Scott Lash (2002) similarly suggests that, in today's world, previously long-lasting and proximal social bonds – such as exemplified by the neighborhood community, the extended family, employees and their colleagues – gradually give way to distanciated *communicational bonds*. Instead of social relationships bounded by space and time, argues Lash, such bonds must rather be seen as forms of communication that are increasingly short-lived, transient and mediated by new, super-fast technologies. Lash sees this development as inevitable and not necessarily detrimental to new forms of community in an information age. Zygmunt Bauman objects to such benevolent readings of the networked potential of contemporary media life, suggesting such more or less benign readings by social theorists "fall victim [to an] internet fetishism fallacy. Network is not community and communication not integration – both safely equipped as they are with disconnection on demand devices."[38]

Where Ito observes a new form of media-enabled sociality emerging among teenagers on the streets of Japanese and American cities, Wittel sees a similar phenomenon at work among new-media workers and freelancers in downtown

London. Ito stresses the creative and performative capacity that media bring to the table when people interact and give their lives meaning, while Wittel laments the unpredictable and unstable nature of mediated engagements. Both scholars recognize the significance of the imagination in how their study participants talk about what they do, in media, together – it is almost as if media open up social relations to intense speculation and intervention by the people involved. What does it mean when someone superpokes you on Facebook? What is the exact social status of a clan membership in *World of Warcraft*? Does the fact that he listens to the same music as I do (as evidenced by his publicly visible audiostream on Last.fm) mean we could be soulmates? Is the communal promise of an online/mobile meeting space a safe substitute for homeliness among marginalized groups such as lesbian, gay, bi-sexual, transgender and questioning youth? Whether hypersociality, network sociality, or perhaps some version of impersonal sociality as reminiscent of a zombified social system, it seems clear that a media life stretches what it means to be sociable, uproots it (at least in part) from essential ties to a specific place or time, and makes it much more messy, and ultimately contingent upon whatever people know about it and subsequently do with it.

Departing from such a co-creative point of view, French media philosopher Pierre Lévy (1997) envisions how people can produce new social bonds through the ongoing development of sophisticated systems of networked communication such as internet, leading to new forms of *collective intelligence* based on bottom-up collaborations between peers rather than top-down expert systems and bureaucracies. This collaborative social system is benchmarked, following Lévy, by the affirmative promise of placeless peer-to-peer connectivity and cooperation driven by interconnected mobile devices. Beyond drawing more people into the sphere of public communication, the kind of sociality engendered by modern-day media has a distinct peer-to-peer personality. Indeed, it is an almost anti-hierarchical sociality, one that tends to bypass traditional conventions and layers of society, including (sometimes) those of language, class and social capital. Similar conclusions are drawn by the scholars involved in the three-year Digital Youth Project (conducted at the University of California, Berkeley, and the University of Southern California), who, in their work of documenting the media lives of young people, emphasize that if teens are not relying on themselves, the next point of call is their peers rather than traditional authorities such as parents, professors or professionals.[39] Beyond connecting to their peers through media, young people sometimes turn to media as a kind of *super-peer* to find information either that is unavailable, or that they are unwilling to seek out, in their peer group (this super-peer theory finds its primary support in studies of the way adolescent boys and girls find out about sex and sexuality using television, magazines and social networking sites). As media become privatized and part of what Canadian communication sociologist Jeffrey Boase (2008) articulates as an individual's *personal communication system* (involving a range of communication technologies as well as in-person contacts that everyone uses in order to stay socially connected), a mediaspace emerges where traditional societal information hierarchies become corrupted, contested and sometimes even abandoned altogether. Considering young people's role as defining users, this would mean that a societal power shift from authorities to ordinary individuals (as they operate in temporary networks and mediated constellations) is going to have significant repercussions, as people learn to make up their own minds, seeking only guidance from their peers rather than to be told what to do. "We are undoubtedly living in an anti-hierarchical age," concludes Ulrich Beck (2000: 150) in an analysis not just about the role of teenagers in society – but indeed about the way all of us (are forced to) make sense of the world and our role in it.

The individualized and peer-based nature of contemporary sociality is not a necessary byproduct or unintended consequence of media – it is a type of sociality that is built into the material infrastructure of networked media. The infrastructure of telephony is decidedly peer-to-peer in that it does not have a privileged center to which callers connect, and the internet is broadly based on end-to-end connectivity, although such innovation-fostering principles get progressively undermined by controlling mechanisms implemented by network providers. Beyond such telecommunications technologies, there exist numerous processes online that follow a peer-to-peer structure, including but not limited to filesharing networks, streaming audio and video services, cloud computing and internet telephony. Even more so, our media devices often run (on) open source software applications: programs that the user can freely "run, copy, distribute, study, change and improve upon, and redistribute."[40] Popular applications are the Firefox web browser, the OpenOffice software suite (for word processing, spreadsheets, presentations, graphics and databases), and the Android operating system for mobile devices.

At the heart of end-to-end (e2e) and peer-to-peer (P2P) standards and applications is the identification of *individual* resources by a network that can be used and acted upon by *everyone* connected to this network. Societies are, like media, a combination of P2P systems – people exchanging news and information at the local market, grocery store or pub – and centralized structures (in technological terms: client-server systems) – like governments, trade unions and other social institutions that individuals and groups can turn to. Belgian information analyst Michel Bauwens (co-founder of the P2P Foundation) goes as far as postulating that P2P should be seen as a template of human relationships, leading to a new kind of social formation.[41] As people bypass traditional social integrators such as neighborhood associations, municipal governments, political parties, amateur sport clubs and houses of worship, it does not necessarily mean they do not get involved with communities any more. It does suggest, however, that people socialize increasingly on their own terms: based on what they (think they) want, grounded in what they (think they) know, prompted by recommendations and reputations of a network of peer relations (connections which may or may not be physically or temporally proximate).

Consolidating general values surveys in 43 countries, political scientist Ronald Inglehart (1997) cofirms a global shift among people in their self-observations as citizens away from traditional social institutions towards a distinctly skeptical, globally interconnected yet deeply personal type of self-determined civic engagement. Other studies, such as those by Robert Putnam in the US, detail broad societal trends toward distinctly individualized and often outright anti-authoritarian attitudes. Austrian sociologist Karin Knorr Cetina (1997) suggests this trend across overdeveloped nations is indicative of an ongoing process of *de-socialization*, in which traditional social structures disintegrate and people seem to relate more to objects – such as mobile phones and online social networking websites – than to other humans. Exactly the fact that in such a social context we are all on our own but at the same time more connected than ever before seems to be the defining feature of society in media. The significance of this trend towards a perhaps more fragile but nonetheless meaningful type of sociality cannot be underestimated. If it is up to us to evaluate on an ongoing basis what and whom to engage with solely on the basis of what we can find out about it or them in media, the urgency of monitoring those around us (whether physically, temporarily or virtually nearby) becomes paramount – just like the necessity of understanding the technological affordances for reciprocal surveillance.

Everyone knows you're (not) a dog

I cannot help but question what kind of society is produced characterized by the ability of everyone to monitor everyone else – to know each other primarily through mediated connections, data storage and transfer, and the sharing of private lives in public archives. This is not necessarily another way of restating the famous 1993 cartoon by Peter Steiner in the *New Yorker*, captioned "On the Internet, nobody knows you're a dog" – it is also its exact opposite: due to the lack of anonymity as we are, for example, continuously captured by our digital shadow, everyone can know you're a dog. Several websites exploit this particular feature of media life to serious and satirical purpose. In February 2010, Dutch social media company Forthehack went live with its website PleaseRobMe.com, featuring a stream of publicly archived tweets by people announcing their location as being other than at home. The goal of PleaseRobMe, according to the developers (Barry Borsboom, Frank Groeneveld and Boy van Amstel), was "Engagement with the online privacy issue and with the brand, Forthehack."[42] As mobile devices, fitted with a wireless internet connection and satellite-based global positioning system, become ubiquitous, companies developing services that combine online presence with offline activities abound. Examples are social networking sites like Loopt and Foursquare, applications such as Google Buzz and Facebook Places, or dedicated location-streaming platforms like Bliin and Jaiku. Another project intended to raise awareness about our tendency to (over-)share our personal information is ICanStalkU.com, a site created by Ben Jackson and Larry Pesce of US security research firm Mayhemic Labs (which went live in May 2010). Collecting information from metadata that publicly posted images generally come embedded with, the service automatically generates tweet-sized stalking reports on the whereabouts of people who upload pictures to social networks such as Twitter. As the developers explain, this way (and often without your consent) anyone can quickly generate information about "where you live, who else lives there, your commuting patterns, where you go for lunch each day, who you go to lunch with," and "why you and your attractive co-worker really like to visit a certain nice restaurant on a regular basis."[43] ICanStalkU comes with a detailed guide to how to disable geotagging in smartphones.

ICanStalkU and PleaseRobMe are based in part on what many people do in media on a daily basis: living their private lives in public, a concept originally experimented with by American media entrepreneur Josh Harris – as documented in *We Live In Public* (2009) by US filmmaker Ondi Timoner. Timoner chronicles the career of Harris, focusing on his experiment with surveillance and oversharing well before social media such as Facebook. In 1999, Harris used millions of dollars earned through his web company Jupiter Communications to furnish a large basement in downtown New York with sleeping pods, bathrooms, a shooting range, an open bar and a dining hall – all fitted with surveillance cameras. In exchange for free room and board, a community of about 100 friends and artists moved into this bunker, everyone dressed in orange jumpsuits and subjecting themselves to questioning by an interrogation artist in a dedicated interrogation room, while being videotaped 24 hours a day. In the end, the underground community broke down completely and on January 1, 2000 the police stepped in and moved everybody out. According to the documentary's companion website, Harris' experiment can be seen as "what to expect as the virtual world inevitably takes control of our lives."[44] In British newspaper *The Sunday Times* (of October 17, 2009), Ondimer "calls it a cautionary tale for our Orwellian, Facebook-addled, Twitter addicted, confessional surveillance age."[45]

Harris possibly gets credit for being among the first to see our life moving into media in terms of a constant and continuous mediatization – but Ondimer's film sees little or no good coming from a near-future hypersocial society in which lives are lived in public, in which everything and everyone can be (and often is) monitored, in which we are all alone yet intricately connected. A networked and peer-based sociality in media produces a society that needs to find out about itself on an ongoing basis in order to socially function. Our tendency to overshare is perhaps best understood as a vital adaptation to a rapidly evolving social mediaspace, rather than a regrettable or generation-specific social problem. In the process of adapting to our co-creative mediated social reality, it becomes crucial to identify and develop skills and competences needed to survive and thrive in a world society benchmarked by permanently recorded, overshared, instantly archived, publicly accessible and redactable computer-mediated communicational bonds.

Survival in the metaverse

One of the first and quite possibly most entertaining analyses of the human condition in cyberspace can be found in the 1992 novel *Snow crash* by American science-fiction writer Neal Stephenson. The book chronicles the experiences of two main characters. The first is Hiro Protagonist, who makes a living as a *Deliverator*: delivering pizza for CosaNostra Pizza (a subdivision of the Mafia), while also having earned the reputation of being one of the first and best hackers of computer code in the world. Beyond delivering pizza and hacking, Hiro earns some money on the side selling information on just about anything and anyone as a freelancer for the Central Intelligence Corporation: a corporate version of what used to be the CIA. The second key figure in the book is Y.T. (short for Yours Truly), a 15-year-old girl working as a skateboard courier. Literally by accident, Hiro and Y. T. become information-sharing partners. In Stephenson's vision of our near-future world, national governments have collapsed and commercial enterprise reigns supreme. The country, and indeed the world, is divided into burbclaves (suburban enclaves) run by competing corporations. In this extremely competitive, frantically paced postnational world – Stephenson calls it *Reality* – the cultural, economic and intellectual elite spends most of its time in the *Metaverse*: a virtual world that people log into and experience via goggles and earphones. In one of the many fascinating quirky details in Stephenson's book, the *Metaverse* seems bound by more rules and regulations than *Reality*:

> When Hiro goes into the Metaverse . . . and sees buildings and electric signs stretching off into the darkness . . . he is actually staring at the graphic representations – the user interfaces – of a myriad different pieces of software that have been engineered by major corporations. In order to place these things . . . they have had to get approval from the Global Multimedia Protocol Group, have had to buy frontage . . . , get zoning approval, obtain permits, bribe inspectors, the whole bit. (2008 [1992]: 25)

In the *Metaverse*, users interact via avatars: pieces of software representing "the audiovisual bodies that people use to communicate with each other in the Metaverse" (36). Stephenson takes credit for coming up with the term "avatar" to denote people's virtual selves, although he acknowledges that he found out after finishing his book that the term was already in use as part of a virtual reality system called "Habitat," created in 1985 by Chip Morningstar and Randall Farmer for Lucasfilm Games. As Morningstar and Farmer elaborate (in a 1990 conference paper), in what can be considered to be one of the first large-scale graphical multi-user virtual environments, "players are represented by animated figures that we call 'Avatars.' Avatars are usually, though not exclusively, humanoid in appearance."[46] Discussing the lessons learned from designing and running their real version of Stephenson's fictional *Metaverse*, Morningstar and Farmer remark that at the core of the debate about virtual worlds is "an unresolved philosophical question: is an Avatar an extension of a human being (thus entitled to be treated as you would treat a real person) or a Pac-Man-like critter destined to die a thousand deaths, or something else entirely?" It is exactly these kinds of questions that Stephenson addresses in his story when he introduces the key plot issue: Hiro and Y.T. attempt to prevent a group of religious fundamentalists unleashing into the world a virus that not only affects computer networks, but also acts on a biological level as it reduces those who come into contact with it to people babbling nonsensically – all in the same language, all slaves to those who can manipulate this primal language. This biolinguistic virus is called Snow Crash, and those who make the mistake of looking at it see "a living wall of light, like a flexible, flatscreened television set, and it's not showing anything at all. Just static. White noise. Snow" (2008[1992]: 3).

Throughout the book, Stephenson's characters make sense of their world (whether it is *Reality* or the *Metaverse*) in terms that confuse, remix and altogether erase the boundaries between software, hardware and the body, living systems and computer systems (cf. *bioware*; 352). Status in these worlds is conferred by technological skills and resources: the more advanced your machine, the faster your network connection, the more qualified you are as a software designer and engineer, the higher you end up on the social ladder. At the top of the pyramid stand computer hackers – those who can actually write the code that constitutes the *Metaverse*, people who live and die by the manipulation of information – the equivalent of digital masters and *femmes digitales*. Nowhere in the book is an explanation offered of what exactly the mind-altering Snow Crash virus is, or what is accomplished at the end of the story when Hiro decapitates the guy planting the virus in the *Metaverse* and installs the right kind of anti-virus software to prevent it from spreading. This apparent lack of context and understanding is picked up by Richard Rorty as an example of contemporary culture giving primacy to "knowingness, or technique, or professionalism" (1998: 134), which is a "state of soul that prevents shudders of awe" and "makes one immune to romantic enthusiasm" (126). According to Rorty, the solution to the issues facing media life provided by a book such as Stephenson's *Snow crash* is one devoid of inspiration, beauty and hope. It is a solution that seems to be premised by just knowing what buttons to push and what kind of program to run. All things considered, it seems exactly the kind of solution that would work for a zombie society.

Using Stephenson's book as a frame of reference, Rorty moves on to proclaim this kind of instrumental rationality as the fundamental problem of how people learn and teach today. It must be said that Hiro Protagonist finds out what he needs to know about the world, the virus and the people (or avatars) who need to be beheaded by regularly consulting a Wikipedia-like virtual encyclopedia (called Earth) that produces neatly packaged information but offers little or no meaningful context. Beyond the observation that *Snow crash* is anything but a heartless piece of writing devoid of passion, desire or wishful thinking, it is important to take note of Rorty's warning about the implications of completely outsourcing the responsibilities for designing and maintaining the contours of our media life to those with knowledge of its code and protocols – or to any kind of machine for delivering information, products and services. Beyond knowing how to properly install anti-virus software on your laptop and effectively manipulating the privacy settings of your online social network profile, one should be able to articulate some sense of value and beauty about the kinds of stories we tell about ourselves and others in media. Before emphasizing media literacy and potentially ending up barring access to an ethical and aesthetical media life to those not so well versed in the idiom and skillset of programming and hacking, we need a sensibility about the kind of society we live in (and inevitably co-create) that enables people to move beyond the binary opposition between media and life. Thinking about what we need to know about media in order to be successful in life therefore needs to be driven by normative as well as playful principles – by a skills toolkit as well as a sense of wonder. At the same time we need to think about media in a fundamental way, a way that deliberately considers its vital materiality. This is what Stephenson also signals in his book: in order to understand and master the machine, one needs to know how it works from the inside out, what its machine language is, how it makes and is made by society. In other words, we need to comprehensively think through how technologies, media, people and nature *intra-act*.

Earlier celebration or apprehension about increasingly intimate human–machine relationships and the fragile future sketched by Stephenson in his assessment of the ongoing fusion of *Reality* and the *Metaverse* perhaps should make way for a more subtle appreciation of inseparable media, in that we overwhelmingly ignore them, take them for granted, accept that they are hardwired into our social systems. In other words, media are essential to the successful survival of human societies and do not necessarily reduce the social to the technological. Hacking, as personified in the character of Hiro Protagonist, is the ultimate survival skill, albeit one not necessarily premised on mastering computer code. Programming and hacking can also be seen as discursive devices – ways of making sense differently from what is expected or predicted. Similar media-life survival tactics would include, as Mimi Ito notes (2005: 31), a practice of media mixing as the technical form of hypersociality, and what Lev Manovich similarly advocates as "people's tactics of bricolage, reassembly, and remix" (2009: 324) in media life. Austrian new-media artist and curator Peter Weibel (writing in 2006) goes as far as suggesting that all current art practice falls subsequent to a *post-media* condition of constant intervention, user innovation and media mixing, which has become the norm for all aesthetic experience:

> Hence in art there is no longer anything beyond the media. No one can escape from the media . . . The set of all media forms a universal self-contained medium . . . The ultimate effect of all this is to emancipate the observer, visitor and user. In the post-media condition we experience the equality of the lay public, of the amateur, the philistine, the slave and the subject. The very terms "user innovation" or "consumer generated content" bear witness to the birth of a new kind of democratic art in which everyone can participate.[47]

Although people may not always realize it, many of their activities in media have a similar creative quality – from the cutting and pasting of texts, the customization of wallpapers and ringtones, the cropping and editing of images, and the building of music playlists to more advanced forms of mixing, editing and otherwise repurposing of media. Advocating a mindful approach to such often-mundane practices, numerous authors and educators enthusiastically embrace a convergence culture as the appropriate ethos of a society in media. Henry Jenkins (2004) is among the more high-profile international advocates for people's right to freely sample and remix media. British media sociologist David Gauntlett takes an additional step by arguing that, with open access to tools to further co-creativity and to platforms to make their voices heard (beyond the constraints of corporately controlled platforms), "people are happier, more engaged with the world, and more likely to develop and learn" (2011: 226). Basing his argument on the works of Austrian philosopher-priest Ivan Illich, Gauntlett passionately advocates a convivial engagement with society in media – not exclusively through the planned process of multimedia conglomerates and commercial software, but through the making, appropriating and, in effect, hacking of tools in order to care for and about others. Offering a more generalized societal perspective, Christian Fuchs (2008) argues that discrete technologies are best seen as being among many media in people's communication repertoire, increasing social trends in two antagonistic directions: cooperation and competition. Under increasingly dominant competitive conditions, the way people use media contributes to an ongoing classification, segmentation and individualization of society in media. On the other hand, those same media can foster a sharing, collaborative and participatory culture, one that Fuchs considers much more in line with the essence of human society.

A blend between people's timeless tendency to make the environment their own by tweaking and adapting it, and contemporary media's qualities of opening their infrastructures, contents and services up to intra-action seems to provide an

encouraging road ahead. In this context people's programming, hacking, remixing and other activities Mirko Schäfer
considers as typical of a *bastard culture* (which is much mess-
ier than Jenkins' rather spotless concept of convergence)
can be considered to be media-life manifestations of Jean
Baudrillard's (1981) call to action in a media-saturated world:
"The more hegemonic the system, the more the imagination
is struck by the smallest of its reversals. The challenge, even
infinitesimal, is the image of a chain failure. . . . Theoretical
violence, not truth, is the only resource left us."[48]

Co-creating and remixing are not just an ontological move –
as in making yourself and making the world your own. These
are also epistemological acts, in that they necessarily involve
the anticatharsis of zombie ways of knowing and doing things:
our media mixing potentially destroys the reigning model
without offering a replacement (Lauro and Embry, 2008: 91,
96). Society in media life is grounded in Weibel's post-media
condition: there is no outside to media. Perhaps in the movies
there is – in *We Live In Public* escape comes at the hands of
the police, and in Romero's films all we need to do is barri-
cade ourselves in shopping malls (or on islands) and fight off
the zombie hordes by shooting them or (as in Stephenson's
novel) chopping their heads off. This escape is, however, an
illusion – just as the Delete key on a computer offers only an
illusion of impermanence. We live in media forever – and in
that eternity, it is up to us as individuals to find a way to hack
the system together by committing, in the first instance, theoretical violence. In other words: by becoming zombies.

CHAPTER SIX

Together Alone

where we are closely connected to endless versions of ourselves

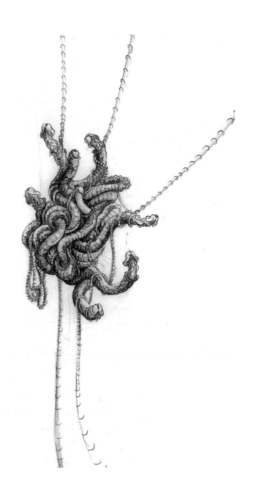

Imagine this: a crowd of 1,000 or more people, moving back and forth, contorting their bodies against each other, waving their hands, sweating and grimacing. Other than the occasional guttural sound or shout, everything takes place in complete silence. Zombies, you presume? Welcome to a silent disco.

A silent disco is "a collective experience in isolated music."[1] Partygoers dance to music received directly into headphones. The music gets broadcast via a restricted FM transmitter with the signal being picked up by wireless headphone receivers worn by the silent party attendees – listening to two or more individualized streams of music while dancing together. The silent disco started in earnest in 2002. In the words of original organizers Dutch disc jockeys Nico Okkerse and Michael Minten:

> In the summer of 2002 two friends organized a secret party on the campsite of Dutch theater festival "De Parade." Apart from the people that joined them, nobody could hear the tunes they were playing, as the party people were wearing wireless headphones. Silent Disco was born . . . As everyone at our show is wearing wireless headsets, only the participants hear the songs and sing-a-long or dance to them, which makes it fun to watch for the people who are not wearing any headphones as well.[2]

In an interview with CNN (published on September 13, 2005) Okkerse and Minten state that "the aim is for people to go wild in silence," suggesting that the success of their privately experienced yet at the same time publicly visible and accessible party is emotional as well as social: "People know that the party is exclusive to them, so it gives a good feeling."[3] Today, the silent disco is a common feature at outdoor events around the world, featuring prominently at high-profile music and arts festivals like Bonnaroo (US), Glastonbury (UK), Big Day Out (Australia) and Pinkpop (Netherlands), attracting thousands of enthusiasts at any one time. Similar phenomena are silent raves, mobile clubs and other gatherings where groups of people dance together while listening to their own personal media on headphones.

Try to remain visible

The notion of being together and generally having a great time, yet still being alone in one's experience of reality captures the notion of a media life, in which people are more connected than ever before – whether through common boundaryless issues such as global warming, terrorism and worldwide migration, or via internet and mobile communication – yet at the same time on their own, securely secluded in a personalized mediasphere. This reality, however individualized, is also inevitably shared. Additionally (and not insignificantly), it is a reality where one can have a lot of fun! Perhaps one could argue that phenomena such as the silent disco offer us the opportunity to act out what Friedrich Nietzsche in *The Dionysian worldview* (1997[1870]) saw as a Dionysian metaphysics of human existence – premised on "the self-forgetfulness of intoxication" (82) through music and dance (and media) – all while maintaining the artificial boundaries between individuals mandated by its opposing Apollonian worldview – consisting of structures, reflexivity, moderation and restraint.

Beyond the silent disco, an even more reflexive form of being together alone in media is UK artist Duncan Speakman's concept of a *subtlemob*, where people gather on street corners at a specific time to jointly listen to pre-recorded soundtracks on their personal media devices. These soundtracks sometimes include instructions on where to look or what to do, including music composed to let people take in their surroundings more deliberately than they normally would, as Speakman explains on his website:

> Imagine walking through a film, but it's happening on the streets you live in. Subtlemobs usually happen in public spaces. . . . It's about integrating with a social or physical

space, not taking it over. The audience listens on headphones, a mix of music, story and instructions. Sometimes they just watch, sometimes they perform scenes for each other . . . Try to remain invisible. . .[4]

In a review of one of these subtlemob events for UK online news magazine *The Londonist*, Tara Sloane writes: "Capricious and profound, the experience definitely captures what it is to escape from the world for a little bit – and then to return and find that you see things just a bit differently. And the fact that others around you may or may not be experiencing the same thing only adds to the surreality" (published November 16, 2009).[5] In interviews about his work, Speakman alludes to the uncanny ability of personal media devices to isolate and connect at the same time, depending on how one perceives such technologies: "Previously I had shunned walkmans because of the way they cut you off from your acoustic space, but I suddenly saw them as an opportunity to make people connect with the world around them."[6] Similar playful performances are organized by New-York-based artist collective Improv Everywhere, whose so-called *Mp3 Experiments* at times involve more than 3,000 participants.[7]

Silent discos, subtlemobs and mp3 experiments are examples of instances, in which the same media that isolate and divide also heighten people's awareness of others, potentially fostering social participation and collective action. Thus, when it comes to who we are as individuals *together alone* in media life, one more boundary needs to be dissolved: between solitude and solidarity. This is a pertinent issue, as countless studies benchmark concerns as well as unbridled enthusiasm about the media's qualities of bringing people together, or driving them farther apart.

As cities grow larger, several studies note how people at times seem to prefer mediated communication to direct face-to-face contact, if anything to avoid some of the complexities of social life. Even though one should always question presumptions of social isolation or cohesion as presumably produced by living in media, a commonsensical approach to the way individuals use media in everyday life does suggest that media do not always seem to ingratiate people with their immediate environment. Indian-American sociologist Sudhir Alladi Venkatesh, for example, remarks (in an op-ed piece for the *New York Times*, published March 28, 2009):

> in today's cities, even when we share intimate spaces, we tend to be quite distant from one another . . . these days, technology separates us and makes more of our communication indirect, impersonal and emotionally flat. With headsets on and our hands busily texting, we are less aware of one another's behavior in public space. Count the number of people with cellphones and personal entertainment devices when you walk down a street. Self-involved bloggers, readers of niche news, all of us listening to our personal playlists: we narrowly miss each other.[8]

Venkatesh's comments resonate deceptively well – which does not mean he is wrong, it is just that he, like so many other observers of the social, is prone to classify people as either together or alone, with an implied aversion to the bereft status and presumed penalty of loneliness. The deception takes place in the form of assuming that wandering in public while wearing headphones is a form of social disconnect. As far as most mobile media artifacts are concerned, this would be a problematic assumption, in that such devices tend to come with interconnected properties. Based on what people do with their personal communication technologies, network architect Kazys Varnelis furthermore suggests that people at the very least inhabit "simultaneously overlapping telecocoons, sharing telepresence with intimates in whom we are in near-constant touch" (2008: 152). Streetwandering while enjoying a personal soundtrack to life can perhaps best be considered as what British media scholar Michael Bull describes as "accompanied solitude" (2005: 343). Bull's research shows how people use mobile sound media to create and maintain a sense of intimacy while moving in-between places (home and work or a bar) and in-between time (killing dead air flanked by meeting colleagues and catching up with friends). Adding the capability of most portable devices to store or make available one's entire music collection through customizable playlists, personal media can be seen as an "auditory identity in the palm of your hand" (Bull, 2006: 145). Our technologically mediated private realms can also be seen as empowering, giving users some level of private control and agency regarding their identity when navigating public spaces that sometimes may not be welcoming of one's presence.

A nuanced take recognizes the complex nature of artifactual capabilities and everyday activities implicated in people's personalized media bubbles. We are not necessarily distant and alone simply by virtue of wearing headphones while walking to school, texting while riding the train, or otherwise fiddling with our personal media in public places. Yet there is a troubling undercurrent to debates about whether media life is either a lonely or (potentially) collective enterprise. This is what political anthropologist Leo Coleman critically addresses as the overused yet ostensibly false dichotomy between solitude and solidarity. Instead, Coleman argues, one should be mindful about forms of *social solitude*, encompassing "places where people go to be alone together" (2009: 758). Such places can be restaurants or bars, airports and shopping malls, as well as online social networks, virtual or synthetic worlds, and any other form of mediated sociality. These spaces are not necessarily filled with lonely people who lack solidarity or cannot form "thick social connections" (769). Instead, the mediapolis can be considered to be a spatial form within which people are alone together in often (but not necessarily) meaningful ways. The supposedly anti-social outcome of the lonely togetherness of mediated interpersonal relationships is expressed forcefully by Sherry Turkle, who, in her aptly titled book *Alone together: why we expect more from technology and less from each other* (2011), introduces what she considers the less-than-ideal consequences of a life completely immersed in media:

Technology is seductive when what it offers meets our human vulnerabilities. And as it turns out, we are very vulnerable indeed. We are lonely but fearful of intimacy. Digital connections and the sociable robot may offer the illusion of companionship without the demands of friendship. Our networked life allows us to hide from each other, even as we are tethered to each other. (1)

In this ever-increasing intimacy between people and machines, Turkle argues, we use media to defend against (13) or even defeat (3) loneliness – which she considers "failed solitude" (288) if it means that without constant connectivity people cannot be meaningfully alone with themselves any more. Her warning is significant, as is the celebration of media's potential to engender collective action (and fun). The extent to which people may feel secure (or forlorn) in media life is a different question altogether. What all these perspectives and examples suggest, then, is the failure of applying the zombie categories of loneliness and collectivity, as well as those of solitude versus solidarity in absolute terms to the ways people live their media life. Media extend social relations into time and space, while at the same time reminding users who they are (supposed to be), or can be.

In media life, who you are may be just as difficult to ascertain as in any other life, with the complication of having many ever so slightly different versions of yourself to pick and choose from. As Matthew Fraser and Soumitra Dutta, both at the business school INSEAD in France, note: "The construction, and maintenance, of multiple identities on social networking sites is rapidly becoming the expected norm. In the online world, the *unitary* self has morphed into the *multiple* self. Identities in cyberspace are multifaceted, splintered, concocted, fluid, negotiated, unexpected and sometimes deceptive" (2008: 32; italics in original).

The individual in media life is like the participant in a silent disco: acutely aware of her own private and personal experience while at the same time living through an involvement with distinct others – with the added unique perspective of being together alone with endless versions of themselves at the same time. In the silent disco of my media life I am, as the British punk-rock band Generation X proclaimed back in 1980, "Dancing with Myself."[9] Mexican philosopher Manuel de Landa (2006) further explores this notion of simultaneous internal and external connectedness, arguing how entities are best understood as never alone or together – they are always versions of both. In De Landa's terms, entities can be individual people, but also social institutions, cities and even entire nations. If someone is alone at home, without media access, this does not necessarily mean that who they are or what they think about at that moment is not in some way influenced by or connected to his or her social relations. Similarly, if a group of people engages in some kind of collective behavior, that would not automatically imply that their individual particularity (for example in terms of their motives and reasons to engage) gets lost.

De Landa's approach indirectly pays tribute (via his greatest inspiration, French philosopher Gilles Deleuze) to the work of German mathematician Gottfried Leibniz, with specific reference to his metaphysical theory of *monadology* (originally published in 1714).[10] Leibniz's aim was to take issue with Descartes' division between mind and matter, instead suggesting that each and every entity in the universe is made up out of monads, which (unlike atoms) have no substance but are all interconnected. He saw every organic body as a "divine machine or natural automaton" and considered the way such machines worked – how all the parts interacted internally as well as externally – as the basis of his theory of monads. For Leibniz, the relations between monads give rise to the substance of all life (including nature, humanity and machines). The supposed constant movement of the monads (acting and being acted upon by all other monads) means every single movement impacts everything else, and change is therefore constant: "this interconnection, relationship, or this adaptation of all things to each particular one, and of each one to all the rest, brings it about that every simple substance has relations which express all the others and that it is consequently a perpetual living mirror of the universe."

The emphasis on continual change also means that nothing is ever – in Leibniz's words – "sterile or dead": everything (whether nature, the body or materiality) is always open to be acted upon, and is therefore contingent. For Leibniz there is no essential distinction between the natural and the artificial – between life and media – as he calls attention to the *divine machines* we all are: infinitely complex and materially plastic entities always inseparably linked. At the heart of his philosophy, Leibniz sought to understand the world in fundamentally biological terms, and therefore introduced a vitalist reading into our understanding of both matter and life. In the context of media life, this would mean that one should always study media in terms of living, while both media and life are constituted through their evolving irreducible interactions. The monadological approach presents a way of thinking about being isolated and connected in media at the same time without this state of being representing some kind of final composite of being alone and together, or being essentially determined by particular technological affordances.

French sociologist Gabriel Tarde deployed Leibniz's metaphysics in his 1893 essay "Monadologie et sociologie" by pointing out how, in the social sciences, specific phenomena – whether an entire society or a behavior particular to an individual person – are in fact always temporary and unstable constellations that exist due to association. There are no individual bodies, Tarde suggests – everything always exists in terms of "unity in the multiplicity of separate elements, interconnected in the same way with the elements of other aggregates."[11] Just as Charles Darwin's theory of evolution shows how every single living being is the result of myriad, complex and ongoing variations and elemental changes, Tarde invokes Leibniz in arguing for a monadological approach to the social, with an emphasis on endless imitation, repetition, differentiation and innovation as the benchmarks for interaction. In effect, both Leibniz and Tarde offer in their work the foundation for a political (and spiritual) ideology of change as made possible through the circulatory interactions between people, nature and machines.

The point of this detour is to point a way out of the morass of considering the individual vis-à-vis society (and nature) in media – by emphasizing how such entities are, like monads, always unfinished and co-constituent. In a way, media make visible the intense interconnectivity between people, social institutions, technologies and the world at large. Monadological metaphysics works in practical terms if people indeed *see* themselves and their environment as affected by each other's actions (or lack thereof). In media life, the monadic hypothesis (as formulated by Tarde) may offer the most important element of being together alone: that of seeing, and being seen. Rather than trying to remain invisible, as in Duncan Speakman's performances of the subtlemob, I would argue the reverse is the key. One thing people can do in media is see themselves live, which in theory allows us to take responsibility for what we witness in (and want of) the world. As William Mitchell posits with reference to no one being on their own in a completely mediated world: "zones of networked interdependence are now growing in rapid, unbounded fashion. As they inexorably fuse into a single global system, they confront us with the challenge of imagining and forming extended social aggregates that are sustained by . . . networks of ethical interconnectivity" (2004: 210–11).

To this, Sherry Turkle adds what she describes as a necessary "*realtechnik* of connectivity culture" (2011: 243; italics in original), referring to a sensibility about our relationships with technology based on the realization that media and life co-evolve, and in this process we have an ethical responsibility to understand who we are and what we are doing in what she calls our *networked life*, which is "always on and (now) always with us" (157). A key difference from previous appeals to a more or less universal and positively pluralistic digital media ethics is perhaps that such a *realtechnik* is a distinctly individual one: it is up to everyone to take responsibility for their own solitude and social engagement. Zizi Papacharissi considers this kind of engagement, powered by "the technological architectures of the private sphere" (2010: 166), as establishing autonomy together with collective action. Seen as such, a mobile phone, for example, is not an instrument of either isolation or solidarity – it is a device in which our solitude and togetherness are embodied, get meaning and provide purpose. A Facebook profile, Twitter account or YouTube channel can enable, but is not required for, political revolution. Beyond *charismatic*, our media are *aspirational*, and thus constituent of collective action as well as social solitude.

In our growing awareness of the inseparably fused relations between technology, body, environment and social role – what James Katz and Mark Aakhus call *apparatgeist* (2003: 301) with specific reference to media, and Damian White and Chris Wilbert (2009) label as *technonatures*, more broadly conceived – one can find pleasure or seek solace in the opportunities and problems of media life. Perhaps the conclusion must be that whoever is capable of successfully sticking to Leibniz's cause of realist–idealist symbiosis may venture farther in understanding the world and their role in it.

Systemworlds, placeworlds, wikiworlds, mediaworlds

To contextualize the various ways in which we, as human beings, make sense of ourselves in the world in media life, one has to do so without making distinctions between mind and matter (including, quite specifically, technology), or between the individual and society. The purpose here is to do justice to the fact that people generally make sense of whatever happens in a particular context (including where they are, what they are doing, what their history is, what people and things they share the moment with), and that this mode of being should be included in any attempt to articulate what life is really like. One of the first attempts to articulate such a point of view comes from Austrian mathematician and philosopher Edmund Husserl, who in 1936 argued how every single individual is part of the world, "as living with one another in the world; and the world is our world, valid for our consciousness as existing precisely through this 'living together'" (1970[1936]: 24). Without directly referencing media, Husserl stresses the intersubjectivity at play when making sense of the world. Regardless of what they do and how they go about doing it, people are always connected to other people (for example through a shared history and cultural memory), to things (including any and all technologies that facilitate or prevent communication) and to nature.

A more deliberate attempt to connect such an understanding of how people are both *in* and *of* the world to the formation and development of modern society as a whole comes from German philosopher Jürgen Habermas, whose theory of communicative action (originally published in 1981) is an expression of his concern with an ongoing colonization of the lifeworld by the systemworld. With the *lifeworld* Habermas, in somewhat similar terms to Husserl, alludes to the background of everyday life and giving life meaning without people being overtly aware of it: our values and beliefs, the influence of (and over) others, shared understandings, desires and aspirations, motives and goals, sense of identity and personality. This realm of everyday experience is something to which no one can take up an extramundane position: it is always familiar, and immediate (1985[1981]: 125). The *systemworld* is the area of society that translates people's values, beliefs, wants and needs into services and institutions that make society work – in a nutshell, these would primarily be the domains of economy (money) and politics (power). What keeps a society together, according to Habermas, is a regular, open and free exchange between systemworld and lifeworld as the two key aspects of existence – which explains why communication is key to the philosopher's ideas. The moment when this *public sphere* of communication gets dominated by money and power, social institutions lose their legitimacy. Sure, market forces and bureaucracies are important for a society to survive and reproduce itself over time – but if that is all there is, it would drain the lifeblood out of society. When the systemworld colonizes the lifeworld, Habermas warns us, people get reduced in their identities to mere citizens and consumers whose communication only gets heard as long as it prolongs the instrumental rationality of political and economic power. As long as we shop and vote, our *affect* – including who we think we are or could be – does not really matter.

Habermas' take on society seems rather bleak, and indeed serves as a word of warning. The Habermasian juxtaposition of systemworld and lifeworld has the qualities of a restrained reworking of Nietzsche's metaphysical distinction between Apollonian and Dionysian worldviews, whereby Nietzsche similarly lamented how his peers (and culture in general) surrendered life's instincts and passions wholesale to the instrumental rationality of the late nineteenth-century machine age. Several prominent scholars noted, at the end of the next century, a similar, but paradoxical, concern: a *recolonization* of the systemworld by the lifeworld. At the forefront are social theorists such as Ulrich Beck, Anthony Giddens, Robert Putnam and Zygmunt Bauman, who note that the ongoing individualization of society (as, for example, expressed in conspicuous consumption, an increasingly unpredictable shifting of political affiliations, and a gradual decline of amateur league bowling) shifts the burden of making sense of the world almost entirely onto the shoulders of the individual. Under such conditions, the self becomes a project, according to Giddens (1991): a transformative force that gives rise to a *life politics* whereby people as individuals, as well as groups or communities, are first and foremost concerned with self-actualization. Although Giddens sees value in such developments – singling out the women's movement as an example whereby a particular group of people's needs become actualized in a social movement that has tremendous political power – others also see a dark side. Belgian sociologist Mark Elchardus (2009) puts forth a pointed argument that all this emphasis on the self should be seen not as a new-found individual autonomy vis-à-vis the systemworld, but rather as a new form of social control mainly exercised through media. What we learn from advertising, in school and by reading self-help books (or going through psychotherapy) are lessons towards the formation of what Elchardus calls an *amenable self* that can take care of itself without relying too much on society's institutions. Social problems thus become problems of the self. The continuing emphasis on the self as a typical modern and rather pitiful phenomenon additionally positions the individual favorably towards media, concludes Elchardus, as "a self that sees itself as a center of decision making . . . is likely to interpret the influence of schooling, media, the world of goods and therapy as forms of self-expression" (155).

As the lifeworld becomes subject to our constant questioning of it – who am I?, what should I do?, how should I be? – it runs the risk of trumping any and all concern we may have for others – including issues of shared and common concern. Ulrich Beck, for example, signals how the shift towards private concerns as benchmarking all public affairs sets the stage for a society where "how one lives becomes the biographical solution of systemic contradictions" (1992[1986]: 137). A fully individualized society, argues Bauman with matching fervor, is one in which "the way individual people define individually their individual problems and try to tackle them deploying individual skills and resources is the sole remaining 'public issue' and the sole object of 'public interest'" (2000: 72). With specific reference to media, Andreas Wittel similarly sees the ongoing individualization of society as a key feature of network sociality, as people seem to make their way in life "defined by a multitude of experiences and biographies" (2001: 65) rather than relying on shared histories and cultural memories. As the lifeworld colonizes the systemworld, suggests Dutch sociologist Henk Vinken, people feel forced to take their life into their own hands, and are thus going to lead a more "biographized life course" (2007: 46), making sense of their lives primarily in their own terms. For Vinken, as for Elchardus and Wittel, media are crucial in this process, forming a powerful mix.

What I would argue in the context of media life is that the Habermasian systemworld (the world of rules) and lifeworld (the world we experience) are not just colonizing or being colonized, but rather should both be seen as collapsing in media. In order to appreciate the ramifications of this, one could consider American philosopher Don Ihde's key work *Technology and the lifeworld* (1990), in which he proposes a de-essentialization of nature, society and technologies, while building an overall argument that, throughout history, human cultures and societies have been technologically embedded and that those technologies transform the human lifeworld. Although Ihde implicitly keeps media and life at some distance from each other, he does emphasize how their relations are mediated through a *technological intentionality* (141). Jos de Mul makes a similar point with specific reference to media in that "every medium carries with it its own distinctive worldview or metaphysics" (2010: 89). For De Mul, the essential worldview we get from our current media mix is based on their key characteristics of being multimedial, interactive and capable of virtualizing reality. In all of this I am once more reminded of how the offline world of practices and experience extends into the realm of media and vice versa, giving shape and form to what Manuel Castells (2010[1996]) describes as a culture of *real virtuality*, where the online world of appearances becomes part of everyday lived experience instead of just existing on our computer and television screens.

Considering media as technologies and institutions of social integration, and as providers of a shared lifeworld (rather than instrumental to alienation and social isolation), is a powerful trope in scholarly work. Directly inspired by Don Ihde, Terje Rasmussen (2003) states how people's wide range of media uses can both reproduce and disintegrate the lifeworld. As media become pervasive and ubiquitous in everyday life, the voguish verbosity on how this may impact the lifeworld – the world taken for granted, every person's horizon of experiences – ratchets up. With specific reference to mobile communication, Ilkka Arminen, for example, attributes an essential role to media in "bridging vastly expanding technological potential and human life-worlds that set the final limits to what will be considered adequate, appropriate and desirable features of ubiquitous communication" (2007: 436). In the field of game studies, the potential of emerging genres of gaming that deliberately blend real-world environments with various forms of mediated gameplay – such as alternate reality games, live-action roleplaying games, location-based and pervasive games – can be seen as similarly benchmarking a fused lived and mediated experience. Virtual worlds scholars Eric Gordon and Gene Koo introduce the concept of *placeworlds* in this context, suggesting that the integration of an online living environment such as *Second Life* with offline activities (such as urban planning involving community feedback) may empower individuals and allow people to form new alliances. As Gordon and Koo argue, "If a lifeworld comes into being when a group of people arrives at a mutual understanding of something, a placeworld arises when people come to a mutual understanding of some*place*" (2008: 206; italics in original).

Using a sociotechnical perspective on media life to stretch arguments about mixing media and lifeworlds even further, Finnish educational philosophers Juha Suoranta and Tere Vadén look forward to the emergence of what they call a *wikiworld*:

> The Wikiworld is built through the "collaborative turn," or
> what is called participatory culture, which includes relatively
> low barriers to civic engagement and activism, artistic and
> other sorts of expression, easy access for creating and shar-
> ing one's outputs with others, peer to peer relations and
> informal mentorship as well as new forms of socialization,
> social connections, collectivism and solidarity. (2008: 1)

For Suoranta and Vadén, it is up to each and every one of
us to take responsibility for the interactive and co-creative
opportunities new media seem to promise. In Paul Taylor's
critical analysis of the literature on digital media and society,
the suggestion is made that the wikiworld point of view is
one among many rather one-dimensional takes on the conditions of everyday experience in "a new mediated lifeworld"
(2009: 95). Often, Taylor laments, people cannot help but
seeing media as either empowering or enslaving, without
thinking through the implications of a lifeworld as affectively
expressed and experienced in media. Interestingly, he points
to hackers and hacktivists (conjoining political activism and
computer hacking) as embracing a more fluent and imaginative engagement with media, in that hackers take media apart,
re-engineer and repurpose them. Taylor's critical yet at the
same time hopeful account represents a distinctly normative
take on what otherwise can be considered a fairly mundane
observation: individuals, communities and any other social
groups can (and indeed should) be seen as living in a world
of ubiquitous media, in which every act of media production
or consumption also constitutes that world. What the point
of these and other scholars invariably comes down to is that
media, as they enter and become fused with the lifeworld,
add certain *qualities* to our individual and shared experience
of life, and in the process dissolve any meaningful distinction
between reality (noumena) and representation (phenomena).
Considering the nature of contemporary media's multiple
and mutual implications in all aspects of everyday life, I would
like to connect these points and extend that line to its logical

end-point: considering the lifeworld as completely mediated, unable to self-actualize in any meaningful or distinctive form outside of media.

The mediated lifeworld

Göran Sonesson offers what is possibly the most far-reaching, yet at the same time comprehensively grounded, take on what life must be like in our mediated lifeworld, suggesting that as media "transform secondary interpretations into significations taken for granted [they] may already be colonizing the lifeworld" (1997: 71). Starting from a consideration of people's lifeworlds as working a bit like magic in that we apply all kinds of rules in our dealings with the world without necessarily being aware of them, Sonesson maintains that our media work in much the same way. Even if we uncover the many rules, rituals and routines that govern the generally taken-for-granted understanding of our living environment, many (if not most) of these processes would not necessarily make a lot of sense – just like the inner workings and protocols that govern media (as artifacts, as activities and as social arrangements) tend to remain unseen and often escape our grasp. All of this "should force us to realize how deeply mediated is our ordinary, unreflected life in the questioned, sociocultural lifeworld" (1997).

Following Sonesson's argument, it is exactly the invisibility of media – their disappearance into natural user interfaces, the vanishing of concrete uses through convergence and portability, and their evaporation as the infrastructures of everyday interactions – that should alert us to their profound prominence. As the ultimate case study of a complete *multi-mediation* of the lifeworld, Sonesson considers the uncanny virtual system proposed in Adolfo Bioy Casares' 1940 novel *The invention of Morel*. Casares was, like Jorge Luis Borges (who wrote the prologue of his book), from Argentina, where he gained prominence as a fiction writer and journalist.

Casares writes *The invention of Morel* as the diary of a young man who, while trying to escape a life sentence (apparently due to an error of justice), crashes his ship on the beach of a "lonely island" (2003[1940]: 10). Yet, for all its loneliness, the island is not empty. In fact, it features a museum (as the protagonist notes, the building could also be a fancy hotel or sanatorium), a swimming pool and a chapel. The basement of the museum even features a working power plant, hidden in a doorless azure-blue tiled room. And then, all of a sudden, the island is not uninhabited either, as its grassy hillsides become crowded with cheerful tourists – even though no form of transportation arrived that would have taken them there. The fugitive, afraid that these people might have come to turn him in, observes them from the marshlands where he has been living for exactly 100 days and nights: "I suppose someone might attribute their mysterious appearance to the effect of last night's heat on my brain. But there are no hallucinations or imaginings here: I know these people are real – at least as real as I am" (11).

He wonders how they do not notice him – as he sometimes takes great risks to get close to them. At times, the dancing of the sharply dressed men and women even goes on during the torrential downpours that are quite common on this island. After observing these people for a while, he desperately falls in love with one beautiful woman – whom others in the group call Faustine. She walks down to the beach near his hideout every day to sit on the rocks and watch the sunset. He is afraid to approach her – although he secretly hopes she will not judge him by his now less than impeccable appearance. So he remains in his hiding place, trembling at the mere sight of her "as if she were posing for an invisible photographer" (26). Even when she suddenly stands up and walks towards him, it seems as if Faustine does not see him at all, a complete detachment from reality which frightens the fugitive. At some point, he thinks he has figured out what is the matter is: she is trying to steer clear of another man who is seeking her attention, a beardy fellow called Morel, who pressures Faustine to accept his advances because – as the fugitive overhears him saying – "We have only a short time left – three days, and then it will all be over" (36).

At this moment in the story, something eerie happens. We take note of the fugitive's account of days passing . . . and after four days go by without meaningful changes to the situation with the people, the buildings, the music and dancing, he again overhears a discussion Morel and Faustine have on his beach, in which Morel asks for her understanding as there are only three days left. The fugitive suspects that they are mocking him, putting on a performance just to make him look ridiculous. He stands up and shouts at them – but they completely ignore his presence. Outraged, he storms up the hill – and finds all the buildings empty, as if no one was ever there. To verify this incredible discovery, he goes down to the basement to turn on the power plant so that all the lights in the museum will go on. Once back upstairs, the people have returned – but still ignore him. Even as he moves among them, lies down next to them, stands in front of them: no response. At this point in his diary, the fugitive starts thinking through every conceivable explanation for what is going on. Nothing seems to make sense. With direct reference to the magical nature of our lifeworld's operations, now uncovered through his experiences with the intruders, he ponders how "The habits of our lives make us presume that things will happen in a certain foreseeable way, that there will be a vague coherence to the world. Now reality appears to be changed, unreal" (65).

In the end, the fugitive witnesses a dinner party with all the tourists present as Morel stands up and formally announces the explanation of everything that is happening. As it turns out, Morel is a scientist obsessed with the idea of overcoming mortality. Considering how various media – radio, television, phonography and the telephone – extend the senses of sight and hearing, Morel has proceeded to develop new

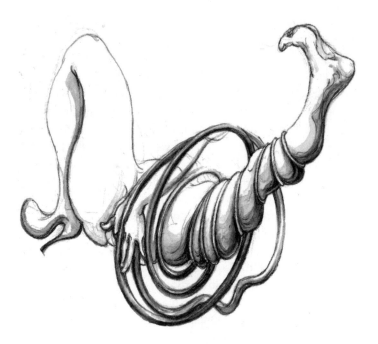

technologies that receive and transmit the senses of smell and touch. He collapsed all these media into a singular device that records a complete and authentic image of a certain person and their reality: "With my machine a person or an animal or a thing is like the station that broadcasts the concert you hear on the radio . . . if you turn all the dials at once, [the recorded person] will be reproduced completely . . . When all the senses are synchronized, the soul emerges" (69, 70, 71).

After testing his machine, Morel indeed finds that people cannot distinguish his recordings from real human beings anymore – raising the possibility of capturing people *forever*. He picks an uninhabited and almost impossible-to-reach island in the middle of nowhere, invites his best friends and closest relatives, and reduces them – without ever telling them what is going on – to "living transmitters" (71). No matter how hard he tries, the people in the room do not seem to believe him. "Don't you see that there is a parallelism between the destinies of men and images?," Morel cries out – but it is in vain. Trembling with anger and disappointment, he asks his friends for forgiveness. Because, like him, they are all dead.

It is because of this spine-chilling story that Casares can take credit for inventing immersive virtual environment technology (commonly referred to as virtual reality) decades before the first computers arrived. More specifically, Morel's invention seems a precursor to a *Star Trek* holodeck. The holodeck, as a virtual reality simulator, has an edge over the island machine: its virtual constructs – people as well as objects – are tangible, and they see you. Today's technologies make such completely immersive and multisensory environments quite feasible, combining the ability of media to project any kind of sensory information (sight, sound, smell, touch and taste) in three-dimensional space with software algorithms that would allow someone to interact with a physical environment (for example, by manipulating a floor to resemble different surfaces: sand, water or rocks). In computer engineering, game design and robotics communities, there is considerable excitement about the possibility of building true lifelike and massively inhabitable environments – which does not seem a far-fetched notion given the availability and popularity of 3D cameras and projection systems (such as the *ZCam* by Israeli developer 3DV Systems, which company advertises its product with the slogan "YOU are the Interface"[12]), augmented-reality applications for personal media devices (such as Layar and Google's Latitude), natural-user interfaces (including touchscreens and motion-sensing technologies like Microsoft's Kinect) and the rapid wiring of the planet for broadband media access (over the air through a wide range of physical transmitters and receivers, in the ground via cables, in open space using satellites[13]).

Early studies of how people experience the increasingly realistic nature of their mediated environments – whether developed for entertainment purposes (cf. massively multiplayer online games) or research (cf. experimental multimedia installations) – find a high level of congruence between virtual- and physical-world experiences. On the other hand, as psychologists Cade McCall and Jim Blascovich (2009) conclude on the basis of a review of their experiments in digital experimental virtual environments (DEVEs), when the DEVE becomes truly realistic, it puts people off – an emotional response of uncanniness similar to when one encounters zombies. The same effect occurs when computer games become all too naturalistic in terms of presence and realism. It seems that Casares anticipated this, describing how the fugitive feels slightly uncomfortable each time the image of a visitor brushes against him (2003[1940]: 79). After his initial disgust, he gradually warms to Morel's invention – not in the least because of his painfully real love for Faustine. In fact, as anthropologist Alex Golub (2010) notes in his study among hardcore players of Blizzard Entertainment's *World of Warcraft*, it is exactly when the fine line between virtual- and actual-world values and experiences is continuously blurred that our understanding of the world becomes immediate – when it truly seems un-mediated to us. For Golub, people's acts, knowledge and experiences in a "bounded sensorially realistic virtual world" spill out into everyday life practices of "[c]reating, spreading, and sharing knowledge," all of which "becomes part of a project which is both real, virtual, and actual" (42).

The lifeworld as a *project* that is at once immediate and mediated raises all kinds of interesting questions about the nature of reality, the essence of self-identity and our experiences of each other. It is perhaps not surprising in this context that Casares' unsettling story also functioned as one of the key inspirations for the popular American television series *LOST* (2004–10). The book features quite literally in episode 4 of season 4, in which one of the characters can be seen reading it.[14] The series follows the lives of more than 40 individuals who survived a plane crash on a tropical island. Their survival is hampered by all kinds of unexplained events – including encountering a mysterious woman (named Danielle) who was shipwrecked on the island 16 years prior to their crash. After 6 seasons and 121 episodes, the show ends with the suggestion that all the survivors have died and reunite, perpetually, in some form of limbo (represented by gathering in a church), where everyone is able to see, recognize and remember everyone else and their lives together.[15] In Casares' original story, the fugitive in the end realizes that he cannot stand the idea of witnessing the same week of images repeat forever – especially given his enduring love for the "artificial ghost" (2003[1940]: 85) Faustine. As she lives in an image for which he does not exist, his love is tragically impossible. In the end, he does the only thing he can do: he faithfully records a week of his experiences on the island into Morel's machine, inserting himself in every scene next to Faustine, appearing as if she is interacting with him. The machine then projects the week eternally – and they all live in media forever.

I could be callous by concluding how all of us are like the tourists on Morel's island, living a mediatized version of our lives. This is not the point of Sonesson's argument, nor does it offer much help in ethically and aesthetically navigating a media life. The key to understanding the significance of media to the lifeworld can be found in what Sonesson considers lacking in Morel's invention: a "double-sided permeability to all senses," which would indeed "break down the limits between the worlds" (1997: 80). Given the developments in media, it is perhaps safe to say that these limits indeed have broken down – our lives in media do not exist independently of the actual (or real) world.

Considering the collapse of media and the lifeworld as a potent pedagogical concept, Canadian e-learning expert Norm Friesen and his Austrian colleague Theo Hug (2009) postulate that media become epistemology – the grounds for knowledge and knowing itself – and therefore call on educators and educational researchers to take seriously what they call the *mediatic a priori*: "the contention that media play an important role in defining the epistemological preconditions or characteristics of cognition, such as the perception of time, space, and the shaping of attention and communication" (73). Friedrich Kittler (2009) raises the stakes to an even higher level of abstraction in this debate, forcefully arguing that media must be considered in ontological terms, for there is nothing we can say about what is, without using some form of media to do it – hence all our expressions of the world are essentially of media. Thinking about media in these terms, the various placeworlds, wikiworlds, media worlds and multimediated lifeworlds can be seen as more or less distinct ontological bubbles or spheres (taking the concept from Peter Sloterdijk's "Sphären" trilogy, published between 1998 and 2004) that exist next to each other, intersect and overlap.

As British geographer Nigel Thrift (2011) suggests, the existence of multiple ontologies is not necessarily problematic if we accept that this introduces opportunities for us to understand things differently, and to come up with new or alternative conceptualizations of how worlds work or should work. In other words: instead of having to settle with a timeless and complete, one and only world, a series of incomplete and permanently under construction worldviews "can live tolerantly side-by-side" (6). What needs to be emphasized here is that an ontologically adventurous perspective is afforded by a media ecology that allows for what John Hartley (2000) describes as a *redactional* sense of society: the experience or expectation of living in a world that can be edited. Don Ihde's perspective on the increasing interdependency between technology and the lifeworld additionally outlines how contemporary mediating technologies of the information age make possible an "essential pluricultural pattern" (1990: 156) in people's understanding of themselves and each other. According to Ihde, our global pluriculture gets established through the various ways in which media expose us to ideas, beliefs, cultures and rituals, up to and including culinary and architectural traditions different from our own. In media we cannot help but see and experience the lives of others (and they can see us). In media life, our world seems intrinsically open to intervention, thriving on our constant remixing and oversharing of it. It is also a world that seems rather unstable and volatile, always escaping the illusion of our (remote) control.

The world is a map in the palm of your hand

Nigel Thrift considers how the information age gradually transforms the way we know and learn about ourselves and the world we live in through new practices of organizing, analyzing, displaying, storing and communicating information. As people's lifeworld is subsumed by technologies in general and media in particular, an ontological reconditioning takes place, according to Thrift, giving rise to "an exaggerated humanity" that looks at its world with a restless and at the same time irresistible "experimental stance" (2011: 7). Our world is "tagged with an informational overlay" (9), which at some point means that maps will be more real than reality. The world becomes an inhabitable map – a world "in which the maps are not just means of colonisation but the colonisation itself" (9). Thrift hints at what is quickly becoming the dominant way most people in overdeveloped countries not just make their way through the world, but also how they see their world: in terms of maps. More specifically, maps such as those that quite literally *live* in media: interactive, real-time and continuously updated, endlessly redacted maps, fueled by satellite-based Global Positioning Systems (GPS), database-driven Geographic Information Systems (GIS) and layer upon layer of information supplied by governments, organizations, companies, communities and individuals. Fascinating examples of such self-organizing maps are Google's Map Maker application, the OpenStreetMap initiative: a community-curated map of the world that lives online and can be ported to all kinds of personal media devices, including laptop computers and smartphones.[16] As John Markoff writes for the *New York Times* (on February 17, 2009):

> With the dominance of the cellphone, a new metaphor is emerging for how we organize, find and use information. New in one sense, that is. It is also as ancient as humanity itself. That metaphor is the map . . . As this metaphor takes over, it will change the way we behave, the way we think and the way we find our way around new neighborhoods.[17]

Looking at the world through the senses of media is not the exception, but the rule in media life. From seeing more of public spaces through the viewfinder of one's cell phone camera to wearable media that augment reality, it is in media that we get more real than reality itself. British sociologist Vincent Miller considers the kind of mapping that goes on in media – specifically on mobile phones, via automotive navigation systems, and indeed anywhere online – a perfect illustration of the colonization of the lifeworld:

> We need maps in order to function relatively efficiently in a society which continues to become more and more sociologically and technologically complex. Within this complexity, our reliance on maps to sort the world out is taken for granted. This taken-for-grantedness hides the fact that maps do indeed have a great influence on how we construct and experience reality. (2010: 21)

The influence of maps does not just come into play because ever so often a mapmaker wants to direct the map user to or away from a particular place (for example, a restaurant on a tourist map, or a celebrity's compound on *Google Earth*); the real power of maps lies in their subtle yet pervasive categorization and thereby normalization of the world. As Stefaan Verhulst, in his capacity as Director of Research for the US-based Markle Foundation, puts it: "in addition to acting as mirrors for the world, maps also act as mediators to the world: they contextualize and frame our perceptions of reality" (2008: 191). If it exists on a map, it must be there (and if it is not, we get quite irate).

Even more so: we can change it on the map in order to produce change in the real world, as in the case of cyberactivists renaming streets in Syrian cities in order to celebrate the 2011–12 uprising against the regime.[18] In an overview of current mapping practices – including art maps, participatory maps and maps as acts of political protest – Jeremy Crampton (2009) calls for a rethinking of cartography, suggesting that we stop looking at maps in terms of how things are, and focus instead on understanding the various ways in which maps are constantly changing and becoming. As we live in a rather complex world and seem to be increasingly on the move – data on international migration gathered by the United Nations consistently shows increasing worldwide mobility patterns – our common reliance on mediated maps liquefies our awareness of not just *where* we are, but also *when* we are (as we may be looking at an earlier version of the map). Thrift suggests that the human condition of living in such a map-driven mediated lifeworld calls for *awhereness*, as people's self-reflection additionally needs a spatial consideration. Do you really know where you are – or do you see your presence (at least to some extent) through the viewfinder of your camera, the GPS locator in your mobile phone, or in the way your friends, the businesses you frequent and all the media you use tag you online? In a media life, your experience of the world has always already been reduced to a series of mediated constructs, bringing some people and places into sharper focus, blurring some to a background, while erasing others altogether. The subtle yet pervasive shift of spatial experience from practice (that is: consciously moving through it, witnessing it deliberately) to experiencing place through abstraction (as in using maps to find your way) transforms our reality to something that is *conceived* before it is *lived* (Miller, 2010: 23). And when reality is experienced in something that has been made, we (think we) can change it.

Crampton makes the case that, until well into the 1980s, the prevailing paradigm in cartography was the production of "the single optimal map" (2001: 236) through ever more advanced means of representation. Ever since then, maps have begun to be seen more as social constructions – either theoretically, or practically because of the intervention of map users in the construction of maps. In a media life, it seems that both goals converge: given the interconnectivity of both hardware and software necessary to create maps, and the permeability of the user–creator relationship in media, it seems we are well on our way towards a single map of everything that everyone is in the process of constantly redacting. One of the prime examples of such a map is *Google Earth* (GE). The program contains a virtual globe, three-dimensional map and geographical information on the world, originally called *EarthViewer* and developed from 1999 onwards by a company called Keyhole (acquired by Google in 2004). One of the lead developers and co-founder of Keyhole, Avi Bar-Zeev, explains on his weblog "RealityPrime" (posted on July 24, 2006) how the Earth program in Neal Stephenson's *Snow crash* (1992) served as a key inspiration for their work: "In fact, early on, before we even launched, I spent some time trying to get Neal Stephenson to visit our offices, for a demo at least."[19] By integrating satellite imagery of the entire globe, Bar-Zeev claims to have come close to the "one best map" ideal, because "Unlike most maps, in GE, you can turn off national boundaries and see the world as it really is." Beyond the single map idea, a powerful feature of GE is the integration of different software layers, each offering options for users to add all kinds of information and functionalities to the map: information about particular places, photos, GIS data and so on. The program can also be partially integrated into users' own websites and services. Considered as such, GE approaches a brilliant conceit by Jorge Luis Borges and Adolfo Bioy Casares of a 1:1 map of the world, as written down in their short story "On exactitude in science" (originally published in 1946):

> In that Empire, the Art of Cartography attained such Perfection that the map of a single Province occupied the entirety of a City, and the map of the Empire, the entirety of

a Province. In time, those Unconscionable Maps no longer satisfied, and the Cartographers Guilds struck a Map of the Empire whose size was that of the Empire, and which coincided point for point with it. The following Generations, who were not so fond of the Study of Cartography as their Forebears had been, saw that that vast Map was Useless, and not without some Pitilessness was it, that they delivered it up to the Inclemencies of Sun and Winters. In the Deserts of the West, still today, there are Tattered Ruins of that Map, inhabited by Animals and Beggars; in all the Land there is no other Relic of the Disciplines of Geography.

Borges and Casares – writing under the single pseudonym "B. Lynch Davis" – seem to allude not so much to the feasibility or impracticality of a map of the territory that is the territory itself, as to the conundrum we face when confronted with *perfect* information without having any external device at our disposal to *verify* such information.

Umberto Eco took on the challenge of Borges and Casares, outlining, in a short essay etitled "On the impossibility of drawing a map of the Empire on a scale of 1 to 1" (originally written in 1982), his take on the possibility of a flawless imperial atlas. After dutifully considering each requirement for achieving a map that would be "one to one, and therefore coextensive with the territory of the empire" (1995[1982]: 96), Eco comes to the conclusion that it must be a transparent map that is permeable, extended and adjustable (101). However, if such a map were indeed created, it would subsume the empire – except perhaps if the map, including faithful representations of all the people in the empire, were endowed with self-awareness. In that case, Eco notes, "such a map (if it were even conceivable) would itself become the empire, while the former empire would cede its power to the map" (106). Jean Baudrillard comes to a similar conclusion in his take on the role of electronic media in people's perception and experience of their reality, suggesting that, ultimately, in a fully mediated existence any relation with an original empire that would have existed before its rendering in media gets destroyed:

> Abstraction today is no longer that of the map, the double, the mirror or the concept. Simulation is no longer that of a territory, a referential being or a substance. It is the generation by models of a real without origin or reality: a hyperreal. The territory no longer precedes the map, nor survives it . . . It is the real, and not the map, whose vestiges subsist here and there, in the deserts which are no longer those of the Empire, but our own. The desert of the real itself.[20]

Baudrillard's dramatic reference to a "desert of the real" is used creatively in the first film of *The Matrix* trilogy, when the character Morpheus introduces the hero Neo to the only part of the world not colonized by machines with the memorable words: "welcome to the desert of the real."[21] With reference to the mediatization of the lifeworld, one could correspondingly argue that a life in media essentially settles on an agential-realist rendering of the real world. *Google Earth* is awesome for achieving its goal of being a single optimal map, while at the same time these kinds of interactive and pervasive maps render our experience of the real subsequent to our redaction of it. Seen as such, the world becomes something we are always in the process of preparing for publication. The implication of collapsing the categories of media and life into the lifeworld is therefore not that there is *no more* reality – it is just that there is always *too much* of it.

In a state of being perpetually together alone and creating, curating and, every so often, curtailing the world we live in through media, one cannot escape the conclusion that perhaps there is too much information available – about ourselves, about others, about all the places we can see. Adapting to a context of seemingly endless variety can be overwhelming, reducing us to people without qualities other than a listless dependency on the outside world to form our character, as Austrian writer Robert Musil originally articulated in the 1930s.[22] Like all other themes in media life, the complicated and potentially problematic nature of information overload is the subject of long-running debates, voiced playfully by American author Gertrude Stein in a piece published posthumously in the *Yale Poetry Review* of December 1947: "Everybody gets so much information all day long that they lose their common sense. They listen so much that they forget to be natural. This is a nice story."[23]

It is safe to say that a media life does not stipulate limits to one's access or exposure to information – in fact, claims about information overload and our brain's limited capacity to process all the images, words and numbers coming at us reign supreme throughout the scholarly and popular literature. American psychologist Kenneth Gergen specifically attributes what he sees as a crisis in contemporary culture to a "massive increment in social stimulation," resulting from "advances in radio, telephone, transportation, television, satellite transmission, computers, and more," leading to the inevitable replacement of "small and enduring communities" by "a vast and ever-expanding array of relationships" (1992: ix). According to Gergen, the *saturated self* in media cannot cope with all this stimulation, making it impossible to find (let alone rely on) accurate generalizations, reason and truth. He sees a new pattern of self-consciousness emerging: "*multiphrenia*, generally referring to the splitting of the individual into a multiplicity of self-investments . . . Someday there may indeed be nothing to distinguish multiphrenia from simply 'normal living'" (73; italics in original). His concerns are echoed by his colleague George Miller (1983) when he labels human beings as *informavores*, who by their very nature are prone to hunt and gather information in order to survive. Unlike Gergen, Miller does not see this foraging for information and scavenging for media as either good or bad for us, considering it a habitual part of a process conducive to our mind's endurance. Former Apple and Microsoft employee Linda Stone remains unconvinced, considering Miller's mental survival skills as detrimental rather than beneficial to us. Indirectly taking her cue from Walter Benjamin's 1930s concerns about the distracting dimensions of media, Stone considers our informavoric life in media as governed by a continuous partial attention disorder, disabling us from being genuinely thoughtful about the world around us:

> To pay continuous partial attention is to pay partial attention – CONTINUOUSLY. It is motivated by a desire to be a LIVE node on the network. Another way of saying this is that we want to connect and be connected. We want to effectively scan for opportunity and optimize for the best opportunities, activities, and contacts, in any given moment. To be busy, to be connected, is to be alive, to be recognized, and to matter. (capitals in original) [24]

Michael Newman historicizes these and other examples of technophobia in an attempt to dismantle their currency, and convincingly shows how the very notion of our attention span, when it comes to media, to a significant extent must be seen as a construct deployed by media producers to validate their work as managing the attention of audiences for the sake of profit. For Newman, this kind of thinking about media negatively affecting attention spans functions to reassert "the superiority of . . . a traditional, establishment culture (print culture, the culture of educational institutions) over a threatening emergent culture (electronic visual culture, educational TV, myriad cable and satellite channels)" (2010: 593).

Newman's argument convinces, but leaves open what we can (or should) do with abundantly available information about anything. In 2010, the US-based science and technology think tank the Edge Foundation asked this question with specific reference to the internet.[25] A total of 172 scientists, artists and entrepreneurs were invited to post their answers online. In her contribution, Esther Dyson talks about media life in terms of our "information metabolism," as she questions the seductive immediacy of the internet in that it provides so many instant answers and responses to our human needs that we may end up only getting empty calories:

> It's sugar . . . Sugar is so much easier to digest, so enticing
> . . . and ultimately, it leaves us hungrier than before. Worse
> than that, over a long period, many of us are genetically dis-
> posed to lose our capability to digest sugar if we consume
> too much of it. It makes us sick long-term, as well as giving
> us indigestion and hypoglycemic fits. Could that be true of
> information sugar as well? Will we become allergic to it even
> as we crave it? And what will serve as information insulin?[26]

Dyson's concerns are echoed by British journalist John Naish, who in his book *Enough: breaking free from the world of more* (2008) signals *infobesity* as a social problem to be reme-died by restricting one's data diet. In a 2010 review of long-term international trends regarding digital media use for the Netherlands Institute for Social Research, Frank Huysmans and Jos de Haan indicate how the lived experience of Too Much Information (TMI) leads to feelings of discomfort and distrust regarding the quality and reliability of informa-tion in general and mediated communication in particular. Huysmans and De Haan consider the rather unstructured and less than deliberate flow of information into the homes and lives of ordinary people, in similar terms to Naish, as leading to *infobesitas* (2010: 19): a rather unhealthy way of living as the result of excessive infocalorie consumption.

Regarding our propensity for infobesity, Naish is par-ticularly worried about our ability to take in relevant and high-quality information, and suggests that a fantastic slogan for the twenty-first century would be "we are so informed that we can't be bothered" (2008: 26). Gertrude Stein's comments about information overload, written in 1946 as a response to a question on what she thinks about the atomic bomb, show that she cannot be bothered by being informed about its destructive powers because "it's the living that are interest-ing not the way of killing them, because if there were not a lot left living how could there be any interest in destruction."

Getting or receiving enough or too much information is not necessarily a key issue of a media life – it is our capacity to do something meaningful with the kind of information we find (if only to be thoughtful about it).

Perhaps the only way to live a richly empowered and meaningful life is to embrace (and add to) the inherent multiplicity of the world through the availability of an excess of information about it. This is the inspiring advice of Italo Calvino in one of his *Six memos for the next millenium* (1993[1985]), emphasizing the necessity of an essentially multiplicitous, polyphonic or carnivalesque worldview in order to do justice to its infinite beauty and complexity. Extending his vision, Calvino suggests our lived experience in media ideally should represent "a network of connections between the events, the people, and the things of the world" (105). To be exposed to that much information about the world (and yourself) is equivalent to changing it, concludes Calvino: "to know is to insert something to what is real, and hence to distort reality" (108). Given the ongoing multiplication of spaces and selves in media, the stakes of figuring out who you really are have been raised beyond the question of whether there is too much information about us available to us. A media life quite possibly forces us to restate that fundamental question altogether.

Who am I and who are you?

Robert Anson Heinlein's short story "All you Zombies. . .," originally published in 1959, documents the experiences of a man who was born a girl as he explores his entire life history with the help of a bartender and a series of time travels. Traveling to previous scenes of his life is made possible by using a device called a Transformer Field Kit, requiring the subject to step underneath a metal net and flip a switch in order to travel through time. After going back and forth a couple of times and piecing the various elements of his life together, the man gradually realizes that all the characters in the story are different versions of himself. As this uncanny insight dawns on him, he thinks "I know where I came from – but where did all you zombies come from?" (2004[1959]: 46). Heinlein's story begs the question of whether all the different versions we are (and once were) are indeed zombies.

In a series of interviews on the topic of identity with Italian newspaper editor Benedetto Vecchi, Zygmunt Bauman remarks that "asking 'who you are' makes sense to you only once you believe that you can be someone other than you are" (2004: 19). Pondering the same question, his German colleague Hans-Georg Gadamer highlights a further problem of asking such a question as "All understanding presupposes an answer to this question, or better, a preliminary insight superior to the formulation of the question" (1997[1973]: 68). Assuming for a moment that a life as lived in media brings with it an inevitable multiplication of selves with whom we are dancing in our very own silent disco, who is it that we are looking for in media when we want to answer the question of who we really are? In his engagement with the dilemma, Gadamer suggests that the "I" in the question "who am I?" is a fisherman who casts a net, over and over again, expecting to catch something (83–4). Like the fisherman, we do everything possible we can to cast the net the right way and in the right place, but ultimately just have to wait and see if something is caught – and whether we catch something or not, we will always have to do it again. Additionally, we have to carefully weigh our options with everything we catch, as we cannot load the net on our lifeboat too lightly or too full – or else it will tip over. Furthermore the catch of the day is always intended for someone – a real or imaginary friend perhaps, an audience, guests at the dinner table, or just for you. Either way, "what lends reality to the I, is the interplay between I and You that promises a catch" (85). Rather than jumping overboard or solely focusing on building more and better contraptions to catch fish (such was the intent of Morel's invention), Gadamer challenges you to consider every confrontation with You as situating you in a space of indeterminacy. Instead of aiming towards controlling all these versions of ourselves into an, at best, temporary illusion of a final and complete mold, we should strive to create as many different versions of ourselves as possible.

It thus can be said that the malleability and endless virtualization of the self in a media life is not so much a function of our media, as the expansion and enhancement of a possible (and intentional) way of thinking about who we are as human beings in conjunction with nature and technology. This perspective can certainly lead to more or less solipsistic, scatterbrained and lonesome attitudes or behaviors. Yet the link between individualization and contemporary society is not *made* in media – in media, the relationship between the self and any kind of social cohesion is just another version of society. Slavoj Žižek engages most explicitly the link between our being together alone and the omnipresence of networked computers and cyberspace, suggesting that media are a "directly universalized form of sociality which enables us to be connected with the entire world while sitting alone in front of a screen" (2008: 34). The life we find in media is therefore just as real and otherworldly unreal as any other life. And, as with any other life, in media life people's primary drive is to stay alive.

CHAPTER SEVEN

In Media We Fit

where living in media provides social and reproductive success

Media can be better than (having) sex. According to a 2008 survey among more than 2,000 US adults, sponsored by technology firm Intel, "nearly half of women (46 percent) and 30 percent of men would rather go without sex for 2 weeks than give up Internet access for the same amount of time."[1] An in-between option would be to mediate sex. Reports on *sexting* – exchanging nude pictures and otherwise sexually explicit messages using mobile phones – among teenagers are common, while the American Association of Retired People (AARP) announced in November 2009 that such behavior is also quite common among those over 50 years of age – as "it makes them feel lively and young."[2] One step further altogether fuses media with sex. Consider, for example, US Inventors Patent 3875932, filed on March 2, 1973 by How Wachspress, for an audiotactile stimulation and communications system:

> Random or controlled electronically synthesized signals are converted to sound waves that are directly coupled to the skin of a life form, such as a human body, to stimulate the skin or internal portions of the life form and to communicate the intelligence, sense or feeling of the sound to the brain . . . The amplified signals then drive an electroacoustic transducer which directs the sound waves through a wave guide to a probe adapted to couple the sound directly to the skin of a life form with a minimum of acoustical radiation.[3]

The device Wachspress proposes here, argues Howard Rheingold (1992), represents a type of *teledildonics*: the use of sophisticated computer and communication technologies for sexual pleasure. "The first fully functional teledildonics system will probably not be a fucking machine. You will *not* use erotic telepresence technology to have sex with machines," argues Rheingold, because "when portable telediddlers are ubiquitous, people will use them to have sex with *other people*" (319; italics in original). Norwegian artist Stahl Stenslie, whose work includes a multisensory bodysuit called "cyberSM" (1993) that simulates tactile interaction between people through an internet connection as they see and touch each other's virtual body on a screen, in this context uses a concept of *teletactility*: human touch mediated through a telepresence machine. In his art and writings, Stenslie explores cybererotics as "sensual communication in computer created space," with what he sees as a new kind of body: "the technologically enhanced telematic body."[4] For German literary scholar Claudia Benthien the promise of teledildonics and Stenslie's exploration of teletactility provide "intimacy without closeness, the intermediation of machines, [and] contact under masks" (2002: 226). Teledildonics, teletactility and cybereroticism seem to be hiding anonymity and self-determination under the cloak of intimacy and connectivity. Discussing teledildonics and other aspects that fall within a more comprehensive conceptualization of cybersex, Finnish cultural theorist Hannu Eerikäinen takes issue with a barely veiled *techno-narcissism* and wishful disembodiment espoused by Rheingold, Stenslie and others about the promise of having sex through and with machines – turning the body into not much more than a "sex-*machine*" (1998: 230; italics in original). As media move into all realms of everyday life and the lifeworld, this confronts us with our notions of sex and reproduction – activities and affections otherwise seen as beholden to our biological bodies. Moving beyond human–machine distinctions, especially in the context of intimacy and sexuality, is not easy.

"I am the one, Orgasmatron"[5]

The history of human sexuality as interfaced in all kinds of fascinating ways with technology is particularly intertwined with the genre of speculative fiction – as it gives its artists considerable freedom to imagine alternate universes, different societies and spectacularly atypical realities. A theme running throughout contemporary speculative fiction is that of technologies providing us with sexual pleasure – such as the *Excessive Machine* in the comic and motion picture *Barbarella*

(1964), an *Orgasmatron* in Woody Allen's film *Sleeper* (1973) and high-tech headgear intended to substitute sexual intercourse in *Demolition Man* (1993, an action movie directed by Marco Brambilla, starring Sandra Bullock, Wesley Snipes and Sylvester Stallone). In all instances, people achieve sexual pleasure by outsourcing their orgasms to machines. Although this makes for fun reading and watching experiences, medical doctor Stuart Meloy and researcher Joan Southern get quite serious about the potential of an orgasmatron, or what they prefer to call Neurally Augmented Sexual Function (NASF), defined as "the production of pleasurable genital stimulation and subsequent orgasm through the application of electrical energy" (2009: 34). In their experiment and clinical practice, Meloy and Southern implanted electrodes into a patient's spine in order to relieve her from chronic pain. In the process, they found that the same kind of therapeutic intervention produced anything from increased vaginal lubrication to full-blown orgasms. Their "precise midline placement" (36) of spinal cord stimulators is reminiscent of the way virtual reality gameplayers in David Cronenberg's movie *eXistenZ* (1990) log in to the gameworld: by attaching organic game consoles to bio-ports located at the players' lower spine.[6] In the film, the lines between reality and virtual reality are crossed so often, that it becomes impossible to tell the two apart. In an interview with *SPLICEDwire* magazine (published on April 14, 1999), Cronenberg elaborates on the link between sex and the body used in the game: "There's no sex really in 'eXistenZ,' except metaphorically. There was an opportunity to have sex scenes, and we were all willing to do that. But as the film evolved, we thought it would be wrong. It would take away from the metaphorical sex, which is all this plugging in and that sort of stuff. That's more interesting."[7]

When our sexual experiences segue to media in one form or another, they indeed may become more interesting. It makes one wonder what the exact appeal of fusing sex with machines is. Beyond noting that such deeply intimate blending confronts people quite literally with the less than stable, finished or absolute nature of their embodied human existence, there often seems a slight unease at work among these and other artists – as exemplified by Bullock's character in *Demolition Man* who appears appalled (as are all other people in her time) by the idea of sexual intercourse *without* media:

> JOHN SPARTAN   [Sylvester Stallone]: Look, Huxley, why don't we just do it the old-fashioned way?
> LENINA HUXLEY   [Sandra Bullock]: Eeewww, disgusting! You mean . . . fluid transfer?[8]

Eerikäinen relates such apparent discomfort with the vulnerable and disorderly human body, and the subsequent deference to media for the communication of intimacy, to the horrifying experience of man–machine fusion in Franz Kafka's short story "In the penal colony" (1914). In this novel, a traveler visits a penal colony to witness the inner workings of a "remarkable apparatus" that needs to be adjusted by hand up to a point, after which "it will work quite of its own accord" (2009[1914]: 75–6). This apparatus is a giant torture and killing machine, a mechanism within which the colony's prisoners are tortured to death with great precision. All of this is eagerly explained to the traveler by an officer responsible for maintaining the machine. He cannot contain his utmost admiration for and devotion to the apparatus, and even refers to its blueprints as Holy Scripture (83, 143). Little do the prisoners who are led up to the apparatus know that its verdict is preprogrammed: "guilt is always beyond question" (80). As the officer elaborates, the machine houses a bed and two rows of needles arranged in a harrow. Once strapped on the padded bed, the sentence gets marked in the prisoner's flesh by the needles, which continue to reinscribe their script deeper and deeper into the flesh until death follows:

> For the first six hours the condemned man is alive almost as before, except that he suffers pain . . . But how still the man becomes at the sixth hour! Understanding dawns upon even

the most stupid . . . nothing further happens; the man simply deciphers the script . . . Admittedly, it is hard work. He needs six hours to accomplish it. Then the process of judgment is at an end. (83–4)

It takes the machine exactly twelve hours to kill. In the analysis of Kafka's story by Canadian digital artist and poet Ollivier Dyens, the prisoner's personal transformation that occurs as the inscriptions of the machine become legible suggests that his body "has to transform itself into something completely free of any human reasoning. The prisoner literally becomes a machine" (2001: 65). For Dyens, it is this man–machine *becoming* that is at the heart of Kafka's telling. In his take on the story, Hannu Eerikäinen similarly emphasizes this "prosthetic redesign of the body" (2001: 60) as central to its premise, putting it in a context of a twentieth-century history wherein "the whole idea of being human became thoroughly redefned in terms of the machine; this was the imperative of the technological: *where I was, there the machine shall become*" (61; italics in original).

The penal colony that Kafka's character of the traveler visits embodies the world as a whole – a vision inspired by the philosophy of negation (privileging an aesthetic distance from the tragic and senseless design of life) of Arthur Schopenhauer, who, in 1818, wrote: "If you want a safe compass to guide you through life, and to banish all doubt as to the right way of looking at it, you cannot do better than accustom yourself to regard this world as a penitentiary, a sort of a *penal colony*" (italics added).[9] In terms of Kafka's take on this advice, it is only by fusing with machines that we can begin to make sense of the world. Whether this is a source of transcendental hope or despair depends on whether one sees technology in general and media in particular as substituting or connecting feelings and sensations of (a)liveness (including sex and erotic intimacy).

The combination of the officer's unbridled techno-fetishism, the social system's surrender of sentencing and punishment to the apparatus, the penetration of machine into man, and a (false) belief in the controlled, automatic and presumably per-fect functions of technology serves as a potent reminder of what could be problematic about the notion of having sex through or with media. Reporting on several studies in Italy, Japan, the US and the UK for the "Sexploration" section of the MSNBC website (on March 27, 2008), Brian Alexander suggests that "laptops, smartphones and big-screen TVs are destroying sex," as such devices are now omnipresent in the bedroom.[10] Although these media artifacts are further removed from our bodies, they similarly seem to herald the end of (bodily, messy, and altogether up-close and personal) sex. On the other hand, the report concludes, it is perhaps not so much that omni-present media are bad (or good) for us, it is just that "we often feel beholden to our technology." The artistic, philosophical, psychological and medical problematizations of mediated sex and sexuality can be seen as part of a broader trend and set of responses regarding what Katrien Jacobs, Marije Janssen and Matteo Pasquinelli dub a *netporn society* (2007), in which technologies infuse people's sex lives in a complex variety of ways. Jacobs, Janssen and Pasquinelli emphasize the con-troversial nature of research into sex and technology, given its focus on an "impetus to air tensions and support a post-utopian quest for pleasure and media awareness" (1) rather than moral panics, narrow-mindedness and porn hysteria. For these authors and activists, mediated sex and sexuality open up all kinds of important spaces for discussion and explora-tion, such as challenging work ethics and gender roles across cultural boundaries, networks and practices of Do-It-Yourself (DIY) cybereroticism, interesting art works and so on. Instead of seeing dangers and disasters everywhere, the various things people do when enacting their sexual desires in media – including "lurking, seducing, up/downloading, chatting, mutual masturbation, dating and orgy-swinging" (2) – can also be celebrated as playful rituals of freedom and excess.

Danish media scholar Adam Arvidsson outlines how, through internet pornography, the act of (largely recreational, non-reproductive) individual fantasy – once demonized as anti-social, then embraced by feminism as a right to control one's own fantasy – has become part of a global sex industry. In this thoroughly mediatized context, people's autoerotic sexuality is anything but private as it relies on fantasies that are shared, collectively produced and augmented through interactive networks online. The bottom line in all of this, according to Arvidsson with specific reference to media life, is the permissive nature of mediated sex as it takes place within the context of technologies and industries that serve to both enhance and enslave people's deepest desires: "the hyper-reality of porn – with its streamlined fashions and standardised practices – is incarnated in the ethically significant, affective reality of real life: porn becomes sex . . . It is ultimately based on the fusion of media and life, and the plasticity that this entails" (Jacobs et al., 2007: 75).

"Take control. Get a divorce."[11]

Beyond automating, circumventing, supercharging, isolating or liberating sexual activities, media can also be seen as moving us through our sex life. At least, this is the premise of the multimedia project *WTFIsUpWithMyLoveLife.com*, an initiative of Jessica Massa and Rebecca Wiegand in an attempt to figure out love and sex in a world dominated by completely mediatized relationships.[12] As Massa blogs at "The Huffington Post" (on September 3, 2010):

> even for those of us who haven't yet embraced the ever-increasing trend towards formalized online dating, the truth is that we're sort of kidding ourselves. We may be holding out against the implication that we need to sign up for one of these sites in order to find love, or that we have no choice but to engage in the Techno-Romance that is shaping our love lives in this post-dating world. But almost all of us are romantically engaging with potential paramours online.[13]

The mediated expression of a post-dating world comes through sites like OkCupid, PlentyofFish and Match. Online and mobile dating is a widespread means of finding a partner in many countries around the world. Reporting on its poll among close to 20,000 online consumers in 18 countries, research firm Global Market Insite found (in 2006) that 23 percent went online to develop a long-term relationship, while 10 percent used online dating to find a marriage partner.[14] According to a 2010 survey among 7,000 married Americans (commissioned by Match), one in six couples married in the preceding three years met each other on a dating website (one of close to 2,000 in the US alone).[15] All of this is unsurprising, Patti Valkenburg and Jochen Peter note in a review of the literature, as in online dating spatial proximity is less relevant (you do not have to be in the same place in order to meet or hang out), meeting people is easier (you can go out any day and any time, and you are not dependent on friends to be introduced to someone), and "the reduced visual and auditory cues that characterize online communication facilitate self-disclosure" (2007: 849). Subsequent studies suggest that the primary allure of online dating is not so much finding a soulmate – as there is no evidence that the matching algorithms of these websites are effective in predicting love – and rather should be understood in terms of people trying to take control of their dating lives in a digital age.[16] Such analyses of the supposed ease and effectiveness of online dating as premised on the intervention of media in processes of personal transformation breathes new life into the critique of cybersexual celebration by Benthien and Eerikäinen. At the same time, the widespead use of online dating and other forms of mediated romantic engagement – including, but not limited to online and mobile social networks – suggests that even when messy bodies are absent, the connection between human beings can be (and often is) profoundly intimate, and it is intimacy we are looking for. In other words, mediated love and sexuality are not necessarily less meaningful or more problematic than interpersonal intimacy experienced without technology.

Patterns in the way people use online and mobile dating services consistently suggest that the way we identify and try to impress mates in media does not differ all that much from our preferred pulling and hook-up methods offline. Researchers of the online dating scene confirm that the redactional trait of media life does not mean that users generally create and maintain completely fake versions of themselves in their pursuit of romance. While deception in online dating profiles is indeed observed, the magnitude of the deceptions is usually small. Christian Rudder – one of the founders and co-owner of the free online dating site OkCupid (started in 2003) – regularly posts research based on the data gathered from the site's users on his *oktrends* blog. In a post entitled "The big lies people tell in online dating" (published on July 7, 2010), Rudder concludes that many, if not most, people lie – making themselves a bit taller and earning a slightly higher income than the US average, additionally appearing to be younger by a year or so (by posting dated profile pictures). "People do everything they can in their OkCupid profiles to make themselves seem awesome," Rudder comments.[17] In their discussion about the soft deception of our mediated selves, Catalina Toma, Jeffrey Hancock and Nicole Ellison point out that people tend to stay true to themselves in the hopes of finding partners who will love them for who they (think they) are, and that they are generally mindful of the possible consequences of future face-to-face interaction and "take advantage of the properties of computer-mediated communication that allow for deception (e.g., editability) but bear in mind its constraints on lying (e.g., recordability)" (2008: 1034).

Beyond noting the formidable challenge involved in forever walking a tightrope between media life's qualities of sheer limitless redactability and recordability, it is crucial to note the flawed assumption that life's move into media causes mating strategies to become deceptive. First of all, as evolutionary psychologist David Buss notes in *The evolution of desire: strategies of human mating* (2004), forms of deception abound in the plant and animal world, and are a constitutive part of all dating situations. Examples of men and women deceiving each other in order to gain sexual access, emotional commitment and investment of resources can be found in the way we dress up (to highlight certain features and disguise what we perceive as physical flaws), how we apply make-up and cover ourselves in lotions and perfumes, drive fancy cars or don expensive luxury items (that we cannot really afford) and so on. It is to be expected that in a media life, more or less active or passive acts of deception are paramount as they are a natural part of the way potential mates relate.

Considering that we essentially face two key struggles in life – the struggle for existence and the struggle for mates – the theory, research and practice of technology and sexuality implies that a media life has evolutionary consequences: living in media means we have way too much sex, or that we just can't be bothered; it also seems to mean that if we do have sex, we are primarily having it with ourselves, or with way too many (more or less anonymous) others. Either way, we're screwed. On the other hand, perhaps a media life is just another evolutionary milestone, something that is a natural part of adapting to our immediate local environment – an environment that today is instantly global, always on, and intrinsically interconnected in media. In evolutionary terms, a key question becomes to what extent a life as lived in media provides us with adaptive cues or advantages in the struggle for survival and procreation. Living a media life can, and perhaps should, be seen as essential for survival.

Darwin among the machines

British philosopher Herbert Spencer must be credited not just with coining the phrase "survival of the fittest" (which he first used in 1862, inspired by Charles Darwin's work), but also with applying the principles of evolution to all aspects of organic and inorganic life – an ambitious approach he described as a "synthetic" philosophy. Like different species of animals and plants, culture and society evolve towards increasing complexity and diversity, Spencer argued. The key to understanding this entire process is Darwin's concept of natural selection, which in subsequent editions of his *On the origin of species* (originally published in 1859) was replaced with Spencer's notion of survival of the fittest. Of course, for Darwin and Spencer, being "fit" does not refer to any prescriptive or physical principle – it just means being adapted to survive in one's immediate, local environment. Although contemporary theorists would (and should) reject Spencer's rather simplistic progressive take on cultural evolution, his influence on Darwin's discourse stimulated much of evolution's take-up among those contemplating the impact on society of technology in general and media in particular.

Shortly after the publication of Darwin's book, British novelist Samuel Butler responded with three written commentaries, published as op-ed pieces in the New Zealand newspaper the *Press* and the London-based *Reasoner*. The second of those pieces, entitled "Darwin among the machines" (published on June 13, 1863), applied Darwin's theory of evolution to the relationships between nature, humanity and technology. In his essay Butler wonders out loud about the direction of mechanical evolution – or what he calls *mechanical life* – awestruck as he is "at the gigantic strides with which it has advanced in comparison with the slow progress of the animal and vegetable kingdom." Applying the principle of natural selection to machines, Butler notes how their ongoing diminution in size attends their development and progress towards ever-increasing independence from humans. To Butler, the emergence of wristwatches is an example of how smaller technologies may replace larger ones – clocks – and thus render them extinct. If technologies have the potential to render each other obsolete, and their evolution moves at a pace far beyond that of nature, Butler proceeds, "We refer to the question: what sort of creature man's next successor in the supremacy of the earth is likely to be." Ultimately, "man will have become to the machine what the horse and the dog are to man. He will continue to exist, nay even to improve, and will be probably better off in his state of domestication under the beneficent rule of the machines than he is in his present wild state." The solution to this evolutionary conundrum, according to Butler, is to wage "war to the death" with machines.

Butler's call to arms can be read as the first among many authors coming to what to them seems an inevitable conclusion of the evolutionary trajectory of media life: sooner or later machines will gain the upper hand. In his provocatively titled book *What technology wants* (2010), Kevin Kelly tackles the same issue from a much more benevolent point of view, arguing that, as technology adapts and evolves in ways increasingly symbiotic with people, it "expands life's fundamental traits," and "amplifies the mind's urge towards the unity of all thought" (359). Carrying such concerns through to their logical conclusion, Ray Kurzweil considers the gradual takeover by machines inevitable, relating this *singularity* to the moment when people can finally leave their obsolete bodies behind. It would be a grave mistake to take with certainty the discussion on the co-evolution of media and life into the territory of all-out conflict or even war between humanity and its machines. The expectation of a singularity misunderstands a basic premise of evolution: it does not equal progress, nor does it move in a neat, linear fashion. Evolution is a messy, kludgy and altogether complicated (if not time-consuming) affair that privileges none – neither humans, plants, animals, nor machines and media.

After publishing his three op-ed columns on Charles Darwin's seminal book, Samuel Butler continued his argument about the development of conscious forms of mechanical life as a probable outcome in the co-evolution of humans and machines – for example in his book *Erewhon*

(1872), about a fictional society that deliberately functions without machines, and where children choose to be born. What Darwin disavowed but what remained central to Butler's analysis of evolution in relation to technology was the notion of intelligent self-creation in organic development. The association of human self-authorship with the remix of technology and nature goes to the heart of the media-life perspective. Consider once more Butler's imaginative argument in 1863: "we are ourselves creating our own successors; we are daily adding to the beauty and delicacy of their physical organisation; we are daily giving them greater power and supplying by all sorts of ingenious contrivances that self-regulating, self-acting power which will be to them what intellect has been to the human race."

Although Butler's comments to some extent read as a first draft of a science-fiction film, his insights embrace an evolutionary view on media life without stepping into the trap of opting for either side of the equation. His recognition of the evolutionary role of technology in the process of human development remains significant to this day – even though we have to recognize how the machines in Butler's time were substantially different from technologies today. Brian Arthur takes up such a historical challenge to consider technology from an evolutionary perspective, in the process suggesting that technologies in the broadest sense affect "our very way of being" (2009: 10). Arthur does not take up a specific normative position in this debate, assured by his conclusion that whatever technology is, it is continually evolving in ever more complex ways – and in the process, it "builds itself organically from itself" (24). The central premise behind such a compound perspective on the nature–technology–humanity relationship is what Nigel Thrift calls an *"active shaping of environments"* (2005: 463; italics in original). Thrift sees our current time in which nature, technology and humanity escape their categorical boundaries (and, in the context of this book, collapse in the mediated lifeworld), as a profound political and ethical challenge to prevent turning the world "into a frenzied roundelay of accumulation of not very much at all" (474). If we stand in a permanently plastic relationship to our world – as noted much earlier by Julien Offray de La Mettrie in 1748 – it is indeed up to us to recognize and retain a principle of messiness (and, I would add, *magic*) over the illusion of control that all too often is associated with technologies.

If war is not the answer, some kind of mastery over our media certainly seems to be. Government research agencies around the world similarly produce regular reports on what tends to be considered as an ongoing digitization of the lifeworld, suggesting that in order to keep up with today's knowledge society people need to be skillful and competent in using and navigating an increasingly complex media environment. The influential theories of Indian economist Amartya Sen are a key point of reference here, in which he emphasizes the responsibility of political and education systems to recognize and advance the capabilities of people to act according to what they value and thus facilitate their quality of life. Nicholas Garnham applies Sen's normative approach directly to the field of media and communication, suggesting that in all modern societies the functioning of social communication is a part of well-being, and that acquiring or using media must to some extent be seen as indices to that effect: "Just as Sen argues that people have different capacities to translate a given food bundle into nutrition and also have different nutritional requirements to reach the same level of functioning, so too in the field of communication it is the real availability of opportunities and the real achievement of functionings that matters" (1997: 32).

It must be clear, then, that a media orientation is much more than owning a really fast personal computer or smartphone, maintaining an online social network profile, and scheduling your daily rituals around mediated connections. It tends to be seen as essential to one's quality of life, to a sense of well-being and belonging, and to one's success in being recognized and achieving life goals. In short: by mediating ourselves and through the multimediation of our lifeworlds we expand and enhance the fitness for our environment.

Media life as survival strategy

Central to claims made about media and (quality of) life are three considerations that can be seen as implying a view on living in media as a necessary survival strategy. First, there is a sense that for people in general (and those growing up in media particularly) a life in media is not so much a choice, as a given. As Margaret Weigel and Celka Straughn of the Developing Minds and Digital Media Project at Harvard University write, "today's youth are the first generation to have lived their entire lives in a world rich with new digital media . . . ripe with the potential to transform young people's experiences."[18] Key to managing these transformations is what researchers of the British Digital Lives Research Project refer to as our ability to safely, authentically and ethically keep track of our lives in media.[19]

A second insight is that our engagement with media today cannot be restricted to the identity of a consumer, but must include what John Hartley (2007) describes as a *multimedia literacy* that includes creative production next to critical consumption of media. As commonly defined, contemporary media competencies tend to include critical and reflective understanding of how media work, how to use different media devices effectively, and how to make your own media. Third, our media life can specifically be seen through a more or less co-creative and participatory lens, thus adding distinct social and productive elements to media literacy. Summarizing findings of a large-scale project identifying new media literacies, Henry Jenkins and colleagues define these as "a set of cultural competencies and social skills that young people need in the new media landscape. Participatory culture shifts the focus of literacy from one of individual expression to community

involvement. The new literacies almost all involve social skills developed through collaboration and networking" (2006: 4).

The assumptions grounding normative approaches to life in the twenty-first century consider media central to people's lives, and relate specific qualities of contemporary media to the requirement of a certain set of skills and competencies that we apparently cannot do without anymore. Using media skillfully as consumer and producer in a more or less co-creative context presumably becomes just as necessary to survival in today's redactional society as finding food and shelter (and a mate). Linking media and survival more explicitly, Norm Friesen and Theo Hug find our immediate and at once local and global, environment to be inseparable from media, because "Just as water constitutes an a priori condition for the fish, so do media for humans" (2009: 66). The metaphysical assertion that we, like fish in water, tend not to question our media has evolutionary consequences: our adaptability for survival today cannot be considered outside of media, and can even be seen as constituted through media. Before we, with Butler, choose to wage war on our machines, a wiser first step in considering media life as a survival strategy is figuring out the exact extent to which our orientation to media provides us with adaptive advantage.

Living a media life is not just having access to all kinds of devices we use to mediate our lives. Nor is it just about knowing how and when to use such equipment. A media life is just as much about our orientation to media as it is about media and what we do with them. It is consequently possible to argue, as media literacy scholars implicitly do, that without orienting ourselves to media, we are not fit for survival. According to German sociologist Niklas Luhmann (2000[1996]), throughout the twentieth-century social systems (such as the political, economic and scientific ones) have increasingly taken seriously the way media depict them. There is not a political party, corporate entity, or non-governmental organization without a dedicated office for media and public relations, or without some kind of media strategy. Luhmann explains how society orients itself to its description in the media, whereas the function of the media as a social institution primarily is to generate descriptions of society. Such circular permanent activity of generating and interpreting information follows a biological pattern of self-organization. Seen in this way, the institutions that make up society through their actions produce information about what society is, and by doing so increasingly rely on (observation and publication in) media for their continued existence and success. Danish media scholar Stig Hjarvard takes up this paramount media orientation as part of a profound *mediatization* of society:

> By the mediatization of society, we understand the process whereby society to an increasing degree is submitted to, or becomes dependent on, the media and their logic. This process is characterized by a duality in that the media have

become integrated into the operations of other social institutions, while they also have acquired the status of social institutions in their own right. As a consequence, social interaction – within the respective institutions, between institutions, and in society at large – take place via the media. (2008: 113)

All institutions are dependent on societal representation, and media are increasingly indispensable as platforms for the publication of their affairs. This means that an institution's success in the media becomes necessary for exertion of influence in other areas of society – in other words, necessary for its successful reproduction and survival. As a result, all functional areas within society have learned to look at themselves through media. Society's institutions – including the family, the temple, the state and the workplace – have, due to the rapid expansion and extension of media undergone a shift towards self-reflective commentary and positioning vis-à-vis the media.

Avatar activism

Not only formal institutions are more or less exclusively oriented towards media – all kinds of groups, networks and communities are, too. Consider, for example, the inhabitants of Bil'in, a Palestinian village located west of the city of Ramallah in the central West Bank. Part of the village farm lands are cut off from the community as a result of expanding Israeli settlements and efforts by the Israeli Defense Force (since 2004) to build a wall around its territory. Since January 2005, the village community has organized weekly protests against the construction of the barrier. These protests take the form of marches from the village to the site of the barrier with the aim of halting construction and dismantling sections already constructed. Israeli forces typically intervene to prevent protesters from approaching the barrier, and violence often erupts in which both protestors and soldiers have been injured. From a media-life point of view, the otherwise tragic plight of the people in this town is fascinating because of the way the community orients itself towards media in order to get support for its cause. Not only does the village operate a professional multi-lingual and multimedia website (www. bilin-village.org), the protests themselves are often staged in mediatized ways. On February 12, 2010, five protestors painted themselves blue and wore bright blue clothes inspired by the Na'vi people in James Cameron's highly successful film *Avatar* (2009). In the movie, the Na'vi are a 10-foot-tall, blue-skinned non-technological species inhabiting the planet Pandora. On this planet, an Earth-based corporation mines for a valuable mineral called "unobtanium," employing a mercenary army to displace the Na'vi who resist the company. A statement on Bil'in's website explained the villagers' choice to dress like the Na'vi people: "Like Palestinians, the Avatars fight imperialism, although the colonizers have different origins. The Avatars' presence in Bil'in today symbolizes the united resistance to imperialism of all kinds."[20] This demonstration in particular garnered worldwide attention and outrage, as pictures and video of blue protestors sprayed with tear gas canisters spread the globe – both through the town's own efforts to upload material to YouTube, and through international news coverage. Writing about the protests in Bil'in for French monthly newspaper *Le Monde Diplomatique* (of September 15, 2010), Henry Jenkins considers the event "a reminder of how people around the world are mobilising icons and myths from popular culture as resources for political speech, which we can call Avatar activism."

The film and themes of *Avatar* are used as a reference in several community initiatives around the world. The Dongria Kondh tribe in the eastern state of Orissa in India, represented by advocacy groups such as Survival International, took out an ad in the Hollywood entertainment magazine *Variety* (of February 2009), stating: "Appeal to James Cameron. Avatar is fantasy . . . and real. The Dongria Kondh tribe in India is struggling to defend their land against a mining company hell-bent on destroying their sacred mountain. Please help the Dongria."[21]

At issue were the plans of British mining company Vedanta Resources to dig up mineral resources around a mountain the tribe considers its homeland. Although Cameron did not directly respond to this appeal, news organizations around the world reported in August 2010 that the tribe had won its case as the Indian government rejected the mining company's proposals. Reporting for CNN, Harmeet Shah Singh and Sumnima Udas wrote about the case with the headline "Indian tribe's 'Avatar' victory over UK mining giant" (on August 24, 2010), stating: "It has been dubbed India's version of the Hollywood blockbuster 'Avatar.' And just like the movie, the indigenous group fighting to save its sacred homeland has won a major fight." The successful movie director did recognize another call for his assistance: this time from a Washington DC-based non-governmental organization called Amazon Watch. This group coordinated a trip for him to visit the Xingu river in the Amazon rainforest (in April of 2010), where he met the Kayapo Indians. The construction of a dam sponsored by the Brazilian government threatens the livelihoods of the indigenous peoples along the Xingu. As Alexei Barrionuevo reported for the *New York Times* (on April 10, 2010), Cameron "encountered the cause . . . after being presented with a letter from advocacy organizations and Native American groups saying they wanted Mr. Cameron to highlight 'the real Pandoras in the world,' referring to the lush world under assault in his movie." Discussing his experience with author Nikolas Kozloff of *The Huffington Post*, Cameron referred to the Kayapo Indians as "real life Na'vi," and to their plight as a "quintessential example of the type of thing we are showing in 'Avatar' – the collision of a technological civilization's vision for progress at the expense of the natural world and the cultures of the indigenous people that live there."[22] He followed up on the campaign by producing a documentary on the dam and its consequences for the Indians, entitled *A Message From Pandora*. The short feature debuted in August 2010 to coincide with the cinematic release of an extended version of *Avatar* (and was included as bonus material on a subsequent DVD release of the film). Alas, Cameron's intervention seems less successful than the victory of the Na'vi: in early June 2011, the Brazilian government granted an installation license for the Belo Monte dam, clearing the way for construction to begin. In response, Cameron told a reporter for Agence France-Presse that "The Kayapo are going to fight," professedly predicting (or premediating) that real-world events would follow the script of his motion picture.[23]

The Bil'in, Dongria Kondh and Kayapo examples are not just instances of media orientation contributing to more or less successful survival. These cases are also relevant because of the various *real-life* claims that are made in reference to (and using physical re-enactments of) media. The experiences of the communities involved become real in the eyes of others – people who use media – because of the references they can make to a mediated reality. Without Cameron's fiction (and the global financial success thereof), their predicaments would quite possibly have gone relatively unnoticed.

It is not just society's institutions, glocalized communities, groups and networks that need to be in media in order to survive – individual human beings face the same adaptive thrust. Perhaps I can elaborate this point best with a personal example. On May 1, 2008, in the midst of the campaign for the Presidential primaries, then-Senator Barack Obama visited the campus of Indiana University in Bloomington, Indiana. He spoke in front of a completely packed Assembly Hall. When we walked up to the venue to catch a glimpse of the Senator, one of his aides approached and asked whether we would like to be on stage with him. This was an offer we could not refuse, and together with about 50 other visitors we were quickly guided to a scaffold in the sports arena. Everyone was supplied with signs – half of them official "Change We Can Believe" placards, the rest consisting of fake (equally professional) make-shift yardsigns painted with various slogans: "Barack Rocks," "Fired Up" and "Obama Oh Yeah." When the Senator finally climbed on stage, the stadium erupted with cheers. Caught in the moment, I could not help myself but cheer along – and take photographs. As we were standing directly behind Obama, the pictures I took showed his back and the upturned faces of the crowd in front of him. Looking back at these pictures, I realized that every single person in that audience carried some sort of (digital) camera. In effect I was taking pictures of other people taking pictures of me. As publics, we were all confirming each other's existence (as in: being there) in the specific terms of how media would signal our presence. The function of these pictures (and amateur videos of the event available online) to a significant extent can be ascribed to being recognized for being authentically part of this otherwise highly stylized and ritualized event. This example, for me, shows how the individual also needs to orient herself to media in order to succeed. Our incessant recording and redacting (and archiving, editing, sharing, forwarding, distributing) of lived experience makes us part of a larger media system that produces reality in terms of the reality it records, redacts, selects and thereby constructs. It is as Juan Miguel Aguado (2009) asserts, building on the work of Luhmann: in a media life, people, groups, networks and institutions observe themselves in the selection terms of media – that is, whether they are relevant and of interest (i.e. deserving attention) to media. In the process, the media's system of reference and criteria for selection gradually come to structure the way we live our lives.

Grooming at a distance

Although plenty of people are doubtful about the omnipresence of media in the lives of others (or themselves), few today are following the call by Samuel Butler to wage war on our machines – for example by deliberately detonating information bombs to create so-called "Technology Free Zones," allowing "direct human–human interaction to flourish while disabling or destroying any and every technological element and/or device within the zone."[24] Alas, it has become a fantasy to be able to avoid media. Anthony Giddens calls attention to the inevitable stretching process of local and faraway interactions made possible (and amplified) through the combination of instantaneous communications and ongoing globalization processes. Both developments are not incidental, argues Giddens, but must be understood as "a shift in our very life circumstances. It is the way we now live" (2003[1999]: 19). No one is outside anymore. Once inside, in media, we seem unable to not participate in the intense interactions across time and space that govern relations between people, social institutions and the world. The best example thereof are consistently exponential growth figures of online and mobile social network use, and the migration of social media into all other consumer electronics. People tell stories about themselves more than doing anything else online. One cannot help but wonder what the adaptive advantage of all of this mass self-communication through media is. What does Darwin's theory of natural and sexual selection have to say about our contemporary tendency to mediate ourselves completely? Researchers in disciplines such as sociobiology, behavioral ecology, evolutionary psychology and cultural science are at the forefront of linking life with media. What is particularly relevant about this kind of work is that it makes us aware of the fact that people are not blank slates when they come into contact with something or someone new – and vice versa. As anthropologist John Tooby and psychologist Leda Cosmides (2005) argue, the nature of our interactions is partly rooted in the design features of evolved mechanisms – patterns of behavior and adaptations to our environment that have been enormously successful over time. In other words: a life as lived in media is not a new, nor necessarily different, life; it could just be another complex adaptation to a constantly changing biological and technological environment – just as that environment stands in adaptive relation to us.

Central to our mediated lives is the shared ability to express ourselves in language. As Neil Postman puts it: "our languages are our media" (1986: 15). The question is, as posed by British anthropologist Robin Dunbar: why (only) humans have language. Throughout his work, Dunbar explores these and other issues deliberately using Darwin's comparative method, gathering evidence from a vast range of sources. At the heart of his conclusions lies the notion that we need language to navigate our way around an increasingly complex and diverse social world. This complexity did not start in the nineteenth century with the first technological media inventions – it began when people formed communities larger than could be sustained through face-to-face communication (which at the time, at least 30,000 years ago, by most accounts consisted mainly of pointing gestures and one-on-one grooming rituals). Dunbar concludes: "For humans, as with all primates, effectively bonded social groups are essential for successful survival and reproduction, and since grooming has a natural limit on the size of group that can be bonded with it, language was necessary to break through this glass ceiling and allow larger groups to evolve" (2003: 14).

Language allows us to talk to several individuals at the same time, and our evolving capacity for storing and recalling all kinds of information contributes to letting other people know what is expected of them, what the rules are and so on. The ability of a social group, community or society to engage in (and maintain some kind of stored archive of) shared story-telling about itself in turn produces such a society. French cognitive scientist Jean-Louis Dessalles similarly suggests that the reason humans use language relates directly to the rapidly increasing size of social groups and coalitions, and our relative ability to show off how we can be seen as valuable members of these (2009: 363).

Beyond signaling our intentions, part of managing one's role and position in social groups is paying close attention to what others are doing in an ongoing process of figuring out what to do under certain circumstances. Paleoanthropologist Richard Leakey makes the case that this monitoring ability confers considerable evolutionary advantage, boosting social intelligence and sharpening self-awareness (1996: 149). Ultimately, Leakey states, those individuals who were particularly good at handling all this information enjoyed greater social and reproductive success, in turn boosting the consciousness of self and others to higher levels. In sum, cooperation and sociality are at the forefront of explanations for the fact that we express ourselves in all kinds of ways, and in turn are generally mindful of each other's expressions. This does not mean that all people use language the same way, or for the same reasons – it just suggests that, as human beings, when faced with an increasingly complex environment featuring an ever-growing number of people (as well as dwellings, tools, plants and animals) to reckon with, we adapted in part by developing language skills, monitoring abilities and a working memory. In terms of media life, adaptive advantage is derived from mass self-communication regarding the management of (belonging to) large social groups, as well as the combined properties of seeing and being seen.

In his book *Grooming, gossip, and the evolution of language* (1998), Robin Dunbar estimates that primates maintain about 50 social ties, while humans, in cultures ranging from tribal groups to modern institutions, maintain social networks of 150 to 200 people. Dunbar's number represents the maximum number of individuals with whom we can have a genuinely social relationship. Facebook, on track to reach more than 1 billion active users worldwide by 2012, reports that the average user has 130 friends.[25] Writing in the *New York Times* magazine (of September 7, 2008), Clive Thompson suggests an update

to the Dunbar number in order to include our *ambient awareness* of others in our online and mobile social networks, as
facilitated by following people's Twitter feeds, Facebook status
updates, and other ways to communicate everything they do.[26]
His suggestion is to double it due to technology. Although statistics certainly show people with online social networks quite
a lot larger than Dunbar's number, reports from companies
such as Facebook show that "the number of people on an individual's friend list with whom he (or she) frequently interacts
is remarkably small and stable" (as reported in *The Economist*
of February 26, 2009).[27] The extension of our social circles in
media thus seems more related to signaling our presence and
monitoring relatively distant others, than to maintaining close
personal ties. Australian interaction design researcher Leisa
Reichelt values this extension of personal networks to include
many more people, describing it as a form of *ambient intimacy*
that enables her "to keep in touch with people with a level of
regularity and intimacy that you wouldn't usually have access
to, because time and space conspire to make it impossible."[28]
Even if people have thousands of friends in media or make do
with only a handful of contacts, humans tend to layer social
networks and prioritize relationships for adaptive advantage.
Although people seem to be spread quite thin when it comes
to the ongoing maintenance of their largely ambient realm of
connections, we do seem to be applying the same rules and
behaviors to a life lived in media as we would when the only
way we could communicate and bond was to sit down and
remove insects, dirt and twigs from each other's skin.

Turkish sociologist Zeynep Tufekci, who puts young people's intense use of social networking sites under the rubric
of social grooming, takes up Dunbar's influential work. For
Tufekci, human behavior at such sites replicates the functions of gossip or social grooming, as people "engage in
these activities in an interlocked dance of community formation" (2009: 547). She argues that the *expressive* internet
– defined as the practice and performance of technologically

mediated sociality – is essential to processes of human bonding, whereas the *instrumental* internet is merely a space of information seeking, knowledge gathering and commercial transactions. It is interesting to see how this instrumental role tends to be privileged in political, economical, and (many) academic accounts of what media are good for, whereas it is the sociality provided in media that explains their attractiveness and success. It certainly sometimes seems that all the status updates, shout-outs, blurbs, tweets, texts, clips and snippets of information people exchange serve no other purpose than to be part of what Vincent Miller (2008) considers an ascendant phatic media culture, based on small communicative gestures that are distinctly social, but are not intended to transmit substantial information. Often, our communications are not about the message we send, but about the process of communication itself: what you are doing and where you are now – which is still one of the most insistent forms of communication in internet chatrooms, text and instant message exchanges, and other new media platforms. This type of communication is, argues Miller, not meaningless, as it implies "the recognition, intimacy and sociability in which a strong sense of community is founded" (395). Judith Donath (2007) similarly considers the evolutionary function of our immersion in online and mobile social networks as enhancing our ability to maintain an immense network – what she calls a *social supernet* – and concludes that "Perhaps the basic pleasure that social network sites provide is endless novelty in the flow of new people and new information, and the knowledge that someone is paying attention to you – social grooming for the information age."[29]

Living in the global mediascape

I want to emphasize how what we do in mediated social networks may be constrained and in part produced by their technological and often commercial infrastructures, and yet all of this should also be seen as providing solutions to enduring evolutionary problems. Beyond romance, sex and social grooming, numerous studies suggest that mass self-communicating online contributes to people's sense of belonging, for example when it comes to maintaining close family ties in an increasingly mobile and diasporic world. Our possibly *post-geographical* and *post-dating* media worlds do not necessarily signify a death of distance, as often proclaimed in the annals of technoculture, nor do they eliminate feelings of fellowship. This comes into sharp relief when considering the everyday experience of different generations of migrants, expatriates, refugees, as well as international travelers. In the context of such extensive worldwide travel and migration, media connections serve as completely mundane yet hugely significant markers for keeping an eye on people and events in one's country of origin (or that of one's parents, close relatives and friends), while at the same time enabling the formation of bonds with the dominant culture in the current place of residence. The kind of belonging produced in media provides a complex and highly dynamic pattern of meaningful relationships, as Arjun Appadurai notes:

> What this means is that many audiences throughout the world experience the media themselves as a complicated and interconnected repertoire of print, celluloid, electronic screens and billboards. The lines between the realistic and the fictional landscapes they see are blurred, so that, the further away these audiences are from the direct experiences of metropolitan life, the more likely they are to construct imagined worlds which are chimerical, aesthetic, even fantastic objects. (1990: 9)

By way of updating Appadurai's argument, global-media scholar Annabelle Sreberny argues how today's media foster even more social complexity by interfacing people with "the world of new diasporas" (2005: 445). This diasporic world is one in which one's sense of belonging is produced as a remix – an ongoing hybridized, magical and messy mixedness of identities, cultures and behaviors primarily derived from constantly and incessantly gazing at each other in media. As Sreberny elaborates, "media channels can maintain, even re-invoke, attachments to old homes, they can encourage involvements with new homes and can support more 'transnational' or diasporic consciousness of multi-sited ethno-cultural attachments" (446). Importantly, her work signals the continued significance of place when considering our sense of belonging – it is just that whatever, whenever and wherever place is seems up for grabs. This in turn amplifies the necessity of social monitoring and active participation in mediated networks in order not only to understand your own place, role and identity, but also to actively create such fundamental aspects of human being. The feedback loop between increasing social complexity, worldwide mobility, globalization and individualization, and our continued immersion in all kinds of media can thus be seen as not necessarily new, nor all that different from how humans adapted to the earliest forms of living together in large groups: by expressing themselves in language, by monitoring each other's communication, and by forming mental archives of behaviors to be used as compasses and roadmaps in order to see and be seen.

CHAPTER EIGHT

Life in Media

where you can see yourself live, and delusion is the way to keep it real

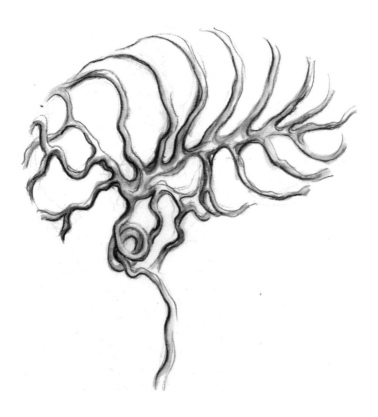

In her book and exhibition *See yourself sensing* (2011), American filmmaker, multimedia artist and architect Madeline Schwartzman documents a wide variety of installations and projects experimenting with the boundaries of our senses, altering the way we experience the world. By augmenting parts of our bodies with all kinds of devices and technological functions – including, but not limited to prosthetic equipment and networked devices added onto body parts (such as eyelashes and teeth) – Schwartzman draws attention to how people, generally speaking, pay little attention to their senses. In a sense, she expects us to feel *more*, not *less*, with and through technologies, machines and media.[1]

Schwartzman's collection of artworks embodies the philosophy of perception as developed prominently by French philosopher Maurice Merleau-Ponty in a series of lectures for French national radio in 1948. Merleau-Ponty's project intends to raise people's awareness about their lifeworld and asks them to take responsibility for it. This is an important call to arms, if only because our embodied senses – like our media – all too often remain largely invisible to us with regard to their inner workings, qualities, and functions: "the world which is revealed to us by our senses and in everyday life, seems at first sight to be the one we know best of all . . . Yet this is a delusion . . . I shall suggest that much time and effort, as well as culture, [are] needed to . . . rediscover the world in which we live, yet which we are always prone to forget" (2004[1948]: 31–2).

What Merleau-Ponty observes about our sensual blindness, Friedrich Kittler (2009) similarly considers as our general blindness to the structuring role of media in what we (can) know about our world. It is safe to say that a life lived in media not just collapses the categories of mediation and the lifeworld – it also presupposes a level of familiarity between media and our embodied existence that seems basically beyond our purview – unless we learn to look at it awry, and allow in the symbiosis of nature, humanity and technology. Such immediate intimacy of media, social and physical reality and everydayness plays out most intensely in the numerous ways in which people (can) see themselves live. Writing in *Forbes* magazine (on May 7, 2007), Sherry Turkle observes how delegating our life to the vast recording, storage and access potential of media primarily allows us – not without consequences – to keep track of ourselves: "People become alienated from their own experience and anxious about watching a version of their lives scrolling along faster than they can handle. They are not able to keep up with the unedited version of their lives, but they are responsible for it . . . Always-on/always-on-you technology takes the job of self-monitoring to a new level."[2]

This new level of self-witnessing, within which solipsism and self-alienation seem to go hand in hand, is established through the devices, practices and emerging digital culture of omnoptic surveillance – a state of being where everyone monitors everyone else (or we presume as much). The work of being watched is done by governments, security establishments (both private and public), businesses, all kinds of social groups, all of us as mass self-communicating individuals, as well as by an emerging internet of things.

Realizing that we can be seen at all times can be considered to be one step towards some kind of critical awareness about the ubiquitous nature of our mediated living environments. Even though people may not be fully aware of this manifest multilateral scrutiny, the intensity with which online and mobile social network users, virtual-world inhabitants and online gamers attend to their multiple selves in media suggests we do share a heightened sense of being watched – of having to perform ourselves in front of diversified yet imperceptible audiences. Considering the current opportunity a media life gives people to create multiple versions of themselves and others, and to endlessly redact themselves (as someone does with their profile on an online dating site in order to produce better matches), we have now a entered a time in which we can see ourselves live.

To picture any image of yourself to yourself

Seeing yourself live is no small achievement. In fact, it is safe to say that up until recently one's ability to witness oneself was limited to only the richest and most privileged members of society – those who could afford to commission artworks such as drawings, paintings, sculptures and plays in their name and about their persona. Although such acts of more or less public self-witnessing are strictly representational, they do mediate otherwise unseen aspects of oneself: certain characteristics and features, particular (and often preferred) expressions and emotions. Perhaps the only way that common people could hope to be able to catch themselves in the act of living was through their reflections in windows and mirrors. In the absence of effective means to self-witness, I tend to act in life based on an unspoken assumption of equivalence based on the supposition that people see me as the person I consider myself to be. The uncanniness of this belief is that we all know it cannot be.

This unknown known of the other leads philosophers to explore or refute the zombic hunch in an attempt to articulate precisely what it is inside of each of us that one would see if we were to go looking for it – but, for most of us, the consequences of critically questioning who we are versus how others see us can be quite devastating, as Italian playwright and novelist Luigi Pirandello considers in *Uno, nessuno e centomila* [translation: *One, no one and one hundred thousand*] (1990[1925–6]). In this novel, a young man – Vitangelo Moscarda – finds out by accident that his wife sees him differently from how he has always seen himself. Catching him in the act of admiring himself in front of a mirror, she reminds him that his nose tilts to the right. After noticing his consternation, she reminds him of other such shortcomings he never noticed: a crooked little finger, a slightly curved left knee. Realizing his blindness to these defects, Moscarda is dumbfounded: "I . . . was made to plunge, at every word addressed to me, at every gnat I saw flying, into abysses of self-reflection and consideration that burrowed deep inside me and hollowed my spirit up, down, and across, like the lair of a mole, with nothing evident on the surface" (4). After verifying the accuracy of his wife's observations, he becomes obsessed "by the thought that for others I was not what till now, privately, I had imagined myself to be" (7). All of these perceptions, however innocent and mundane, nonetheless send Moscarda into a downward spiral, propelled by his desire to be truly alone – that is: to be *"without myself"* (11; italics in original).

Pirandello touches on a fundamental insight here, finding that "Solitude is never with you; it is always without you" (11). The protagonist in this disturbing and strangely comical novel comes to the conclusion that the only way to see himself live is to find a way to cancel himself out while witnessing his own actions. His distress stems from his inability to accomplish this task: "I was unable, while living, to picture my self to myself in the actions of my life; to see myself as the others saw me; to set before me my body and see it live . . . When I stood before a mirror, a kind of arrest took place inside me; all spontaneity vanished, my every movement seemed artificial, an imitation" (12–13).

This observation highlights a crucial aspect of performing oneself to (more or less invisible) others and media: when acting the part that is ascribed to us in everyday life, to what extent can we be expected to *keep it real*? It is important to note that, while recognizing that the precarious balance between one's sense of true self and whatever version of ourselves we present to others is not unique to media life, the opportunity a mediated existence offers to instantaneously juggle and maintain multiple versions of the self serves to heighten our awareness of Pirandello's true-self dilemma.

Studies documenting people's mass self-communication in media find that, when doing so, people tend to approximate their normal selves. Perhaps even more so than in face-to-face communication, suggest John Bargh, Katelyn McKenna and

Grainne Fitzsimons on the basis of experimental research: "compared to face-to-face interactions, people are better able to present, and have accepted by others, aspects of their true or inner selves over the Internet" (2002: 45). The work of Danish e-learning experts Thomas Ryberg and Malene Larsen corroborates how most people consider identity work in media primarily in terms of their real lives and selves, generally striving "to construct themselves with an identity that appears as sincere and real as possible" (2008: 108).

In a comprehensive study of the degree of realness of people's online social network profiles, German personality psychology researcher Mitja Back and his colleagues (2010) find that people, generally speaking, maintain *extended real-life* (rather than *idealized-virtual*) persona when adding, editing or deleting personal information in media. The participants – students at German and American universities – were asked to first "describe yourself as you ideally would like to be" (373). These self-reports were then correlated with personality descriptions of them by four of their closest friends. In a separate stage of the project, research assistants perused the personal profiles of the participating students, rating them on the basis of a personality inventory. After correlating the scores of these three reports, Back's team found a high degree of accuracy in the reports of the research assistants, without evidence of self-idealization in the case of students' self-reports, leading them to conclude that "[online social networking sites] might be an efficient medium for expressing and communicating real personality, which may help explain their popularity" (374).

Much like today's social networking website users, Pirandello's protagonist initially endeavors to live up to the version of him others see in order to figure out who he really is. As people spend most of their time in social media communicating their selves to real (yet imagined, inasmuch as invisible) others, our efforts in this regard can be seen as so many attempts to project and live up to one or more versions of our selves that we create and have co-created in media. In essence, we predominantly are what communication researchers Mor Naaman, Jeffrey Boase and Chih-Hui Lai (2010) label as *Meforming* in media: continuously posting messages, publishing and publicizing information exclusively related to our self or our thoughts. As Naaman and colleagues suggest, "although the Meformers' self focus might be characterized by some as self-indulgent, these messages may play an important role in helping users maintain relationships with strong and weak ties" (50). Our constant communication about the self therefore is just as much about projecting a true self as it is about living up and through the multiple versions of our selves. However, we generally do not consciously, or deliberately, see this process taking place, nor do we necessarily reflect on it as Pirandello's protagonist does.

Vitangelo Moscarda's quest to see himself live is a heroic effort. He sets out to discover the endless versions of him that live in the eyes and minds of others (including his wife) through interrogation and research, proceeding "to destroy them one by one" (1990[1925–6]: 49). It is in this act of willful destruction that Moscarda's heroism lies, as most people halt their attempts to see themselves live at managing the version of self that they feel most comfortable with, or that seems most in line with social expectations. In a whirlwind combination of mass self-communication, an explosion in self-help media appealing to personal amenability and self-disciplining regimes, and do-it-yourself advocacy (as for instance espoused regarding making your own media as a roadmap to personal liberation in the work of David Gauntlett), the call to become and be yourself in media life is paramount. The process of such mediatized self-making on a mass scale accelerated in the late nineteenth century with the emergence of marketing and advertising as distinct disciplines, and can be extended to the current popularity of reality television in general, and competitive talent search shows (such as the *Idols* format worldwide) and makeover series in particular.

After analyzing thousands of hours of American makeover TV, featuring bodies, trucks, finances, relationships, kids and homes, Brenda Weber (2009) finds that what all these wildly popular genres have in common is the notion that, in order to uncover your true self, you must be reinvented. As this act of mediated (re)creation is inscribed with the morals and values of others (friends and family members, adumbered audiences, mainstream experts and jurors), the self-making individual inevitably metamorphs into a consensus-based version of everyone else. Weber's German colleague Tanja Thomas reaches somewhat similar conclusions after aggregating the findings of studies on reality television and online dating services in her country. She suggests how the kind of self-actualization supposedly feasible in media life can be seen as a mode of socialization that requires "self-control, self-surveillance, and self-responsibility" (2009: 268), rather than relying on membership of, or allegiance to, social institutions such as the family, organized religion or the state. The hyper-exhibitionist essence of a life lived in media potentially goes hand in hand with hyper-conformism, Thomas argues, because such self-expressive individualization requires much more work to be done by the individual towards active social integration. Moscarda, in a very real sense, is ahead of his time as he forces himself to radically answer the questions every individual shares in a hyper-individualized society without surrendering to the certainty of conformity implicit in the act of public self-reinvention.

Following Pirandello's argument, the process and practice of self-identification, self-branding and subsequent self-creation in media inevitably ends up with someone becoming the person everybody else expects them to be. Moscarda, however, takes a step farther: rather than trying to become more or less comfortable with the one (or 100,000) Moscarda/s created for him, he rebels. One by one, he disassembles the realities made outside any will of his own: his family history, his body and physical being-in-the-world, his class and position as conveyed to him by his background and social context – in other words, he comes to realize how his identity is in fact not his, nor did he make it so. So many others gave his summary features to him, as he has "as many realities as the people he knows" (1990[1925–6]: 61). Moscarda's rebellion takes the form of performing acts "contrary to himself and incoherent" (76). The people around him respond puzzled, disconcerted, and at times follow him around "like . . . robots" (89), dumbfounded by his out-of-character performance of himself. After these "necessary follies" (49), his friends and colleagues, the local townspeople, even his wife (and her best friend) turn against him, seeing in him a madman – "All because I wanted to prove that, for the others too, I could be someone different from the man I was believed to be" (95).

After alienating everyone, Moscarda finally feels he has become one (rather than no one or 100,000). At first glimpse, his obsessive behavior seems not just rather self-indulgent, but – as noted by German-American political theorist Hannah Arendt in her influential work *The human condition* (1958) – also an excellent example of people's exclusive concern with the self as the inescapable byproduct of the modern age. After several centuries of scientific discovery, philosophical sophistication, political professionalization and the rise of a global economy, the individual is, quite literally, left all alone with herself. Arendt discusses how modernity has thus turned into a general process of both external and internal world alienation. First, through the exploration and subsequent mapping of the planet, "all earthly space has become small and close at hand" (1998[1958]: 250), thereby reducing the immensity of our external experience of the world to something that can be brought "into our living rooms" (251). Arendt refers to a globe here, but could in this context just as well been invoking the television or a personal computer with an internet connection. Second, through the Reformation and industrial revolution, our bodies and minds diverged, turning our inner world into something entirely on its own, rather than contained in a material being. In essence, both the physical world and our lifeworld transformed from something unknown, epic and (therefore) awe-inspiring into spaces to be conquered and consequently colonized.

Hannah Arendt argues how the twin processes of planetary exploration and psychological self-discovery put a decisive distance between whoever we are and whatever we are looking for. Instead of reverting back to a time where noblemen and the clergy provided answers (or direction), in modern times this void remains empty – waiting to be filled by no one else but the individual. Instead of man being thrown back upon the world in the face of the relentless pace of change in modern times, Arendt suggests that people are thrown back upon themselves. The eventuality of this exclusive focus on the self, according to Arendt, is "the eclipse of a common public world" and an emerging "lonely mass man" (257). In Pirandello's final analysis, Moscarda indeed experiences "the eternity and the chill of this infinite solitude" (1990[1925–6]: 122). Stripped of all his worldly possessions – and to him that includes his name – he finally becomes one for himself and one for all, in part by completely ignoring everyone else and looking at the world each day as if for the first time: "And the air is new. And everything, instant by instant, is as it is, preparing to appear . . . This is the only way I can live now. To be reborn moment by moment . . . I die at every instant, and I am reborn, new and without memories: live and whole, no longer inside myself, but in every thing outside" (160).

The beauty of Pirandello's final paragraphs for a thinking through of a life in media lies in Moscarda's insistence, established earlier in the novel, that every time you capture and see yourself in media (he talks specifically about a camera and photographs), you die, "[b]ecause you have to arrest the life inside you for an instant, to see yourself" (148). Ultimately, Moscarda's insight reveals the omnipotence of the immediate and instantaneous nature of life as lived *in* media: each moment captured and caught onto itself, without context, lost as well as archived forever. By letting go of holding on to his life as it is or could be seen by others, Moscarda rebels against the constructed make-up of his reality, and focuses completely on what he calls the *God in me*: "the very one who constructed" (144). In other words: Vitangelo Moscarda finally embraces the premise of a reality that can be made, rather than one we somehow have to respond or live up to. This is the essence of a reality as experienced in media life. This reality is, by virtue of its mediatization, connected to everything and everyone else, as well as seeming rather lonely.

It's all about me

As numerous observers note, while people using media are at once and instantaneously connected with generally large and multiple dynamic groups and networks, they are also increasingly ascribed with a deeply individualized and self-centered value system. American author and educator Thomas de Zengotita (2005) is a particularly poignant pundit to this effect, suggesting how the universal "mediated self" (7) lives in a "little MeWorld" (75), automatically attuned to the solipsistic idea that everyone has their own reality. Australian media researchers Yangzi Sima and Peter Pugsley (2010) signal in this context the rise of a distinct *Me Culture* in China, engendered by an increased emphasis on self-expression and identity exhibition in media. According to De Zengotita, this mediated self is in fact a flattered self (2005: 7), endlessly stimulated by at least the possibility of being incessantly addressed in media. Interpellation in media, for example, happens by being liked, poked and tagged on Facebook, or by being singled out in advertisements geared towards *you*.

It seems that the media that connect people also stimulate us to look more or less exclusively at ourselves. American psychologist David Downing argues how "such ostensible connectedness is, in actuality, with a machine that is, in circular fashion, a projected externalization of our own desires and phantasies with which we are in narcissistic relation" (2007: 991–2). In a series of studies on the various combinations of self-focus and other-focus in everyday media life, social psychologist Sarah Konrath shows how people who feel their online identities – as, for example, expressed in a game avatar or a social network profile – are central to their sense of self are indeed chronically influenced by these mediated versions of themselves.[3] Writing with a team of researchers spread across several American universities, Konrath documents rising levels of self-centeredness, assertiveness, agency, self-esteem and extraversion among young people in particular, suggesting that "media activities may have promoted an increase in narcissism" (Twenge et al. 2008: 892).

Instead of destroying the multiple versions of ourselves, it seems that a common tactic in media life is to fall in love with a specific, often preferred version of the self that can be both *found* and *made* in media. Today's youngsters are apparently also absorbed with fitting in – a contemporary personality trait Downing recognizes in an "overvaluation of normality and a hyperconformist orientation toward the world and self" (2007: 1005), as powerfully represented in the fate of outcasts, loners and altogether alien others in popular movies like *The Matrix*, *Dark City*, *eXistenZ* and *The Truman Show*. To Downing, these films manifest "disquieting intrapsychical dilemmas" (993) with which individuals seem to be increasingly (albeit unconsciously) preoccupied, all relating to a profound uncertainty vis-à-vis one's identity and sense of self. By this account, in a society of multiplied selves, media become all-powerful as agents of oppressive blandness and self-similar collectivity, encouraging an even more deeply felt need to fit in.

Rather than being seen as either hyperconformist, supremely solipsist or hyper-exhibitionist narcissistic, the nature of people's mass self-communication can perhaps better be contextualized by a long-term and subtle shift in almost all industrial societies around the world from survival values towards an increasing emphasis on self-expression values as comprising the major area of concern to people in such societies. Ronald Inglehart maps this trend between 1970 and 2006 (and predominantly in Western Europe, North America and Japan, but also in Australia, New Zealand, Uruguay, Colombia, Mexico and South Africa), suggesting how this major cultural change reflects "a process of inter-generational change linked with rising levels of existential security" (2008: 145). Our quest to figure out who we are and who others (think we) are thus can be seen as amplified by media in their capacity to present a smorgasbord of self-expressive options, while at the same time constrained by those very same media in that they can contribute to a process of losing ourselves in front of a (real or perceived) absent present audience. While performing different versions of yourself in everyday life is not exactly a new phenomenon, the publicness of our performances (and those of others not necessarily connected to who or where you are) is. Through the ongoing performance of what Zizi Papacharissi calls "public displays of social connections" we in fact get to "authenticate identity and introduce the self through the reflexive process of fluid association with social circles" (2011: 304–5). The very notion of publicness thus may provide a media life some kind of stability in an otherwise potentially fragmented and plastic experience of identity.

People compare themselves with everyone else through media, and in doing so become used to adding performative and redactable elements to their everyday mediated interaction. It could be argued that, until recently, people's identity negotiations chiefly took place under conditions of proximity – as was the case in the town of Richieri where Vitangelo Moscarda decomposed his personality in a hopeless search for a unified identity. The influence of the family, the local community and nearby social institutions such as school or places of worship has always been a key frame of reference for figuring out who you are (and what you may become). In media, this situation transforms if one considers the acceleration and amplification of finding similarities and differences with others anywhere. As Zygmunt Bauman notes, "we are presently moving from the era of pre-allocated 'reference groups' into the epoch of 'universal comparison', in which the destination of individual self-constructing labours is endemically and incurably underdetermined" (2000: 7). Mark Poster (1999) suggests that it is exactly such *underdetermination* that is a typical feature of today's media. Our identities and experiences in an increasingly interconnected and networked mediaspace are always open to intervention, to redaction, to being altered in all kinds of different ways – often by others who, like the material conditions of media, remain unseen.

If figuring out who you are indeed is a lifelong project and the more or less exclusive concern of the modern age, the question is how living *in* media offers a meaningful roadmap for navigating our lived experiences, in terms of what Anthony Giddens (1991: 35ff.) calls our ontological security (knowing who you are and how you relate to the world) and existential anxiety (permanently questioning what to believe in and whom you should become). To some extent, the very presence of media in all facets of life provides a paradox for the individual, as machines amplify and extend human capabilities while the same technologies alienate us from the world. It is therefore no surprise that some would advocate a complete disconnect from media – and live, like Moscarda in Pirandello's novel, as no one. As neither disconnection nor dehumanization can be complete in media life, one thing to take note of is how people, when wielding the weapons of mobile communication and constant connection, seem to have little or no problem with putting themselves out there in media. The practice of both making and maintaining multiple versions of yourself is a significant element of media life – especially if one considers the delicate balancing act this requires: what do I share, which profile is more like the real me, how much weight do I give to each site, channel and device that asks for my personal information? This is not a tug-of-war between human beings and technologies – one that would require considering media as external to human being. As Asle Kiran and Peter-Paul Verbeek (2010) point out, such externalization of technologies to the self supposes all we are doing is either relying on media to structure our everyday life, or acting suspicious towards media as potentially dehumanizing us and our social relations. Instead, Kiran and Verbeek propose a third point of view, premised on what they call "a fundamentally non-transparent human–technology relation" (419). Given the fact that media have become so central to all elements of everyday life, our individual relationship with technologies is not only governed by the juggling of reliance versus suspicion, but can also be understood as a matter of "trusting ourselves *to* technologies" (409; italics in original). The philosophers suggest that, rather than giving up freedom, this would be a way to create freedom, understanding freedom as "a free relation to the forces that help to shape our selves" (425). For Kiran and Verbeek, trust in this context has the quality of confidence. Such an optimistic take on media life demands that individuals be able to take responsibility for their many co-creative and complex relations with technologies, especially insofar as these affairs pertain to the multiple versions of the mediated self and the correspondingly countless imaginings of mediated reality. In essence, Kiran and Verbeek ask us to become Moscarda without disconnecting from media and the world.

Keeping it real

In Tom McCarthy's novel *Remainder* (2007), a man who, after suffering a terrible accident (of which the reader learns almost nothing else but that it involves technology), desperately tries to reconnect with his life and the reality of his surroundings. Recovering from his accident, he feels disconnected from life, struggling to understand himself, the world around him, the way people seem to go about their daily lives. The nameless protagonist questions the authenticity of his existence as he

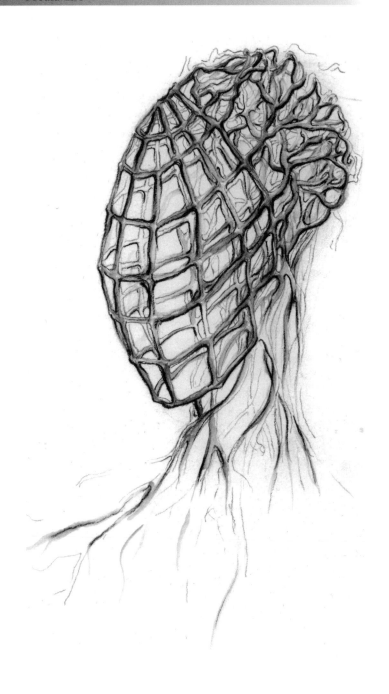

considers himself "plastic" (24) and "malleable," much like a movie actor (McCarthy references Robert de Niro in this context). After receiving a vast sum of money as compensation for his suffering, he proceeds to stage and film memories of his (past) life, hiring as characters the people around him. The farther he progresses into ever more extreme mediated retellings of experiences, the less he feels certain of the reality of his own existence. Instead of calling into question reality as such, McCarthy aims to make our experience of life instant, immediate: "to be real – to become fluent, natural, to cut out the detour that sweeps us around what's fundamental to events, preventing us from touching their core: the detour that makes us all second-hand and second-rate" (264).

McCarthy's protagonist keeps it real by recreating his life in media, and in the process the fine line between life and media gets lost. In *Remainder*, the invention of Morel gets created in real-time with the added benefit of interaction. What the book shows as a runaway rendering of reality can also be seen as a faithful articulation of what a permanently impermanent and yet ever so slightly malleable reality seems to be in media life. Jos de Mul suggests that we should not question whether such a mediated reality is real or not – instead advocating that we should focus on media life as constituting "a different type of being-in-the-world" (2010: 151), and question how these experiences relate to each other. From a media-life point of view, it is exactly through and *in* media that reality can come back into focus. By way of example, digital game developer Jesse Schell notes how many of the most recent developments in computer and video games – such as achievement point systems for game consoles, games specifically designed for social media (such as Zynga's *Farmville* for Facebook) and games based on embodied interaction between people and technology (such as the *Guitar Hero* franchise) – can be characterized by the fact that they are breaking through into reality.[4] Speaking at the 2010 conference of the Academy of Interactive Arts & Sciences, Schell extends his observation to all kinds of everyday experiences in media life: watching television has become a daily ritual of zapping from one reality genre to another, going to the grocery store one finds aisle upon aisle featuring genuine products (variously labeled as organic or otherwise branded as environmentally friendly) and frequenting fast-food places has become a pilgrimage to acquire real food (featuring fresh fruit and vegetables, certified meats). To explain this sudden rush to reality, Schell suggests that "all this virtual stuff that has been creeping up to us . . . has really cut us off from nature . . . we live in a bubble of fake bullshit, and we have this hunger to anything that is real." In the end, he offers the narrative of James Cameron's movie *Avatar* as a case in point of people connecting back to reality through technology.

It seems Schell is on to something – something similar to the conceptualization of media cities and of media life in general: it is only through media that we can come back to who we really are and what reality really is. In order to move beyond everlasting questions of whether a mediated reality – any mediated reality – is real, whether such mediatization is good or bad for us, and whether whoever we think we are in media is fake or authentic, we may have to delude ourselves into believing that *everything* is real, and that we all have a role to play in collaboratively maintaining the principal plasticity of our reality.

The *Truman Show* delusion

In a review piece for the *International Journal of Cultural Studies*, Henry Jenkins wonders what could happen if someone who realizes that his mediated world is not entirely real did not decide to run away from it, but instead turned to his media with an eye to change his reality:

> I am struck by the ending of The Truman Show [. . .] All the film can offer us is a vision of media exploitation, and all its protagonist can imagine is walking away from the media and

slamming the door. It never occurs to anyone that Truman might stay on the air, generating his own content and delivering his own message, exploiting the media for his own purposes. (2004: 36–7)

Jenkins rightfully questions the escape clause of the movie as unsatisfying. The media-life perspective applied to the theory and empirical evidence of how most people generally use media raises the issue that our lived reality is not separate, or outside of media. Metaphorically speaking, we are now all living inside our very own reality show (referring to the 1998 movie *The Truman Show* by Australian director Peter Weir): a world characterized by pervasive and ubiquitous media that we are constantly and concurrently deeply immersed in, that we are the stars of, and that remix and shape all aspects of our everyday life. Importantly, in this world it is also up to each of us to navigate the largely unwritten rules and hidden passages of an ocean of media on our own.

In the film, Canadian-American actor Jim Carrey portrays the life of a man – Truman Burbank – who does not know his entire life is one big reality-television show, watched by millions all over the world.[5] In the course of the movie, it becomes clear that the only way out for Carrey's character will be his individual ability, as the only *true man*, to figure out whether the people in his life are actors (and to what extent they act), and where the fine line between the studio (i.e. Burbank, where part of the film was shot) and the real world (the community of Seaside in Florida[6]) can be drawn. As in the contemporary individualized society, the solution to this vexing dilemma can only be found by the individual on the basis of their personal biography, all the time aware of at least the possibility of being constantly monitored and recorded. The ominous *The Truman Show* metaphor is perhaps only appropriate insofar as it addresses people's complex, interconnected yet often-solipsistic engagement with reality in media. When asked how the show can be so successful in convincing Truman that his world is real even though it so clearly features a fake reality, the director of Truman's reality show (named Christof in the film, a not-so-subtle reference to the divine authority of a God-like director) answers: "We accept the reality of the world with which we are presented."[7] It is important to note the implication of this narrative, as it does not seem to be premised on a notion that Truman's world is unreal – it just means that the protagonist of such a world is unaware of being on camera at all times. *The Truman Show* is just another version of the real, one that is carefully staged, consensus-driven (and therefore depressingly conformist) and completely mediated. This staged reality bears semblance to Plato's "Allegory of the cave" (written as the introduction to one of the books in the Greek philosopher's work *The Republic*, published around 380 BC), as the people in the cave, watching the puppets, like Truman, were unaware of any other lifestyle or world other than the one which they were shown. Using *The Truman Show* as a metaphor for living a media life, one must additionally note that the ending of the movie – Truman escapes from the studio – might in fact be the only truly unreal aspect of the film's story, as, in our fully mediated existence, escape is impossible.

During the summer of 2008, psychiatrists Joel and Ian Gold made headlines around the world with their diagnosis of a new condition found in five of their patients. The brothers suggested that the combination of pervasive media, classical syndromes such as narcissism and paranoia, and an emerging media culture in which the boundaries between the physical and virtual worlds are blurring produces a new type of psychosis: a *Truman Show Delusion* (TSD).[8] People who suffer from TSD are more or less convinced that everything around them is a décor, that the people in their lives are all actors, and that everything they do is monitored and recorded. In an interview with Canadian newspaper the *National Post*, McGill University's Ian Gold attributes TSD to "unprecedented cultural triggers that might explain the phenomenon: the pressure of living in a large, connected community can bring out the unstable side of more vulnerable people [. . .] New media is opening up vast social spaces that might be interacting with psychological processes" (published on July 19, 2008). In a follow-up interview with *Newsweek*, his brother (who is affiliated with the Bellevue Hospital Center in New York) suggests that TSD "is the pathological product of our insatiable appetite for self-exposure" (August 11, 2008). Earlier that week, in a special report on the *WebMD* site, Joel Gold links TSD more generally to the role media play in people's lives: "We've got the 'perfect storm' of reality TV and the Internet. These are powerful influences in the culture we live in."[9] TSD additionally contains a belief that one's life has ceased being spontaneous, as one is always aware of (the possibility of) the scripted and broadcasted nature of everything one does. In a special report about TSD on the website of the American Psychological Association one year later (on June 6, 2009), the brothers identify specific features of modern culture – "warrantless wiretapping and video surveillance systems . . . widely accessible technology . . . reality TV shows and MySpace" – as squaring with the *Truman Show*'s basic premise.[10]

In the APA report and in an earlier background story in the *International Herald Tribune*, several experts are quoted who confirm the possibility of TSD, suggesting that "One way of looking at the delusions and hallucinations of the mentally ill is that they represent extreme cases of what the general population, or the merely neurotic, are worried about" (August 30, 2008, p. 7). Writing in the *British Journal of Psychiatry*, Paolo Fusar-Poli and colleagues confirm the diagnosis of their American colleagues, describing the common symptoms of TSD as:

> First, there is the sense that the ordinary is changed or different, and that there is particular significance in this. This is coupled with a searching for meaning, which, in this case, results in the "Truman explanation." The third feature is a profound alteration of subjective experience and of

self-awareness, resulting in an unstable first-person perspective with varieties of depersonalization and derealization, disturbed sense of ownership, fluidity of the basic sense of identity, distortions of the stream of consciousness and experiences of disembodiment. (2008: 168)

In an online response to this article, the Gold brothers argue that "while the forms of delusion appear to be constant across cultures, the content of delusional beliefs are sensitive to local culture, including technology."[11] The work on TSD is part of a broader project on the role that culture and social life play in psychoses, as documented in their book *Suspicious minds: madness, society, and the limits of neuroscience* (2013). Suggesting that the field of psychiatry often underestimates or ignores external influences on people's minds and sense-making faculties, Ian Gold emphasizes how technologies, as part of the living environment we create and therefore always somewhat familiar (yet at the same time potentially alienating), act as extensions of the way we think.[12] As one of their inspirations Gold refers to Austrian psychoanalyst Victor Tausk's 1933 paper "On the origin of the 'influencing machine' in schizophrenia." In this paper, Tausk (a student and, later on, colleague of Sigmund Freud) discusses how psychotic patients often delude themselves into thinking that their thoughts and behaviors are controlled by an external machine – an influencing machine that makes them see pictures, wields its power unseen to the human eye, and stimulates all kinds of intense emotions and bodily sensations. As the boundaries between the patient's sense of self and the influencing machine break down, the person actually *becomes* the machine. Like the prisoners in Franz Kafka's penal colony, the self gets lost as it is absorbed into the machine.

As we become media, do we necessarily lose ourselves to media? And, if so, is that all there is to it? Or would it be possible to propose that it is exactly by living *in* media we can find reality (and therefore be able to take responsibility for it)? Because it seems that the significance of the analysis by

Joel and Ian Gold, insofar as they relate TSD to the broader contemporary human condition, is a realization that such a delusion can perhaps best be understood as an amplification of a distinct sense of uncanniness and unsettlement in the population at large – amplified by the social context of today's hyperindividualized society, a technological context of rapidly proliferating portable and networked media, and a political context of increasing uncertainty. Whereas the delusion of living inside your own *Truman Show*, in psychiatric practice, is a source of suffering for the individual, a more or less optimistic bias towards the world and its social reality as having a certain plasticity may in fact be beneficial to happiness. As Woody Allen remarks in an interview with the *New York Times* (published on September 14, 2010): "This sounds so bleak when I say it, but we need some delusions to keep us going. And the people who successfully delude themselves seem happier than the people who can't."[13]

The problem, however, is that we keep convincing ourselves and others that elements of our life in media are either good or bad for us, failing to witness what is already taking place. In other words: people experience the ongoing mediation and mediatization of their lives, but seem to remain blind to its profound potential. First, most people spend the majority of their time with media, generally not aware nor overtly mindful of this constant and concurrent media exposure. Second, most of the time spent with media today is taken up by some combination of consuming (primarily watching television) and producing (engaging in social media and, to a much lesser extent, creating one's own media), behaviors which are, increasingly and inevitably, mutually implicated as media devices, platforms, industries and services converge and become networked. Our media use and the capabilities of media devices thus become part of a feedback loop whereby it is indeed possible to argue that media mediate more and more by virtue of the fact that they mediate. Third, as people use media on a continuous basis, the boundaries between their previously partitioned aspects of everyday life – such as school, work and play – blur beyond meaningful recognition to themselves and others. The belief that one's media presence can be managed or maintained in multiple coherent selves is not just highly questionable, but profoundly unrealistic. Fourth, as mediated communication provides the benchmark for social relationships in all aspects of life – within and between families, circles of friends and colleagues, loved ones and anyone else – people's social reality only comes into being insofar as it is produced in terms of media; it therefore, intrinsically, becomes real and unreal at the same time. This is indeed a world governed by the rules of *The Truman Show* (cf. Christof and his cameras), where hacking or destroying the technologies that run the show presents the only way out.

"The best of all possible worlds"[14]

What if living inside your own *Truman Show* can be considered to be a positive bias towards life? This seems an attractive idea – but I venture that is only so if it includes a sense of ethical and aesthetical responsibility towards our being-in-the-world. Considering the key properties of media life, we need to think differently about its promises. In a 1990 essay, Ray Funkhouser and Eugene Shaw outline the social and cultural implications of a completely mediated experience of the world. Considering the "growing prevalence of synthetic experience" (1990: 83) in the world, the two American communication researchers hypothesized that people would be less tolerant of inactivity as well as the general messiness of real life, have heightened expectations of perfection (in each other) and the potential for quick and neat solutions of problems, and have "limited contact with, and a superficial view of, their own inhabited environment" (84). Less than thrilled about such prospects, Funkhouser and Shaw lament how media will distort "entire cultural world views via synthetic experience" (85) as the reality of everyday life shifts from something about which we *"know* that it is real" (76; italics in original) to something we experience – and therefore becomes subject to manipulation. In essence, Funkhouser and Shaw lament the transition of living *with* a map to living *in* a map – a map that people can co-create in media.

Important as this work is, it begs the question what really happens to a society wholly immersed in media and realizing its own complete mediatization. This would be a society with an active awareness that everything and everyone is or can be known (because all is archived); that has (or expects) instantaneous access to all the information there ever was and will be. This is the de facto narrative of "The Library of Babel" (1941), a short story by Jorge Luis Borges, documenting the fate of a society living inside "an indefinite, perhaps infinite number of hexagonal galleries" (2000[1941]: 65) that some consider to be the universe, and others call the Library. This Library contains all possible books in all known languages, comprising all possible combinations of the letters of the alphabet, the comma, the period and the space (whereas each book has 410 pages). Borges writes that some people claim there exists a circular book with a continuous spine at the center of the Library, and that cyclical book is God; as narrator, he proclaims the entire Library "the handiwork of a god" (67), and there are those who remain convinced there is a librarian, somewhere in the universe, who has seen "the cipher and compendium of *all other books* . . . this librarian is analogous to a god" (71; italics in original).

In his story, Borges explores what happens to a society when confronted with the irrefutable evidence that they live in a universe of complete information. At first, people were ecstatic. "All men felt themselves the possessors of an intact and secret treasure. There was no personal problem, no world problem, whose eloquent solution did not exist – somewhere in some hexagon" (69). But this exalted state was also the problem: faced with the presence of all possible books containing all possible information, how to find the right information? And even if someone, somewhere could indeed find a readable and coherent book: how can you know whether the knowledge contained in that work is correct, or good? Naturally enough, Borges writes, "That unbridled hopefulness was succeeded . . . by a similar disproportionate depression" (70). Some proposed destroying all or part of the library – perhaps only the worthless books. Yet, as the Library is total, "any reduction by human hands must be infinitesimal" (71). Some people went insane, others started worshipping the Library or specific rows of books in some gallery. Many committed suicide, faced with the horrible knowledge that everything one can say has already been foreseen and contained in a book somewhere in the Library. In the end, the narrator concludes that, while the human species may become extinct, "the Library – enlightened, solitary, infinite, perfectly unmoving, armed with precious volumes, pointless, incorruptible, and secret – will endure" (73). Borges finds elegant hope in the realization that the Library is periodic: that at some point the Library ends, and then proceeds to repeat itself in the same disorderly fashion.

For all its endlessness, the Library is not infinite. In fact, it may only contain two strips of text, as American logician Willard Van Orman Quine, in 1987, remarked in his take on Borges' tale. For this to work, one would have to reduce all the characters of language into machine-readable language – for example, into the dots and dashes of Morse code. Quine concludes his short essay with a startling reflection:

> The ultimate absurdity is now staring us in the face: a universal library of two volumes, one containing a single dot and the other a dash. Persistent repetition and alternation of the two is sufficient, we well know, for spelling out any and every truth. The miracle of the finite but universal library is a mere inflation of the miracle of binary notation: everything worth saying, and everything else as well, can be said with two characters. It is a letdown befitting the Wizard of Oz, but it has been a boon to computers.[15]

The combination of Borges' exploration and Quine's conclusion point towards a distinct material aspect of our mediated reality: a life in media potentially exposes us to all the information about anything and anyone we want, and at the same time all of this knowledge is or can be reduced to the zeros and ones of computer code. In fact, it is the expectation of completeness neatly achievable by the reduction of the real into binary code that remains the ultimate fallacy.

Daniel Dennett, in his discussion of Borges' narrative and Quine's take on it, suggests that in the Library "this *logical* space is so Vast that many of our usual ideas about location, about searching and finding and other such mundane and practical activities, have no straightforward application" (1996: 110; italics and capitals in original). Fusing Borges' library with Richard Dawkins' work, Dennett moves on to consider the implication of a library containing all possible genomes (DNA sequences) – and concludes that the vast majority of these permutations "are surely gibberish, recipes for nothing living at all" (113). He concludes that there are many more ways for organisms to be dead (or not living) than ways of being alive. Dennett's remarks seem applicable to finding our own way in media life, as it seems to be up to us as individuals to make sense of and take responsibility for it all – even though whomever we will find in media when we go looking for ourselves will not be special, as there will always be other ways of being alive (and dead) in media. The beauty of (media) life is not its superficial promise of disembodiment, order and perfection – it can be found in its much more powerful reminder of the messy, loopy and ever so slightly delusional nature of everydayness.

The art of media life

At the heart of the process of media life, people know (or are being told) that everything they do in life gets recorded, archived, edited, redacted and publicized on a continuous basis. With people's lives playing out in digital and networked archives, the need for more or less stable cultural memories gets gradually erased – which in turn makes for a world that can only live in the moment of recording itself. Paraphrasing Vilém Flusser, our electronic memories are simulations that exaggerate a few aspects of the original while disregarding all the rest. This superior yet selective permanent rendering of history can be quite liberating, argues Flusser, potentially unleashing human creativity and transforming a person from a mere worker (*homo faber*) to "an information processor, a player with information (*homo ludens*)" (1990: 399; italics in original). As the outcome of this process, the philosopher hopes that we will realize that:

> there is no hard core within each of us which somehow mysteriously governs that process, but that the process of acquiring, storing and transmitting information flows through us and involves not only all of present and past society but also the whole of what we call "the world". We are but knots within a universal network of information flux that receive, process and transmit information. (399)

Flusser does not take aim at our quest to find out who we are, but hopes we will be able to move beyond considering ourselves as somehow singular, stable and coherent individuals. Instead of finding the One (or Neo) in all of us, a media life opens up the potential of being one and everything around you. In modern times, being one with and within yourself is a paramount charge to the self – which does not make the process of searching for self pointless, but trying to find it anywhere else but in the network of relations that constitute us will be futile. In short, what will truly free us from the shackles of *weak media* – that is, considering media as external agents having effects and needing to be switched off (at times) – is a postulate of *strong media*: media that are us, as we stop obsessing about ourselves (as individuals), and start living along the lines of the networks and relations that connect all of us. Perhaps this is the most vital application of the zombie metaphor to the contemporary human condition: we need the impersonal sociality of zombies to form, maintain and strengthen our sense of community and society (including its materiality), while "breaking out of the shell of individuality" (399) that would otherwise make us suffer and go mad, as it did with Vitangelo Moscarda.

In media, we are Gods. Our life, our social and physical reality, is open source. As we render our lives completely in media, we end up dancing with many multiple selves in a silent disco. As media zombies, we perform and play in front of real or imaginary omnoptic surveillance cameras to enact our very own *Truman Show*. At the same time . . . we can see ourselves live. We have the ability to put our life at a distance – which opens the world up to intervention. Instead of attempting to reduce the plasticity of the real by hopelessly searching for a true self, people should embrace the co-creative nature of being, and take responsibility for it. Media offer tremendous potential for collective action – not because of today's technologies like smartphones, the internet or spy chips, but because of what media truly are: us, producing a sensemaking lived experience of who we are as more than just *me, myself* and *I*.

Our social and physical reality or essence, as human beings, is not immutable, locked in to our physical presence, our cognition and behaviors. This is not an atomized, fragmented and depressing worldview. Our world – as in our sense of self – in a media life perhaps must be seen as a world in which we truly have individual and collective control over reality, if only we would be at peace with the perpetual plasticity of that reality. This is not to say that a life lived in media is a life lived without all kinds of constraints, limitations and boundaries. Society governed by media life is one where reality is, like every single website, permanently under construction – *not only* by unseen yet all-powerful guardians in the panoptic fortresses of governments and corporations that seek to construct a relatively cohesive and thus controllable reality, *but also* by all of us.

It is the privilege of our times to use media to make art with life. As Michel Foucault asks: "Why should the lamp or the house be an art object, but not our life?" (1984: 350). Indeed, suggests Zygmunt Bauman, "we are all artists of our lives – knowingly or not, willingly or not, like it or not" (2009: 125). Both raise an issue powerfully exploited by Friedrich Nietzsche throughout his work, in which the philosopher, from an early age, passionately called on people to "fashion an unquivocal work of art out of one's own life," (Safranski, 2003: 89) in order to set oneself free from the indifference of the world. In this massively self-communicated work of art, people are always on their own but never alone.

In his book *The revolution of everyday life* (1967), Belgian poet and philosopher Raoul Vaneigem writes:

> the search for new forms of communication, far from being the preserve of painters and poets, is now part of a collective effort. In this way the old specialization of art has finally come to an end. There are no more artists because everyone is an artist. The work of art of the future will be the construction of a passionate life.[16]

In this book I insist on adding media to such a life. The consequence of such a hopeful conclusion is that we have to let go of seeing media as influence machines that will eventually make us disappear, instead considering media as part of our lives to the extent that they will make us visible (again). When we, like Truman Burbank, navigate our ocean of media to what we think will be the door leading beyond the studio, we will see what Patrick Bateman – the imaginary serial killer in Brett Easton Ellis' novel *American Psycho* (1991) – saw on the door of a place that could be anywhere in his world: "a sign and on the sign . . . are the words THIS IS NOT AN EXIT" (399).

Notes

I MEDIA LIFE

1 www.sterneck.net/musik/bey-immediatism.
2 http://records.viu.ca/~johnstoi/Nietzsche/history.htm.
3 www.spiegel.de/international/0,1518,451392,00.html.
4 www.akiba.or.jp/english.
5 www.mediacityuk.co.uk.
6 www.dubaimediacity.com.
7 www.media-city-leipzig.de.
8 www.mediacityberlin.de.
9 www-personal.umich.edu/~mmmc/BOOKS/
   AboutAmbientCommons.pdf.
10 http://test.qosmo.jp/press/nbuilding.php; via: http://rhizome.
   org/editorial/3285.
11 www.popkalab.com/ramblershoes.html.
12 www.wired.com/wired/archive/5.05/ff_cronenberg_pr.html.
13 www.pewinternet.org.
14 www.kff.org/entmedia.
15 http://ec.europa.eu/public_opinion/index_en.htm.
16 www.usatoday.com/news/health/2010-02-10-igeneration10_
   CV_N.htm.
17 www.nytimes.com/2010/01/20/education/20wired.html.
18 http://en.wikipedia.org/wiki/The_Man_That_Was_Used_Up.
19 www.fln.vcu.edu/hoffmann/sand.html.
20 www.nytimes.com/2010/11/25/technology/
   personaltech/25pogue.html.
21 www.primesense.com.
22 www.indiana.edu/~tisj/readers/abstracts/12/12-1%20Winner.
   html.
23 http://informatics.indiana.edu/rocha/i-bic/lec02.html.
24 www.inteco.cl/articulos/006/doc_ing.htm.

2 MEDIA TODAY

1 www.sequentpartners.com/publications/medialife.pdf.
2 http://blogs.wsj.com/law/2009/10/07/the-human-sacrifice-channel-crush-video-arguments-get-creative.
3 http://en.wikipedia.org/wiki/Clarke's_three_laws.
4 http://powazek.com/posts/2842.
5 www.theonion.com/video/sony-releases-new-stupid-piece-of-shit-that-doesnt,14309.
6 www.marxists.org/reference/subject/philosophy/works/ge/benjamin.htm.
7 www.pewinternet.org/Reports/2009/5-The-Mobile-Difference--Typology.aspx.
8 http://blogs.nyu.edu/projects/materialworld/2010/09/polymedia.html.
9 As reported in the *New York Times* of June 6, 2010: www.nytimes.com/2010/06/07/technology/07brainside.html.
10 www.wired.com/wiredscience/2009/02/attentionlost.
11 I am referring in particular to the "Middletown Media Studies" at Ball State University in Indiana (US); see: http://cms.bsu.edu/Academics/CentersandInstitutes/CMD/InsightandResearch/Capabilities/ProjectGallery/MiddletownMediaStudies.aspx.
12 www.ubiq.com/hypertext/weiser/UbiHome.html.
13 www.genderchangers.org.

3 WHAT MEDIA DO

1 http://hydra.humanities.uci.edu/kittler/eno.html.
2 www.inmotionmagazine.com/eno1.html.
3 Although Norbert Wiener represents a different approach to matters of machines and mankind, his overall perspective embraces a similar premise, benchmarking his work with the thesis "that society can only be understood through a study of the messages and communication facilities which belong to it" (1988[1954]: 16).
4 www.scienceandsociety.org/web/Library_files/A.Digital.Life.pdf.
5 http://techcrunch.com/2010/09/07/eric-schmidt-ifa.
6 Source of quotes from Bush's article "As we may think": www.theatlantic.com/magazine/archive/1969/12/as-we-may-think/3881.
7 http://en.wikipedia.org/wiki/Knowledge_Navigator.

8 http://gapingvoid.com/2006/11/24/seth-godins-unforgiveable-manifesto.

9 www.nytimes.com/2010/07/25/magazine/25privacy-t2.html.

10 Source of quotes: http://classics.mit.edu/Plato/phaedrus.html.

11 www.google.com/about/corporate/company.

12 www.ruanyifeng.com/calvino/2008/12/world_memory_en.html.

13 Google alluded directly to Borges when, on August 24, 2011, it marked the 112th anniversary of the author's birthday on its homepage: www.google.com/logos/logos11-3.html.

14 www.gutenberg.org/files/15000/15000-h/vol1.html.

15 www.bbc.co.uk/pressoffice/pressreleases/stories/2005/05_may/16/imp.shtml.

16 Original video and a collection of other Martini video advertisements are catalogued at: wn.com/martini_ad.

17 Quote is from Nintendo President Satoru Iwata at the first presentation of the Wii remote, as reported by *Gamespot* on September 15, 2005: www.gamespot.com/news/6133389.html.

18 http://elupton.com/2009/10/skin.

19 See for a video report: http://vimeo.com/7815225.

20 www.chrisharrison.net/projects/skinput.

21 www.wright.edu/cola/Dept/PHL/Class/P.Internet/PITexts/QCT.html.

22 www.rogerclarke.com/DV/CACM88.html.

23 http://go.iu.edu/4BE.

24 http://trendwatching.com/trends/LIFE_CACHING.htm.

25 The concept was pioneered in the early 1990s by Steve Mann, who roamed his university's campus with a portable computer hooked up to a digital camera and visor, posting everything he saw live to his website. Source: http://en.wikipedia.org/wiki/Steve_Mann.

26 http://wearcam.org/glogs.htm.

27 www.kk.org/thetechnium/archives/2007/02/lifelogging_an.php.

28 www.reuters.com/article/idUSN0828582220090908.

29 http://eu.techcrunch.com/2010/08/23/germany-to-outlaw-employers-checking-out-job-candidates-on-facebook-but-googling-is-ok.

30 www.youtube.com/watch?v=RR1n_7GN2.

31 www.nytimes.com/2009/03/28/your-money/28shortcuts.html.

32 Full video at: www.colbertnation.com/the-colbert-report-videos/263253/february-02-2010/the-word---cognoscor-ergo-sum.

33 www.getty.edu/art/exhibitions/devices/flash.

34 www.v2.nl/archive/articles/intro-information-is-alive.
35 www.cscs.umich.edu/~crshalizi/LaMettrie/Machine.

4 NO LIFE OUTSIDE MEDIA

1 Jill Magid is quoted here from an interview with Amativa Kumar in his 2010 book *A foreigner carrying in the crook of his arm a tiny bomb*.
2 www.jillmagid.net/LOVE-web.php.
3 www.jillmagid.net/SurveillanceShoe.php.
4 www.notbored.org/the-scp.html.
5 http://guerrillageography.blogspot.com.
6 http://felix.openflows.com/html/priv_surv.html.
7 www.n5m.org/n5m2/media/texts/deleuze.htm.
8 www.readwriteweb.com/archives/top_trends_of_2011_frictionless_sharing.php.
9 See https://www.teensurance.com.
10 Similar arguments are made in greater detail by authors such as Peter Weibel and Slavoj Žižek in in the 2002 "CTRL [SPACE]" exhibition catalogue, published by MIT Press; see http://ctrl-space.zkm.de/e.
11 www.ucl.ac.uk/Bentham-Project/journal/cpwpan.htm.
12 http://cartome.org/panopticon2.htm.
13 http://en.wikipedia.org/wiki/Telescreen.
14 http://en.wikipedia.org/wiki/1984_(advertisement).
15 http://cartome.org/panopticon2.htm.
16 danah boyd makes this comment in a blogpost for the Digital Media and Learning Research Hub at the University of California, Irvine, at http://dmlcentral.net/blog/danah-boyd/public-default-private-when-necessary (published on January 25, 2010).
17 www.123people.com/blog/2011/01/28/international-data-privacy-day-survey-reveals-surprising-and-troubling-consumer-undertones.
18 www.surveillance-studies.net.
19 As reported by *BBC News* on April 4, 2007; http://news.bbc.co.uk/2/hi/uk_news/england/6524495.stm.
20 As reported at *WashingtonCityPaper.com* on July 7, 2006: www.washingtoncitypaper.com/districtline/2006/speakers0707.html.
21 www.itu.int/osg/spu/publications/internetofthings.
22 For these and other RFID and internet-of-things examples, see

science-fiction author Bruce Sterling's blog at *Wired*: www.wired.
com/beyond_the_beyond/category/arphid-watch ("arphid" is a
way to pronounce RFID).

23 www.techforltc.org/product.aspx?id=4477.

24 www.guardian.co.uk/science/2005/jan/16/theobserver.
theobserversuknewspages.

25 www.msnbc.msn.com/id/19904543.

26 www.loe.org/shows/segments.htm?programID=10-P13-
00048&segmentID=2.

27 www.pwc.com/us/en/technology-innovation-center/lifestyle-
media.jhtml.

5 SOCIETY IN MEDIA

1 http://pewresearch.org/pubs/1830/social-networking-computer-
cell-phone-usage-around-the-world.

2 www.comscore.com/Press_Events/Presentations_
Whitepapers/2011/2010_Europe_Digital_Year_in_Review.

3 http://globalwebindex.net

4 www.wired.com/magazine/2010/03/ff_tablet_
essays/4#mcluhan.

5 http://gawker.com/#!5187060/what-kind-of-media-zombie-are-
you.

6 http://mediacartographies.blogspot.com/2010/07/zombie-
media-on-art-methods-and-media.html.

7 www.step-initiative.org; the US partnership is detailed at the EPA
website: www.epa.gov/international/toxics/ewaste.html.

8 www.time.com/time/magazine/article/0,9171,1890384,00.html.

9 www.eurekalert.org/pub_releases/2011-10/esr-uba102611.php.

10 As posted to the Nettime-L mailing list on October 31, 2011,
archived at www.nettime.org/Lists-Archives/nettime-l-1110/
msg00106.html.

11 www.theatlantic.com/technology/archive/2010/06/evaluating-
irans-twitter-revolution/58337.

12 www.time.com/time/world/article/0,8599,2044142,00.html.

13 www.foreignpolicy.com/articles/2011/03/30/the_youtube_
revolutions.

14 www.politicsdaily.com/2011/02/01/mobs-and-democracy-the-
facebook-twitter-youtube-revolution.

15 http://rabble.ca/columnists/2011/11/occupy-movement-making-
world-more-web.

16 http://io9.com/5875897/did-zombie-flash-mobs-help-pave-the-way-for-occupy-wall-street.

17 Daniel Dennett (1999) The zombic hunch: extinction of an intuition? Royal Institute of Philosophy Millennial Lecture; online text at: http://ase.tufts.edu/cogstud/papers/zombic.htm.

18 http://ase.tufts.edu/cogstud/papers/msgisno.htm.

19 http://zombieresearch.org.

20 www.bt.cdc.gov/socialmedia/zombies_blog.asp.

21 www.zombiephiles.com/zombies-ate-my-brains/zombie-outbreak-ten-worst-things-to-do.

22 www.theaa.com/public_affairs/reports/zombie-cyclists.html.

23 "Truthiness" is a word introduced by US comedian Stephen Colbert (meaning, in his words: "truth that comes from the gut, not books"), and was named 2006 Word of the Year by Merriam-Webster: www.merriam-webster.com/info/06words.htm.

24 http://mobithinking.com/mobile-marketing-tools/latest-mobile-stats.

25 www.worldenergyoutlook.org/electricity.asp.

26 Quote from page 9 of the 2008 report, available at: www.educause.edu/ECAR/TheECARStudyofUndergraduateStu/163283.

27 Quote from page 7 of the 2010 report, available at: www.educause.edu/Resources/ECARStudyofUndergraduateStuden/217333.

28 http://news.bbc.co.uk/2/hi/8548190.stm.

29 Report available at: www.contextresearch.com/context/study.cfm.

30 http://blog.vodafone.de/2009/07/08/wer-ist-die-generation-upload.

31 http://trendwatching.com/trends/GENERATION_C.htm.

32 Report available at: http://us.yimg.com/i/adv/tmde_05/truly_madly_final_booklet.pdf.

33 www.dumbestgeneration.com.

34 www.forrester.com/empowered/tool_consumer.html.

35 www.antropologi.info/blog/anthropology/2009/digital-anthropology-report.

36 http://pewinternet.org/topics/Technology-user-types.aspx.

37 www.mediaonderzoek.nl/1295/kobalt-typeert-nieuwe-mediagebruiker.

38 Personal e-mail from Zygmunt Bauman to the author, Monday, June 5, 2006.

39 http://digitalyouth.ischool.berkeley.edu.

40 www.fsf.org.

41 http://p2pfoundation.net/Manifesto.
42 www.forthehack.com/press-release-engagement-thats-all.
43 http://icanstalku.com/why.php.
44 www.weliveinpublicthemovie.com.
45 http://weliveinpublic.blog.indiepixfilms.com/category/theatrical-release.
46 www.crockford.com/ec/lessons.html.
47 www.medialabmadrid.org/medialab/medialab.php?l=0&a=a&i=329.
48 www.egs.edu/faculty/jean-baudrillard/articles/simulacra-and-simulations-xviii-on-nihilism.

6 TOGETHER ALONE

1 A news report by David Quick for Australian rural newspaper *Lakes Mail* (published on May 26, 2011): www.lakesmail.com.au/news/local/news/general/silent-disco-is-a-big-hit/2176032.aspx.
2 http://silentdisco.com/v2/about-2.
3 http://edition.cnn.com/2005/TECH/09/01/spark.disco/index.html.
4 http://subtlemob.com/?p=21.
5 http://londonist.com/2009/11/review_subtlemob.php.
6 Quote from an interview with blogger Jeff Watson (published October 7, 2010), at http://remotedevice.net/blog/subtlemob-creator-duncan-speakman-on-framing-everyday-realities.
7 http://improveverywhere.com/missions/the-mp3-experiments.
8 www.nytimes.com/2009/03/29/opinion/29venkatesh.html
9 http://en.wikipedia.org/wiki/Dancing_with_Myself.
10 The version I use is its 2003 translation by George Martin Duncan: www.marxists.org/reference/subject/philosophy/works/ge/leibniz.htm.
11 http://davidbacker.com/2011/06/11/english-translation-of-gabriel-tardes-monadology-and-sociology.
12 http://3dvzcam.com.
13 www.telegeography.com.
14 http://en.wikipedia.org/wiki/Eggtown.
15 http://en.wikipedia.org/wiki/The_End_(Lost).
16 www.openstreetmap.org.
17 www.nytimes.com/2009/02/17/science/17map.html.
18 http://ogleearth.com/2012/01/google-conspiring-for-regime-change-in-syria-through-maps-hardly.

19 www.realityprime.com/articles/notes-on-the-origin-of-google-earth.
20 www.egs.edu/faculty/jean-baudrillard/articles/simulacra-and-simulations.
21 www.imdb.com/title/tt0133093/quotes.
22 http://en.wikipedia.org/wiki/The_Man_Without_Qualities.
23 http://writing.upenn.edu/~afilreis/88/stein-atom-bomb.html.
24 http://lindastone.net/qa/continuous-partial-attention.
25 www.edge.org.
26 www.edge.org/q2010/q10_2.html#dysone.

7 IN MEDIA WE FIT

1 www.intel.com/pressroom/archive/releases/2008/20081215corp.htm.
2 www.aarp.org/relationships/love-sex/info-11-2009/sexting_not_just_for_kids.html.
3 www.wikipatents.com/US-Patent-3875932/audiotactile-stimulation-and-communications-system.
4 www.stenslie.net/stahl/txt/cyberotics.html.
5 Quote taken from the 1986 song "Orgasmatron" by UK metal outfit Motörhead; http://lyrics.rockmagic.net/lyrics/motorhead/orgasmatron_1986.html.
6 http://en.wikipedia.org/wiki/EXistenZ.
7 http://splicedwire.com/features/cronenberg.html.
8 www.imdb.com/title/tt0106697/quotes.
9 The link between Schopenhauer and Kafka is established in the introduction of Joyce Crick's translation of several of Kafka's stories (2009b: xxvi). Schopenhauer's original essay is available online, and directly accessible at http://ebooks.adelaide.edu.au/s/schopenhauer/arthur/pessimism/chapter1.html.
10 www.msnbc.msn.com/id/23749828.
11 www.lifeshortgetadivorce.com.
12 www.wtfisupwithmylovelife.com.
13 www.huffingtonpost.com/jessica-massa/youre-online-dating-and-y_b_705548.html.
14 www.gmi-mr.com.
15 Full report at: http://cp.match.com/cppp/media/CMB_Study.pdf.
16 www.psychologicalscience.org/index.php/publications/journals/pspi/online-dating.html.
17 http://blog.okcupid.com/index.php/the-biggest-lies-in-online-dating.

18 www.goodworkproject.org/research/dm2.
19 www.bl.uk/digital-lives.
20 www.bilin-village.org/english/articles/testimonies/Bilin-weekly-demonstration-reenacts-the-Avatar-film.
21 http://newsblaze.com/story/20100209133850zzzz.nb/topstory.html.
22 www.huffingtonpost.com/nikolas-kozloff/talking-the-amazon-with-c_b_571326.html.
23 http://amazonwatch.org/news/2011/0623-james-cameron-warns-of-violence-over-brazil-dam.
24 www.eiu.org/experiments/i-bomb.
25 www.facebook.com/press/info.php?statistics.
26 www.nytimes.com/2008/09/07/magazine/07awareness-t.html.
27 www.economist.com/node/13176775?story_id=13176775.
28 www.disambiguity.com/ambient-intimacy.
29 http://jcmc.indiana.edu/vol13/issue1/donath.html.

8 LIFE IN MEDIA

1 See also www.we-make-money-not-art.com/archives/2011/07/see-yourself-sensing-redefinin.php.
2 www.forbes.com/forbes/2007/0507/176.html.
3 http://konrath.socialpsychology.org.
4 www.g4tv.com/videos/44277/dice-2010-design-outside-the-box-presentation.
5 Andrew Niccol's *Truman Show* script is available at www.imsdb.com/scripts/Truman-Show,-The.html.
6 See URL: www.seasidefl.com.
7 See URL: www.reellifewisdom.com/reality_we_accept_the_reality_of_the_world_with_which_we_are_presented.
8 http://en.wikipedia.org/wiki/The_Truman_Show_delusion.
9 Source URL: www.webmd.com/mental-health/features/truman-show-delusion-real-imagined?page=2.
10 Source URL: www.apa.org/monitor/2009/06/delusion.html.
11 http://bjp.rcpsych.org/cgi/eletters/193/2/168.
12 Ian Gold in a phone interview with the author (recorded on March 7, 2011).
13 www.nytimes.com/2010/09/15/movies/15woody.html.
14 http://en.wikipedia.org/wiki/Best_of_all_possible_worlds.
15 http://jubal.westnet.com/hyperdiscordia/universal_library.html.
16 http://library.nothingness.org/articles/SI/en/display/67.

References

Aguado, Juan Miguel (2009) Self-observation, self-reference and operational coupling in social systems: steps towards a coherent epistemology of mass media. *Empedocles* 1(1), 59–74.

Altheide, David (1984) The media self. In: A. Fontana and J. Kotarba (eds.), *The existential self in society*, 476–90. Chicago: University of Chicago Press.

Altheide, David, and Robert Snow (1991) *Media worlds in the postjournalism era*. New York: Walter de Gruyter.

Anderson, Benedict (2006[1983]) *Imagined communities*. London: Verso.

Andrejevic, Mark (2002) The work of being watched: interactive media and the exploitation of self-disclosure. *Critical Studies in Media Communication* 19(2), 230–48.

Andrejevic, Mark (2009) *iSpy: surveillance and power in the interactive era*. Lawrence: University Press of Kansas.

Ang, Ien (1995) *Living room wars*. London: Routledge.

Appadurai, Arjun (1990) Disjuncture and difference in the global cultural economy. *Public Culture* 2(2), 1–24.

Apter, Michael (1992) *Dangerous edge: the psychology of excitement*. New York: Free Press.

Arendt, Hannah (1998[1958]) *The human condition*. Chicago: University of Chicago Press.

Arminen, Ilkka (2007) Mobile communication society? *Acta Sociologica* 50(4), 431–37.

Arthur, W. Brian (2009) *The nature of technology*. New York: Focal Press.

Auster, Paul (1990[1986]) *The New York trilogy*. New York: Penguin.

Back, Mitja, Juliane M. Stopfer, Simine Vazire, et al. (2010) Facebook profiles reflect actual personality, not self-idealization. *Psychological Science* 21(3), 372–74.

Barad, Karen (2004) Posthumanist performativity. *Signs* 28(3), 801–31.

Barad, Karen (2007) *Meeting the universe halfway*. Durham: Duke University Press.

Bargh, John, and Katelyn McKenna (2004) The internet and social life. *Annual Review of Psychology* 55(1), 573–90.

Bargh, John, Katelyn McKenna and Grainne Fitzsimons (2002) Can you see the real me? Activation and expression of the "true self" on the internet. *Journal of Social Issues* 58(1), 33–48.

Baudrillard, Jean (1998[1981]) Simulacra and simulations. In: Mark Poster (ed.), *Jean Baudrillard, selected writings*, 166–84. Palo Alto: Stanford University Press.

Bauman, Zygmunt (2000) *Liquid modernity*. Cambridge: Polity.

Bauman, Zygmunt (2004) *Identity*. Cambridge: Polity.

Bauman, Zygmunt (2005) *Liquid life*. Cambridge: Polity.

Bauman, Zygmunt (2007) *The consuming life*. Cambridge: Polity.

Bauman, Zygmunt (2009) *The art of life*. Cambridge: Polity.

Bauman, Zygmunt (2010) *44 letters from the liquid modern world*. Cambridge: Polity.

Bausinger, Hermann (1984) Media, technology and daily life. *Media, Culture & Society* 6, 343–51.

Baym, Nancy (2010) *Personal connections in the digital age*. Cambridge: Polity.

Beck, Ulrich (1992[1986]) *Risk society*. London: Sage.

Beck, Ulrich (2000) *The brave new world of work*. Cambridge: Polity.

Beck, Ulrich (2002) *Power and countervailing power in the global age*. Cambridge: Polity.

Beck, Ulrich (2009[2007]) *World at risk*. Cambridge: Polity.

Bell, Gordon, and Jim Gemmell (2006) MyLifeBits: a personal database for everything. *Communications of the ACM* 49(1), 88–95.

Benhabib, Seyla (1992) *Situating the self*. Cambridge: Polity.

Bennett, Jane (2010) *Vibrant matter*. Durham: Duke University Press.

Bennett, Sue, Karl Maton and Lisa Kervin (2008) The "digital natives" debate: a critical review of the evidence. *British Journal of Educational Technology* 39(5), 775–86.

Benthien, Claudia (2002) *Skin*. New York: Columbia University Press.

Best, Kirsty (2010) Living in the control society. *International Journal of Cultural Studies* 13(1), 5–24.

Bijker, Wiebe, Thomas Hughes and Trevor Pinch (eds.) (1989) *The social construction of technological systems*. Cambridge, MA: MIT Press.

Boase, Jeffrey (2008) Personal networks and the personal communication system. *Information, Communication & Society* 11(4), 490–508.

Bolter, Jay, and Richard Grusin (1996) Remediation. *Configurations* 4(3), 311–58.

Borges, Jorge Luis (1998[1944]) The Aleph. In: *The Aleph and other stories*, 118–33. New York: Penguin.

Borges, Jorge Luis (2000[1941]) The library of Babel. In: *Fictions*, 65–74. New York: Penguin.

Briggs, Asa, and Peter Burke (2009) *A social history of the media*. Cambridge: Polity.

Brownell, Blaine (2011) *Matter in the floating world*. New York: Princeton Architectural Press.

Buckingham, David (2000) *After the death of childhood: growing up in the age of electronic media*. Cambridge: Polity.

Bull, Michael (2005) No dead air! The iPod and the culture of mobile listening. *Leisure Studies* 24(4), 343–55.

Bull, Michael (2006) Investigating the culture of mobile listening. In: Kenton O'Hara and Barry Brown (eds.), *Consuming music together*, 131–50. Dordrecht: Springer.

Calvino, Italo (1993[1985]) *Six memos for the next millennium*. New York: Vintage.

Canguilhem, Georges (1992[1947]) Machine and organism. In: Jonathan Crary and Sanford Kwinter (eds.), *Incorporations*, 45–69. New York: Zone.

Cardoso, Gustavo, Angus Cheong and Jeffrey Cole (eds.) (2010) *World Wide internet: changing societies, economies and cultures*. Macau: University of Macau.

Carey, James (1989) *Communication as culture: essays on media and society*. Boston: Unwin Hyman.

Cartmill, Matt (1993) *A view to a death in the morning: hunting and nature through history*. Cambridge, MA: Harvard University Press.

Casares, Adolfo Bioy (2003[1940]) *The invention of Morel*. New York: New York Review Books.

Castells, M. (2010[1996]) *The rise of the network society*. Malden: Blackwell.

Castronova, Ted (2005) *Synthetic worlds*. Chicago: University of Chicago Press.

Chayko, Mary (2008). *Portable communities*. Albany: SUNY Press.

Clarke, Arthur C. (1964) *Profiles of the future*. New York: Bantam.

Clynes, Manfred, and Nathan Kline (1995[1960]) Cyborgs and space. In: Chris Gray (ed.), *The cyborg handbook*, 29–34. New York: Routledge.

Coleman, Beth (2011) *Hello avatar*. Cambridge, MA: MIT Press.

Coleman, Leo (2009) Being alone together: from solidarity to solitude in urban anthropology. *Anthropological Quarterly* 82(3), 755–78.

Couldry, Nick, and Anna McCarthy (eds.) (2004) *Media/space*. London: Routledge.

Crampton, Jeremy (2001) Maps as social constructs: power, communication and visualization. *Progress in Human Geography* 25(2), 235–52.

Crampton, Jeremy (2009) Cartography: performative, participatory, political. *Progress in Human Geography* 33(6), 840–8.

Cubitt, Sean (2005) *Eco media*. Amsterdam: Rodopi.

Davis, Erik (1999) *Techgnosis*. London: Serpent's Tail.

De Botton, Alain (2001) *The consolations of philosophy*. London: Penguin.

De Jong, Alex, and Marc Schuilenburg (2006) *Mediapolis*. Rotterdam: 010 Publishers.

De Landa, Manuel (2006) *A new philosophy of society*. New York: Continuum.

De Mul, Jos (2009) The work of art in the age of digital recombination. In: Marianne van den Boomen, Sybille Lammes, Ann-Sophie Lehmann, Joost Raessens and Mirko Tobias Schäfer (eds.), *Digital material*, 95–106. Amsterdam: Amsterdam University Press.

De Mul, Jos (2010) *Cyberspace odyssey*. Newcastle upon Tyne: Cambridge Scholars Publishing.

De Souza e Silva, Adriana (2004) From simulations to hybrid space: how nomadic technologies change the real. *Technoetic Arts* 1(3), 209–21.

De Souza e Silva, Adriana, and Daniel Sutko (eds.) (2009) *Digital cityscapes*. New York: Peter Lang.

De Zengotita, Thomas (2005) *Mediated*. New York: Bloomsbury.

Dennett, Daniel (1996) *Darwin's dangerous idea*. New York: Touchstone.

Dessalles, Jean-Louis (2009) *Why we talk*. Oxford: Oxford University Press.

Dick, Philip K. (1987) *The Philip K. Dick reader*. New York: Citadel Press.

DiMaggio, Paul, Eszter Hargittai, Russell Neuman and John Robinson (2001) Social implications of the internet. *Annual Review of Sociology* 27(1), 307–36.

Donath, Judith (2007) Signals in social supernets. *Journal of Computer-Mediated Communication* 13(1), article 12.

Dourish, Paul, and Genevieve Bell (2011) *Divining a digital future*. Cambridge, MA: MIT Press.

Downing, David (2007) Paranoiac visions and neo-realities in the recent cinema. *Psychoanalytic Review* 94(6), 991–1006.

Doyle, Richard (2003) *Wetwares*. Minneapolis: University of Minnesota Press.

Dunbar, Robin (1998) *Grooming, gossip, and the evolution of language*. Cambridge, MA: Harvard University Press.

Dunbar, Robin (2003) The social brain: mind, language, and society in evolutionary perspective. *Annual Review of Anthropology* 32, 163–81.

Durkheim, Émile (1997[1893]) *The division of labor in society*. New York: Free Press.

Dyens, Ollivier (2001) *Metal and flesh*. Cambridge, MA: MIT Press.

Dyson, George B. (1997) *Darwin among the machines*. New York: Perseus Books.

Eckardt, Frank, Jens Geelhaar, Laura Colini, Katherine Willis, Konstantinos Chorianopoulos and Ralf Hennig (eds.) (2008) *MEDIACITY: situations, practices and encounters*. Berlin: Frank & Timme.

Eco, Umberto (1995[1982]) On the impossibility of drawing a map of the Empire on a scale of 1 to 1. In: *How to travel with a salmon*, 95–106. New York: Harcourt.

Eco, Umberto (1998[1983]) The multiplication of the media. In: *Faith in fakes*, 145–50. New York: Vintage.

Eerikäinen, Hannu (1998) Cybersex. In: Sam Inkinen (ed.), *Mediapolis: aspects of texts, hypertext and multimedial communication*, 203–42. New York: Walter de Gruyter.

Eerikäinen, Hannu (2001) Love your prosthesis like yourself. In: Anu Koivunen and Susanna Paasonen (eds.), *Affective encounters*, 55–74. Turku: University of Turku.

Elchardus, Mark (2009) Self-control as social control: the emergence of symbolic society. *Poetics* 37, 146–61.

Ellis, Brett Easton (1991) *American psycho*. New York: Picador.

Ellul, Jacques (1964[1954]) *The technological society*. New York: Vintage Books.

Elmer, Greg (2004) *Profiling machines*. Cambridge, MA: MIT Press.

Erikson, Kai (2004[1966]) *Wayward puritans: a study in the sociology of deviance*. Boston: Allyn & Bacon.

Ernest-Jones, Max, Daniel Nettle and Melissa Bateson (2010) Effects of eye images on everyday cooperative behavior. *Evolution and Human Behavior* 32(3), 172–8.

Fidler, Roger (1997) *Mediamorphosis: understanding new media*. Thousand Oaks: Pine Forge Press.

Firestone, Matthew (2008) *Lonely Planet Tokyo city guide*. London: Lonely Planet.

Florida, Richard (2002) *The rise of the creative class*. New York: Perseus.

Floridi, Luciano (2007) A look into the future impact of ICT on our lives. *The Information Society* 23, 59–64.

Flusser, Vilém (1990) On memory (electronic or otherwise). *Leonardo* 23(4), 397–9.

Flusser, Vilém (2002[1993]) The future of writing. *Yale Journal of Criticism* 6(2); reprinted in Andres Ströhl (ed.), *Writings*, 63–9. Minneapolis: University of Minnesota Press.

Fortunati, Leopoldina (2001) The mobile phone: an identity on the move. *Personal and Ubiquitous Computing* 5, 85–98.

Fortunati, Leopoldina (2005) Is body-to-body communication still the prototype? *The Information Society* 21, 53–61.

Fortunati, Leopoldina (2009) Theories without heart. In: A. Esposito and R. Vích (eds.), *Cross-modal analysis*, 5–17. Berlin: Springer-Verlag.

Foucault, Michel (1995[1975]) *Discipline and punish*. New York: Vintage.

Foucault, Michel (1984) On the genealogy of ethics. In: Paul Rabinow (ed.), *The Foucault reader*, 340–72. London: Penguin Books.

Fraser, Matthew, and Soumitra Dutta (2008) *Throwing sheep into the boardroom*. Malden: Wiley.

Freeman, Eric (1997). The Lifestreams software architecture. Doctoral dissertation, Yale University. Available at www.cs.yale.edu/homes/freeman/dissertation/etf.pdf.

Freud, Sigmund (1961[1930]) *Civilization and its discontents*. New York: W.W. Norton & Company.

Friesen, Norm, and Theo Hug (2009) The mediatic turn. In: Knut Lundby (ed.), *Mediatization*, 64–81. New York: Peter Lang.

Fuchs, Christian (2008) *Internet and society: social theory in the information age*. London: Routledge.

Fukuyama, Francis (1996) *The end of history and the last man*. New York: Free Press.

Fulk, Janet (1993) The social construction of communication technology. *Academy of Management Journal* 36(5), 921–50.

Funkhouser, Ray, and Eugene Shaw (1990) How synthetic experience shapes social reality. *Journal of Communication* 40(2), 75–87.

Fusar-Poli, Paolo, with Oliver Howes, Lucia Valmaggia, Philip McGuire (2008) "Truman" signs and vulnerability to psychosis. *British Journal of Psychiatry* 193, 168.

Gadamer, Hans-Georg (1997[1973]) *Gadamer on Celan*. Albany: SUNY Press.

Gane, Nicholas (2006) Speed up or slow down? Social theory in the information age. *Information, Communication & Society* 9(1), 20–38.

Gane, Nicholas, and David Beer (2008) *New media*. Oxford: Berg.

Garnham, Nicholas (1997) Amartya Sen's "capabilities" approach to the evaluation of welfare and its application to communications. *Javnost / The Public* 4(4), 25–34.

Gauntlett, David (2011) *Making is connecting*. Cambridge: Polity.

Gergen, Kenneth (1992) *The saturated self*. New York: Basic Books.

Giddens, Anthony (1991) *Modernity and self-identity*. Stanford: Stanford University Press.

Giddens, Anthony (2003[1999]) *Runaway world*. London: Routledge.

Gitelman, Lisa (2006) *Always already new: media, history, and the data of culture*. Cambridge, MA: MIT Press.

Golub, Alex (2010) Being in the world (of warcraft). *Anthropological Quarterly* 83(1), 17–45.

Gordon, Eric, and Gene Koo (2008) Placeworlds. *Space & Culture* 11(3), 204–21.

Grahame-Smith, Seth (2009) *Pride and prejudice and zombies*. Philadelphia: Quirk Books.

Gray, Mary (2007) Face value. *Contexts* 6(2), 73–5.

Green, Stephen (1999) A plague on the Panopticon. *Information, Communication & Society* 2(1), 26–44.

Greenfield, Susan (2009) *Tomorrow's people: how 21st-century technology is changing the way we think and feel*. London: Penguin.

Grossberg, Lawrence (1988) Wandering audiences, nomadic critics. *Cultural Studies* 2(3), 377–91.

Grusin, Richard, and Jay Bolter (2004) Premediation. *Criticism* 46(1), 17–39.

Habermas, Jürgen (1985[1981]) *The theory of communicative action*, volume II: *Lifeworld and system*. Boston: Beacon.

Habuchi, Ichiyo (2005) Accelerating reflexivity. In: Mizuko Ito, Daisuke Okabe and Misa Matsuda (eds.), *Personal, portable, pedestrian: mobile phones in Japanese life*. Cambridge, MA: MIT Press.

Hansen, Mark (2003) Affect as medium. *Journal of Visual Culture* 2(2), 205–28.

Haraway, Donna (1990) *Simians, cyborgs, and women*. London: Routledge.

Hardt, Michael, and Antonio Negri (2000) *Empire*. Cambridge, MA: Harvard University Press.

Harper, Richard, Abigail Sellen, Tim Kindberg, Phil Gosett and Kaisa Väänänen-Vainio-Mattila (2004) The myth of the Martini solution. In: Stephen Brewster and Mark Dunlop (eds.), *MobileHCI*, 536–37. Berlin: Springer.

Hart, Keith (2009) An anthropologist in the world revolution. *Anthropology Today* 26(6), 24–5.

Hartley, John (2000) Communicational democracy in a redactional society. *Journalism* 1(1), 39–47.

Hartley, John (2007) "There are other ways of being in the truth": the uses of multimedia literacy. *International Journal of Cultural Studies* 10(1), 135–44.

Harvey, David (1990) *The condition of postmodernity*. Malden: Blackwell.

Hay, James, and Jeremy Packer (2004) Crossing the media(n). In: Nick

Couldry and Anna McCarthy (eds.), *Media/Space*, 209–32. London: Routledge.

Hayles, N. Katherine (1999) *How we became posthuman*. Chicago: University of Chicago Press.

Hayles, N. Katherine (2009) Waking up to the surveillance society. *Surveillance & Society* 6(3), 313–16.

Hayles, N. Katherine (2012) *How we think: digital media and contemporary technogenesis*. Chicago: University of Chicago Press.

Heinlein, Robert A. (2004[1959]) All you zombies. In: Orson Scott Card (ed.), *Masterpieces: the best science fiction of the twentieth century*, 36–46. New York: Ace.

Hjarvard, Stig (2008) The mediatization of society. *Nordicom Review* 29(2), 105–34.

Hobsbawn, Eric, and Terence Ranger (1992[1983]) *The invention of tradition*. Cambridge: Cambridge University Press.

Hoffmann, E. T. A. (1992[1816]) The sandman. In: *The golden pot and other tales*, 85–118. Oxford: Oxford University Press.

Hofkirchner, Wolfgang, Christian Fuchs and Bert Klauninger (2005) Informational universe: a praxeo-onto-epistemological approach. In: Eeva Martikainen (ed.), *Human approaches to the universe*, 75–94. Helsinki: Luther-Agricola-Seura.

Honoré, Carl (2008) *Under pressure: rescuing our children from the culture of hyper-parenting*. New York: HarperOne.

Huhtamo, Erkki (1997) From kaleidoscomaniac to cybernerd: notes toward an archaeology of media. *Leonardo* 30(3), 221–4.

Husserl, Edmund (1970[1936]). *The crisis of European sciences and transcendental phenomenology*. Chicago: Northwestern University Press.

Huysmans, Frank, and Jos de Haan (2010) *Alle kanalen staan open: de digitalisering van mediagebruik*. Den Haag: SCP.

Ihde, Don (1990) *Technology and the lifeworld: from Garden to Earth*. Bloomington: Indiana University Press.

Illouz, Eva (1997) *Consuming the romantic utopia: love and the cultural contradictions of capitalism*. Berkeley: University of California Press.

Inglehart, Ronald (1997) *Modernization and postmodernization*. Princeton: Princeton University Press.

Inglehart, Ronald (2008) Changing values among Western publics from 1970 to 2006. *West European Politics* 31(1–2), 130–46.

Ishii, Kenichi (2006) Implications of mobility: the uses of personal communication media in everyday life. *Journal of Communication* 56, 346–65.

Ito, Mizuko (2005) Technologies of the childhood imagination: Yugioh, media mixes, and everyday cultural production. In: Joe Karaganis and Natalie Jeremijenko (eds.), *Structures of participation in digital culture*. Durham: Duke University Press.

Jacobs, Katrien, Marije Janssen and Matteo Pasquinelli (eds.) (2007) *C'lick me: a netporn studies reader*. Amsterdam: Institute for Network Cultures.

Jameson, Fredric (1991) *Postmodernism*. Durham: Duke University Press.

Jenkins, Henry (2004) The cultural logic of media convergence. *International Journal of Cultural Studies* 7(1), 33–43.

Jenkins, Henry (2006) *Convergence culture*. New York: New York University Press.

Jenkins, Henry, Katie Clinton, Ravi Purushotma, Alice Robison and Margaret Weigel (2006) *Confronting the challenges of participatory culture*. Chicago: MacArthur Foundation.

Jensen, Jakob Linaa (2007) The internet omnopticon. In: Henrik Bang and Anders Esmark (eds.), *New publics with/out democracy*, 351–80. Frederiksberg: Samfundslitteratur Press.

Johnson, Steven (1997) *Interface culture*. New York: Perseus Books.

Jung, Heekyoung, Youngsuk Altieri and Jeffrey Bardzell (2010) SKIN: designing aesthetic interactive surfaces. In: *Proceedings of the 4th International Conference on Tangible, Embedded, and Embodied Interaction*, 85–92. New York: ACM.

Kafka, Franz (2009[1914]) In the penal colony. In: *The metamorphosis and other stories*, 75–99. Oxford: Oxford University Press.

Katz, James, and Mark Aakhus (eds.) (2003) *Perpetual contact: mobile communication, private talk, public performance*. Cambridge: Cambridge University Press.

Kelly, Kevin (2010) *What technology wants*. New York: Viking.

Kiran, Asle, and Peter-Paul Verbeek (2010) Trusting our selves to technology. *Knowledge, Technology & Policy* 23(3–4), 409–27.

Kittler, Friedrich (1996[1988]) The city is a medium. *New Literary History* 27(4), 717–29.

Kittler, Friedrich (1999[1985]) *Gramophone, film, typewriter*. Palo Alto: Stanford University Press.

Kittler, Friedrich (2009) Towards an ontology of media. *Theory, Culture & Society* 26(2–3), 23–31.

Knorr Cetina, Karin (1997) Sociality with objects: social relations in postsocial knowledge societies. *Theory, Culture & Society* 14(4), 1–30.

Koskela, Hille (2000) "The gaze without eyes": video-surveillance and the changing nature of urban space. *Progress in Human Geography* 24(2), 243–65.

Krahmann, Elke (2010) *States, citizens and the privatization of security*. Cambridge: Cambridge University Press.

Krämer, Sybille (1998) Das Medium als Spur und als Apparat. In: Sybille Krämer (ed.), *Medien, Computer, Realität*, 73–94. Frankfurt am Main: Suhrkamp.

Lash, Scott (2001) Technological forms of life. *Theory Culture Society* 18(1), 105–20.

Lash, Scott (2002) *Critique of information*. London: Sage.

Lash, Scott (2010) *Intensive culture*. London: Sage.

Latour, Bruno (1993[1991]) *We have never been modern*. Trans. Catherine Porter. Cambridge, MA: Harvard University Press.

Lauro, Sarah, and Karen Embry (2008) A zombie manifesto. *boundary 2* 35(1), 85–108.

Leakey, Richard (1996) *The origin of humankind*. New York: Basic Books.

Lefebvre, Henri (1987) The everyday and everydayness. *Yale French Studies* 73, 7–11.

Lefebvre, Henri (1991[1974]) *The production of space*. Malden: Blackwell.

Levinson, Paul (2009) *New new media*. Boston: Allyn & Bacon.

Lévy, Pierre (1997) *Collective intelligence: mankind's emerging world in cyberspace*. New York: Perseus.

Lewis, Thomas, Fari Amini and Richard Lannon (2001) *A general theory of love*. New York: Vintage.

Licoppe, Christian (2009) Recognizing mutual "proximity" at a distance: weaving together mobility, sociality and technology. *Journal of Pragmatics* 41(10), 1924–37.

Lievrouw, Leah, and Sonia Livingstone (eds.) (2004) *Handbook of new media*. London: Sage.

Livingstone, Sonia (2002) *Young people and new media: childhood and the changing media environment*. London: Sage.

Livingstone, Sonia (2009) On the mediation of everything. *Journal of Communication* 59(1), 1–18.

Luhmann, Niklas (2000[1996]) *The reality of the mass media*. Cambridge: Polity.

Lupton, Ellen (2002) *Skin: surface, substance and design*. New York: Princeton Architectural Press.

Lyon, David (2001) *Surveillance society: monitoring everyday life*. Milton Keynes: Open University Press.

Lyon, David (2007) *Surveillance studies*. Cambridge: Polity.

Lyotard, Jean-François (1984) *The postmodern condition*. Minneapolis: University of Minnesota Press.

Manovich, Lev (2009) The practice of everyday (media) life. *Critical Inquiry* 35, 319–31.

Martin, Gus (ed.) (2010) *Terrorism and homeland security*. London: Sage.

Massey, Doreen (2005) *For space*. London: Sage.

Massey, Doreen (2007) *World city*. Cambridge: Polity.

Massumi, Brian (2002) *Parables for the virtual: movement, affect, sensation*. Durham: Duke University Press.

Mathiesen, Thomas (1997) The viewer society: Michel Foucault's "Panopticon" revisited. *Theoretical Criminology* 1(2), 215–34.

Mattelart, Armand (2010[2007]) *The globalization of surveillance*. Cambridge: Polity.

Mayer-Schönberger, Victor (2009) *Delete: the virtue of forgetting in the digital age*. Princeton: Princeton University Press.

McCall, Cade, and Jim Blascovich (2009) How, when, and why to use digital experimental virtual environments to study social behavior. *Social and Personality Psychology Compass* 3(5), 744–58.

McCarthy, Tom (2007) *Remainder*. New York: Vintage.

McCullough, Malcolm (2005) *Digital ground*. Cambridge, MA: MIT Press.

McGlotten, Shaka (2011) Dead and live life: zombies, queers, and online sociality. In: Stephanie Boluk and Wylie Lenz (eds.), *Generation zombie*, 182–93. Jefferson, NC: McFarland.

McKenna, Katelyn, and John Bargh (2000) Plan 9 from cyberspace: the implications of the internet for personality and social psychology. *Personality and Social Psychology Review* 4(1), 57–75.

McLuhan, Marshall (2004 [1964]) *Understanding media*. Cambridge, MA: MIT Press.

McLuhan, Marshall, and Quentin Fiore (1967) *The medium is the massage*. New York: Touchstone.

Meloy, Stuart, and Joan Southern (2009) Neurally augmented sexual function in human females. *Neuromodulation* 9(1), 34–40.

Merleau-Ponty, Maurice (2004[1948]) *The world of perception*. London: Routledge.

Miller, Daniel (2011). *Tales from Facebook*. Cambridge: Polity.

Miller, Daniel, and Mirca Madianou (2012) *Technologies of love*. London: Routledge.

Miller, George (1983) Informavores. In: Fritz Machlup and Una Mansfield (eds.), *The study of information*, 111–13. Malden: Wiley.

Miller, Vincent (2008) New media, networking and phatic culture. *Convergence* 14(4), 387–400.

Miller, Vincent (2010) Mapping and the colonization of the lifeworld. *Lo Squaderno* 15, 21–5.

Minsky, Marvin (2006) *The emotion machine.* New York: Simon & Schuster.

Mitchell, William (2004) *Me++.* Cambridge, MA: MIT Press.

Miyata, Kakuko, Barry Wellman and Jeffrey Boase (2005) The wired – and wireless – Japanese. In: Rich Ling and Per Pedersen (eds.), *Mobile communications*, 427–50. Berlin: Springer.

Montgomery, Kathryn (2007) *Generation digital.* Cambridge, MA: MIT Press.

Moore, Charles (2004[1967]) Plug it in, Rameses, and see if it lights up, because we aren't going to keep it unless it works. In: Kevin Keim (ed.), *You have to pay for the public life*, 151–61. Cambridge, MA: MIT Press.

Moores, Shaun (2005) *Media/theory.* London: Sage.

Morley, David (2007) *Media, modernity and technology.* London: Routledge.

Mumford, Lewis (1961) *The city in history.* New York: Harcourt.

Naaman, Mor, Jeffrey Boase and Chih-Hui Lai (2010) Is it really about me? In: *Proceedings of the 2010 ACM Conference on Computer Supported Cooperative Work.* New York: ACM.

Naish, John (2008) *Enough.* London: Hodder & Stoughton.

Nass, Clifford, and Youngme Moon (2000) Machines and mindlessness: social responses to computers. *Journal of Social Issues* 56(1), 81–103.

Neff, Gina, and David Stark (2004) Permanently beta. In: Leah Lievrouw and Sonia Livingstone (eds.) (2004) *Handbook of new media*, 173–88. London: Sage.

Newman, Michael (2010) New media, young audiences and discourses of attention. *Media, Culture & Society* 32(4), 581–96.

Nietzsche, Friedrich (1997[1890]) The Dionysian worldview. Trans. Claudia Crawford. *Journal of Nietzsche Studies* 13(1), 81–97.

Noll, Michael (2006) *The evolution of media.* Lanham: Rowman & Littlefield.

Norris, Pippa (2002) The bridging and bonding role of online communities. *Harvard International Journal of Press/Politics* 7(3), 3–13.

Nowak, Martin, and Karl Sigmund (2005) Evolution of indirect reciprocity. *Nature* 437, 1291–8.

Ohanian, Melik, and Jean-Christophe Royoux (2005) *Cosmograms.* New York: Lukas & Sternberg.

Ong, Walter (1982) *Orality and literacy.* London: Routledge.

Ophir, Eyal, Clifford Nass and Anthony Wagner (2009) Cognitive control in media multitaskers. *PNAS* 106(37), 15583–7.

Palfrey, John, and Urs Gasser (2008) *Born digital*. New York: Basic Books.

Papacharissi, Zizi (2010) *A private sphere: democracy in a digital age*. Cambridge: Polity.

Papacharissi, Zizi (ed.) (2011) *A networked self*. London: Routledge.

Parikka, Jussi (2010) *Insect media*. Minneapolis: University of Minnesota Press.

Perry, Mark, and Jackie Brodie (2005) Virtually connected, practically mobile. In: Erik Andriesson and Matti Vartiainen (eds.), *Mobile virtual work*, 97–127. Berlin: Springer.

Pinch, Trevor (2010) The invisible technologies of Goffman's sociology. *Technology and Culture* 51(2), 409–24.

Pirandello, Luigi (1990[1925–6]) *One, no one and one hundred thousand*. New York: Marsilio Publishers.

Poe, Edgar Allen (1981[1839]) The man that was used up. In: *The complete tales of mystery and imagination*, 364–70. London: Octopus Books.

Poster, Mark (1990) *The mode of information*. Cambridge: Polity.

Poster, Mark (1999) Underdetermination. *New Media & Society* 1(1), 12–17.

Poster, Mark (2004) The information empire. *Comparative Literature Studies* 41(3), 317–34.

Postman, Neil (1986) *Amusing ourselves to death*. New York: Penguin.

Purcell, Patrick (ed.) (2006) *Networked neighbourhoods*. Berlin: Springer.

Quandt, Thorsten, and Thilo von Pape (2010) Living in the mediatope. *The Information Society* 26(5), 330–45.

Qvortrup, Lars (2003) *The hypercomplex society*. New York: Peter Lang.

Rasmussen, Terje (2003) On distributed society. In: Gunnar Liestøl, Andrew Morrison and Terje Rasmussen, (eds.), *Digital media revisited*, 445–68. Cambridge, MA: MIT Press.

Reder, Sheri, Gwen Ambler, Matthai Philipose and Susan Hedrick (2010) Technology and Long-term Care (TLC): a pilot evaluation of remote monitoring of elders. *Gerontechnology* 9(1), 18–31.

Reeves, Byron, and Clifford Nass (1996) *The media equation*. Stanford: CSLI Publications.

Rejali, Darius (2009) *Torture and democracy*. New York: Princeton Architectural Press.

Resnick, Paul, Richard Zeckhauser, Eric Friedman and Ko Kuwabara (2000) Reputation systems: facilitating trust in internet interactions. *Communications of the ACM* 43(12), 45–8.

Rheingold, Howard (1992) *Virtual reality*. New York: Touchstone.

Rorty, Richard (1998) *Achieving our country*. Cambridge, MA: Harvard University Press.

Rosen, Christine (2005) The age of egocasting. *The New Atlantis* 7, 51–72.

Rosenbaum, James (2000) In defense of the DELETE key. *The Green Bag* 3(4), 393–6.

Rothenbuhler, Eric (2009) Continuities: communicative form and institutionalization. In: Knut Lundby (ed.), *Mediatization: concept, changes, consequences*, 277–92. New York: Peter Lang.

Rushkoff, Douglas (2003) *Open source democracy*. London: Demos.

Rybczynski, Witold (1983). *Taming the tiger: the struggle to control technology*. New York: Viking Press.

Ryberg, Thomas, and Malene Larsen (2008) Networked identities. *Journal of Computer-Assisted Learning* 24, 103–15.

Safranski, Rüdiger (2003) *Nietzsche: a philosophical biography*. London: Granta.

Sassen, Saskia (2006) *Cities in a world economy*. Thousand Oaks: Pine Forge Press.

Schäfer, Mirko Tobias (2011). *Bastard culture!* Amsterdam: Amsterdam University Press.

Schmitt, Cannon (2004) Materia media. *Criticism* 46(1), 11–15.

Sennett, Richard (1998) *The corrosion of character*. New York: W.W. Norton & Company.

Sennett, Richard (2006) *The culture of the new capitalism*. New Haven: Yale University Press.

Silverstone, Roger (2002) Complicity and collusion in the mediation of everyday life. *New Literary History* 33(4), 761–80.

Silverstone, Roger (2007) *Media and morality*. Cambridge: Polity.

Sima, Yangzi, and Peter Pugsley (2010) The rise of a "me culture" in postsocialist China. *Gazette* 72(3), 287–306.

Simmel, Georg (1895) The problem of sociology. *Annals of the American Academy of Political and Social Science* 6, 52–63.

Sloterdijk, Peter (2004) *Sphären*. Berlin: Suhrkamp Verlag.

Sonesson, Göran (1997) The multimediation of the lifeworld. In: Winfried Nöth (ed.), *Semiotics of the Media*, 61–78. New York: Mouton de Gruyter.

Spigel, Lynn (2001) Media homes: then and now. *International Journal of Cultural Studies* 4(4), 385–411.

Sreberny, Annabelle (2005) "Not only, but also": mixedness and media. *Journal of Ethnic and Migration Studies* 31(3), 443–59.

Stephens, Mitchell (1998) *The rise of the image, the fall of the word*. Oxford: Oxford University Press.

Stephenson, Neal (2008[1992]) *Snow crash*. New York: Bantam Spectra.

Stiegler, Bernard (2009[1996]) *Technics and Time, 2: Disorientation*. Palo Alto: Stanford University Press.

Suoranta, Juha, and Tere Vadén (2008) *Wikiworld*. Tampere: University of Tampere.

Tapscott, Don (2008) *Grown up digital*. New York: McGraw-Hill.

Taylor, Charles (2002) Modern social imaginaries. *Public Culture* 14(1), 91–124.

Taylor, Paul (2008) From mit-sein to bit-sein. *Information, Communication & Society* 11(6), 781–98.

Taylor, Paul (2009) Critical theory 2.0 and im/materiality: the bug in the machinic flows. *Interactions* 1(1), 93–110.

Taylor, Paul (2010) *Žižek and the media*. Cambridge: Polity.

Thacker, Eugene (2003) Data made flesh: biotechnology and the discourse of the posthuman. *Cultural Critique* 53, 72–97.

Thacker, Eugene (2004) *Biomedia*. Minneapolis: University of Minnesota Press.

Thomas, Graham, and Sally Wyatt (1999) Shaping cyberspace – interpreting and transforming the Internet. *Research Policy* 28, 681–98.

Thomas, Tanja (2009) Social inequalities: (re)production through mediatized individualism. In: Knut Lundby (ed.), *Mediatization*, 263–76. New York: Peter Lang.

Thompson, John (2005) The new visibility. *Theory, Culture & Society* 22(6), 31–51.

Thrift, Nigel (2005) From born to made: technology, biology and space. *Transactions* 30, 463–76.

Thrift, Nigel (2011) Lifeworld Inc – and what to do about it. *Environment and Planning D* 29, 5–26.

Toma, Catalina, Jeffrey Hancock and Nicole Ellison (2008) Separating fact from fiction: an examination of deceptive self-presentation in online dating profiles. *Personality and Social Psychology Bulletin* 34(8), 1023–36.

Tomlinson, John (2007) *The culture of speed: the coming of immediacy*. London: Sage.

Tooby, John, and Leda Cosmides (2005) Conceptual foundations of evolutionary psychology. In: David Buss (ed.), *The handbook of evolutionary psychology*, 5–67. New York: Wiley.

Tufekci, Zeynep (2009) Grooming, gossip, Facebook and MySpace. *Information, Communication & Society* 11(4), 544–64.

Turkle, Sherry (2005[1984]) *The second self*. Cambridge, MA: MIT Press.

Turkle, Sherry (2011) *Alone together*. New York: Basic Books.

Turow, Joseph (2005) Audience construction and culture production.

The Annals of the American Academy of Political and Social Sciences 597, 103–21.

Twenge, Jean, Sara Konrath, Joshua Foster, Keith Campbell and Bard Bushman (2008) Egos inflating over time: a cross-temporal meta-analysis of the Narcissistic Personality Inventory. *Journal of Personality* 76(4), 875–901.

Valkenburg, Patti, and Peter Jochen (2007) Who visits online dating sites? Exploring some characteristics of online daters. *CyberPsychology & Behavior* 10(6), 849–52.

Valkenburg, Patti, and Peter Jochen (2009) Social consequences of the internet for adolescents: a decade of research. *Current Directions in Psychological Science* 18(1), 1–5.

Van den Boomen, Marianne (2009) Interfacing by material metaphors. In: Marianne van den Boomen, Sybille Lammes, Ann-Sophie Lehmann, Joost Raessens and Mirko Tobias Schäfer (eds.), *Digital material*, 253–66. Amsterdam: Amsterdam University Press.

Varnelis, Kazys (ed.) (2008) *Networked publics*. Cambridge, MA: MIT Press.

Verhulst, Stefaan (2008) Linked geographies. In: Joseph Turow and Lokman Tsui (eds.), *The hyperlinked society*, 191–205. Ann Arbor: University of Michigan Press.

Vinken, Henk (2007) Changing life courses, new media, and citizenship. In: Peter Dahlgren (ed.), *Young citizens and new media*. London: Routledge.

Virilio, Paul (1997[1995]) *Open sky*. New York: Verso.

Virilio, Paul (2006[1998]) *The information bomb*. New York: Verso.

Virilio, Paul (2008[2005]) *The original accident*. Cambridge: Polity.

Weber, Brenda (2009) *Makeover TV*. Durham: Duke University Press.

Webster, Frank (2011) Information and democracy. In: Stylianos Papathanassopoulos (ed.), *Media perspectives for the 21st century*, 21–41. London: Routledge.

Weiser, Mark (1991) The computer for the 21st century. *Scientific American* 265(30), 94–104.

Wellman, Barry (2002) Little boxes, glocalization, and networked individualism. In: Makoto Tanabe, Peter van den Besselaar and Toru Ishida (eds.), *Digital Cities II*, 10–25. Berlin: Springer.

White, Damian, and Chris Wilbert (eds.) (2009) *Technonatures*. Waterloo: WLU Press.

Wiener, Norbert (1988[1954]). *The human use of human beings*. Cambridge: Da Capo Press.

Wittel, Andreas (2001) Toward a network sociality. *Theory, Culture & Society* 18(6), 51–76.

Yee, Nick, Jeremy Bailenson and Nicolas Ducheneaut (2009) The Proteus effect: implications of transformed digital self-representation on online and offline behavior. *Communication Research* 36(2), 285–312.

Žižek, Slavoj (2008) *In defense of lost causes.* New York: Verso.

Index